D0216684

Identity and stability in marriage

Identity and stability in marriage

JANET ASKHAM
Research Fellow, University of Aberdeen

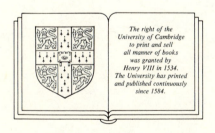

The right of the
University of Cambridge
to print and sell
all manner of books
was granted by
Henry VIII in 1534.
The University has printed
and published continuously
since 1584.

CAMBRIDGE UNIVERSITY PRESS

Cambridge
London   New York   New Rochelle
Melbourne   Sydney

HQ
618
.A84
1984

Published by the Press Syndicate of the University of Cambridge
The Pitt Building, Trumpington Street, Cambridge CB2 1RP
32 East 57th Street, New York, NY 10022, USA
296 Beaconsfield Parade, Middle Park, Melbourne 3206, Australia

© Cambridge University Press 1984

First published 1984

Printed in Great Britain at the University Press, Cambridge

Library of Congress catalogue card number: 83-26150

British Library Cataloguing in Publication Data

Askham, Janet
    Identity and stability in marriage.
    1. Marriage
    I. Title
    306.8'1   HQ728

    ISBN 0 521 25996 7

BO

SEP 25 1984

Contents

Preface

❯❯

The idea for this study was born in the mid-1970s, a time when there was much discussion, but little research, on new forms of intimate relationship: cohabitation, serial monogamy, group marriage, sexual freedom within marriage. The problem for the researcher at that time – and still the problem now – is that there was very little systematic evidence about the nature of 'ordinary' marriage (if there is such a thing) with which to compare any changes that might be occurring. Apart from the occasional light thrown upon aspects of the relationship between wives and husbands (for example, whether they have joint or segregated roles, whether they are dependent upon each other or upon outsiders for help and companionship, whether one partner has more power to impose his or her wishes than the other), the internal lives of married couples have remained obscure. Marriage is a very private matter. This has deterred much research, but those few brave enough to persevere have been able to obtain useful findings. The aim of the study which forms the substance of this book was a further contribution to this understanding of what takes place within marriage.

Since the aim was to explore some of the complexities of the joint lives of married couples it was decided that it should be a small-scale investigation. It was small in the sense that it relied upon a sample of twenty wives and their twenty husbands; in that it was carried out by the author alone; and in the sense that it was confined to couples living in just one geographical area, namely Aberdeen. It is not, however, a study of marriage in north-east Scotland; it is a study which happened to be carried out there because it was where the author lived. There is no reason to suppose that Aberdeen marriages are atypical of marriages anywhere else in provincial Britain. There is no way of knowing how representative any sample of twenty couples is, whether selected in

Aberdeen or elsewhere in Britain. What a small-scale study can do is explore its subject in greater detail than can be achieved by the larger-scale survey. It is hoped that the findings presented here will provide a useful way of looking at marriage and suggest new approaches for understanding such aspects of people's behaviour as why they get married, their levels of satisfaction with marriage, and their reasons for disenchantment and conflict. It is hoped that these new approaches will encourage others to re-examine and develop the findings through further investigations.

Single-handed research is often a solitary pursuit. I obtained much enjoyment from this study, however, through the friendliness and co-operation of the men and women who agreed to be interviewed, to whom many thanks are due. I would also like to thank my colleagues at the Institute of Medical Sociology in Aberdeen for their help and encouragement.

1

~~▶▶▶~~

Prologue

The nature of marriage

Marriage in Britain today is a fascinating but bewildering subject. This is partly because so much of a marriage relationship takes place in private, because its character varies from couple to couple, because it is extremely complex, and because it has been subjected to a great deal of change in recent years. These four themes require some expansion.

Whether or not a marriage is a legally constituted one, there is usually public recognition of its existence: the couple's relatives, friends and acquaintances know that they are married or living together. But beyond this fact it is probable that most people will know little about the relationship between the two people involved, for example what they talk about when they are together, even whether they talk at all, what their sexual relationship is like, what if anything they disagree about and how violently, how if at all they share tasks around the house and in the care of children, who takes what sort of decisions, who gives in to whom, and what interests if any they share. Their habits will usually only explode into public view when something abnormal occurs (such as severe marital discord) and outsiders gain information about them through the couple's need to talk or to seek advice or help. Of course some marriages are less private than others, but it is generally true in our society that most of the interaction between a wife and husband is carried on in their own home and away from the public gaze, and that they will not usually discuss with other people most of the intimate details of their lives together. If one wants to understand other people's marriages, all one usually has to go on is a vast array of tiny clues, but with most of the major pieces missing. It may therefore be hard to reach an answer to the question of what marriage is like, for one will know little about any marriages except those of which one is either a close observer or a participant.

1

Marriage is also bewildering because, even though it may be hard to obtain detailed information about any one marriage, it is clear that there are many different styles or ways of being married. Even without the categories identified by researchers (see chapter 2) everyone has heard of marriages in which the husband dominates, or of those dominated by the wife, of the couple who are always rowing but appear quite content, of those who seem constantly on the verge of splitting up, of those who appear to spend most of their time together to the exclusion of other people, of those who seem to lead quite separate lives, of relationships which never seem to change as against those apparently in constant flux; and so on and so on. Explanations of why marriages have the character they do are therefore also complex and varied; there are cultural, structural, psychological, even physiological explanations. No individual marriage can be explained by any single factor, and therefore no one can easily predict the form a marriage will take.

The difficulty of understanding marriage is of course compounded by its complexity and by the way in which it pervades the lives of the married: marriage is not just one aspect of their lives, but hundreds. It is usually the building up and maintenance of a home, and all the goods that go with it and in it (garden, furniture, car, pets, television); it is (usually) the bearing and rearing of children; a sexual relationship; being company for each other, and giving and receiving comfort, advice, criticism, anecdotes, useful information; looking after each other when sick; joining in hobbies, pastimes or games together; helping to provide each other's daily comforts and requirements (for example, providing clean clothes, growing vegetables, fetching or cooking food); helping to look after or entertain each other's friends and relations; and perhaps assisting with each other's occupation. Although there is considerable variation it is probably true to say that, outside working hours, most of the time of most married people is spent doing or thinking about the things involved in being married. An enterprise of so many facets seems a difficult thing to fulfil well: after all not everyone can be good at, or enjoy, all aspects; and it seems likely that, unless they are rigidly compartmentalised, difficulties in one area may well affect other areas. It makes one wonder how such a large-scale enterprise can be built on the back of such a seemingly small and fragile thing as a relationship between two people.

Finally, of course, marriage behaviour is changing. What makes this bewildering is the difficulty of predicting what will happen in the future. The three main directions of marital change are towards more cohabitation, more symmetry between the roles of husband and wife, and more divorce. The latter change is the most evident: over the last twenty years there has been a 400% increase in the divorce rate, and it is estimated that about one in four of the couples marrying today will end that marriage in divorce (Rimmer 1981); if present trends continue, of course, the proportion will become even higher. There are no single factors that distinguish those who divorce from those who do not, so it is hard to predict future trends. Another consideration is the effect upon young people's own marriage behaviour of their parents' divorce and of subsequent periods in a household with a single parent or a stepparent; data from the U.S.A. show a weak association, but we do not yet know whether the same will be true for Britain (Thornes and Collard 1979). Cohabitation is also on the increase. It has been estimated that 'of all marriages taking place between 1977 and 1979 nearly a third were preceded by cohabitation compared with only one in twenty of all marriages that took place between 1961 and 1970' (Office of Population Censuses and Surveys 1981). The proportion of couples living together before first marriages was 20% by the end of the 1970s, and for second marriages it was as high as 60%. If these trends continue, obviously a period of cohabitation before marriage will eventually become the norm (though the proportion for whom cohabitation is an alternative to marriage still appears to be small). As far as the relationship between the partners within marriage is concerned, there have undoubtedly been considerable changes outside marriage in the post-war period which have in turn led to changing attitudes towards marital roles. Factors such as the growing acceptability of, and demand for, equality of opportunity and treatment of all sections of the population; the development of the women's movement, producing greater public awareness of the position of women, and its efforts to alter attitudes towards women; the expanded labour market compared with the pre-war period, which has improved the economic position particularly of married women; these have all contributed to bring about an alteration in role distribution within marriage. Thus it is now more likely that a wife will contribute to earning the household income, and that a husband will help with or even share the household tasks or childcare (see chapter 2). Complete symmetry, however, is still far away, except among a minority of couples (Mansfield 1982), and again one cannot know whether the present trend will continue and, if so, how rapidly further change will occur.

The continued existence of the more traditional forms of behaviour alongside the newer means that a far greater degree of choice is available to couples today: the choice of whether or when to have a legal marriage ceremony, whether to stay married for ever or not, and whether to organise marital roles symmetrically or not. Having the opportunity to make choices may be preferable to having no choice, but it does in some ways make life more difficult than mere adherence to universally accepted standards.

These four characteristics of marriage (its private, varying, complex and changing nature) all make it a fascinating subject for research, but they also make it a difficult subject. In particular, its private nature means that a marriage relationship may not be easy for an outside investigator to study. There is for this reason relatively little research on the topic (see chapter 2). However, the nature of marriage today makes it more than ever an interesting subject for research, the questions frequently asked being, first, what is it that makes marriage difficult nowadays (and thus helps to explain the rising divorce rate), and second, if it is difficult, why do people still want to marry, either for a first or even for a second time.

Few people would disagree that marriage is difficult. The kind of phrases people use when one interviews them about their marriages are, for example, 'it's a struggle', 'you've got to stick it out', 'you've got to learn to adjust', 'you can't do just what you want', 'you've got to learn to take responsibility', 'all couples have their disagreements'. Yet even though it may be difficult, people still get married. They must therefore hope that it will bring important gains. What they are trying to achieve is thus an interesting and important question. The main aim of this book is to examine two possible answers. They were suggested partly by a previous answer proposed in a well-known article by the American sociologists Berger and Kellner (1964). Before discussing new answers one should therefore look briefly at theirs.

'Marriage and the Construction of Reality'

Berger and Kellner make the important point that, in order to give us the certainty that the world and our own identity within it really are as we ourselves see them, we need the knowledge that other people see them in the same way. It is thus through interaction with other people that what they call the 'validation' of the social world is carried out. They go on to say that some validations are more significant than others (namely, the validation of one's own personal identity and place in the world) and that these can only be carried out through interaction with truly significant others (that is, those with whom we have an important or close relationship) in a continuing conversation. Having said this they then assume that marriage, being the relationship with a truly significant other *par excellence*, is an identity-building relationship. This then is the essence of the answer provided by Berger and Kellner to the question posed above about what people may be trying to achieve within marriage. However, the way in which they continue their analysis of marriage shows that it presents features which are likely to act against, or conflict with, the creation of identity. A confusing picture is thus presented, probably resulting from the fact that the authors fail to analyse the conditions necessary for identity creation and neglect an examination of the other kinds of activity carried out in intimate relationships (for another critical review see Morgan 1981).

Thus, they say that it is in the private sphere (i.e. within marriage) that the individual may obtain 'power'. This is a world in which 'he is *somebody* – perhaps even, within its charmed circle, a lord and master'. It is a world of 'individual choice' and 'autonomy'. However, if one partner in a marriage has power and is 'the master', then presumably the other undergoes a diminution of his choice and autonomy, and thus perhaps also a loss of identity. (He need not, of course, necessarily feel a sense of identity constraint: the identity of 'servant' may be fully congruent with his own sense of self.)

In assuming that marriage is an identity-creating relationship Berger and Kellner also overemphasise the autonomy which partners to a marriage have. An identity-creating relationship needs autonomy, 'its own controls', etc. But marriage is not necessarily able to function in this fashion. There are numerous rules with widespread public acceptance of how 'wives' and 'husbands' should behave. These rules may well impose an identity on individuals which is not congruent with their previous or potential sense of identity. Berger and Kellner do admit that the wider society provides the pair with 'certain standard instructions as to how they should go about this task' (i.e. creating a marriage), but they also say that beyond these instructions it is up to the pair to construct the world in which they live. However, is it not likely that in many cases these 'instructions' may inhibit the couple's task of the creation of their *own* world?

Again, Berger and Kellner convincingly state that reality and identity creation are continuing processes in which both persons play an active part. It is 'a continual and endless conversation'. But how many marriages conform to such a pattern? Marriage is – as Berger and Kellner admit – a precarious relationship, and it may well be that whole areas of conversation have to be avoided in order that it may continue to exist.

The authors also convincingly state that it is likely that within marriage reality becomes more definite and more *stable* and that there is a narrowing of the future projections of each partner – 'both world and self thus take on a firmer, more reliable character for both parties'. But does this not involve a narrowing or constraining of the sense of identity? It would seem likely that as reality becomes firmer and narrower the sense of *stability* would be increased; however, one's sense of *self* may become less real, as also may one's sense of the other's identity. For if, as Berger and Kellner admit, the conversation about outsiders is one-sided ('the husband typically talks with his wife about his friend, but not with his friend about his wife') then one's sense of the other's identity comes to depend solely on the conversation one has with the partner, and is not enriched by conversation about one's partner with outsiders. In other words, two people rely largely on what they tell each other about their identity. Outside marriage it is more usual for us to make up our minds about the identity of another person from conversation with several others, from which we are able to piece together several dimensions of his identity. If this conversation is denied (as it typically appears to be within marriage), then the partner may come to be perceived as having a 'two-dimensional' identity. If this happens, one's own identity is threatened, for our partner will perceive us as having a two-dimensional identity. Thus this is how we will come to perceive ourselves, if it is true that it is partly from others' views of us that we see our own identity.

It seemed that, without fully realising it, Berger and Kellner were discussing two different and conflicting activities carried out within marriage: not only the creation of a sense of identity but also that of a sense of stability. The theme of stability creation is a strong one throughout the article: for example, when they say that people do not apprehend the process of reality construction which occurs within marriage, but merely think they have discovered something that was always there. This feeling, as Berger and Kellner say, enhances the stability of the world, and reduces the anxiety which accompanies the feeling that reality is sustained only by oneself.

The narrowing and solidifying of reality, the autonomy which one partner may have, the instructions the pair receive about how to go about the task of creating a marriage, all these seem likely to enhance a sense of stability. But each of them, as described above, also seems likely frequently to inhibit the creation of an individual's sense of identity, which may require more fluidity and freedom of choice so that the 'continual and endless conversation' can be carried on.

The concepts of identity and stability, and the conflict between them

A reading of Berger and Kellner encouraged two tentative answers to the question of what people may be trying to achieve within marriage; but some closer examination of the concepts seemed necessary before one could consider exploring them through empirical research (see Askham 1976 for an earlier version of the following section).

To return to the concept of identity: individuals within our society perceive themselves and others to have a wide variety of identities. These may be divided broadly, as Zicklin (1969) suggests, into three categories: macro-identities, which are revealed on cursory inspection and may involve 'sex, colour, occupation if a uniform is worn, and physical appearance'; micro-identities, which are only revealed to the other after a certain degree of acquaintance and which may involve 'name, family relationship, marital status, friendship ties, occupational role, socio-economic position, religious affiliation' etc.; and character attributes, which necessitate an even greater degree of acquaintance by the other and which involve 'personality and character traits, moods, habits, values, interests, attitudes and tastes'. Similarly, identities can be perceived as ranging from the most general types of classification which the individual shares with thousands of others (such as 'woman', 'white person', 'adolescent'), through those which are more and more restricted (such as 'unmarried mother', 'retired policeman', 'collector of butterflies'), to that in which the individual perceives himself to be unique (the 'I-myself' who is different from all other human beings).

For whatever reason, individuals in our society tend to want to develop and maintain a sense of this unique, personal identity. First, it is perhaps partly because doing so enables them to give form and direction to various types of social behaviour. For example, one may envisage the concept of personal identity as assisting the individual to make sense of the multitude of more specific identities which he performs. Thus he has a conception of how to behave for each of the roles he performs; yet these roles could frequently contradict one another or be incapable of being performed simultaneously. A sense of personal identity will aid him in his decision as to which role should be given priority in which situation, and will also help him to modify his behaviour so that two or more roles become less contradictory. For example, instead of saying to herself that a woman is someone who does X, while a schoolteacher is someone who does Y, the individual may say: 'I am the kind of person who does Y even though I am a woman.' (Of course this is not the only strategy individuals can use to resolve role conflict; for example, there may be an acceptable way of ordering roles so that the individual knows which one should be given priority without having to refer to his self-conception.)

Second, in cases in which the individual has a choice of action, a sense of self may aid him in deciding between a variety of different goals or motives for action. In other words, as Turner (1968) states, it may 'supply a stable and workable direction to action by providing a criterion for selective attention to the social consequences and reflections of ego's behaviour'.

Third, and similarly, a sense of personal identity may give meaning to one's past and guide one's future behaviour. This is stated in Zicklin's article in which he says that the sense of identity is the individual's experience in trying to do two things: 'to make meaning out of past events in which the individual has participated', in other words, to seek behavioural consistency; and 'to delineate a certain character for himself which will guide his behaviour in future interaction'.

Assuming that people do want a sense of personal identity, the next question is how it is developed and maintained. First, of course, it can only be created if the individual interacts with others. Without this he is not a human being at all. As Mead (1934) states:

The individual experiences himself as such, not directly, but only indirectly, from the particular standpoints of other individual members of the same social group or from the generalised standpoint of the social group as a whole to which he belongs. For he enters his own experience as a self or individual, not directly or immediately, not by becoming a subject to himself, but only insofar as he first becomes an object to himself just as other individuals are objects to him or are in his experience; and he becomes an object to himself only by taking the attitudes of other individuals toward himself within a social environment or context of experience and behaviour in which both he and they are involved.

We learn through interaction, therefore, that we are man or woman, coal-miner or sociologist, stamp collector or poet, and how to act within these identities. However, as we switch from more generalised to more specific or unique identities we need a special type of 'other' with whom to interact – or rather a special kind of interaction – in order to create such identities. Because we are formulating the more intimate self we need a more intimate relationship, and another to whom we can reveal, and who will aid us in creating, the complexities of our unique self. For, as Turner says, unless they take place within an intimate relationship, 'interpretations at other than face-value, and especially at the diagnostic level, are regarded as invasions of personal privacy and attacks on personal dignity'. On the other hand, he goes on to say, 'Relationships of intimacy . . . carry with them not only license but obligation for a limited amount of mutual empathic interpretation.'

However, along with this intimate relationship, we also need – in order to create and maintain a sense of identity – certain periods of privacy. However intimate the relationship 'my' behaviour is always modified by 'yours' and by my expectations of you, and to this extent I cannot be 'myself'. I need my privacy in order to reflect upon past interaction and behaviour and upon potential future behaviour, and to produce order out of what may be conflicting identities. It is a necessary part of a mutual process of identity creation for two people – the coming together to create each other, the withdrawing in order to reflect on what may be a turbulent, disturbing or problematic period of inter-action, and then a further period of interaction to continue working on the identity creation, using the reflections one has had in private. As Zicklin states:

Alone, we may engage in speculation and reflection upon all sorts of identities of which we have felt ourselves possessed. Once engaged in face-to-face interaction a certain focussing of attention and awareness takes place, and we fashion ourselves into a certain kind of person, again depending on with whom we are interacting.

The development of a sense of identity then seems to be an evolving process in which the individual is aided by his intimate others but from whom he also periodically withdraws.

The concept of stability is very different. It can be likened to that of the home as described by Schutz (1971) who suggests that individuals tend to seek a home environment which will provide them with 'an unquestionable way of life, a shelter and a protection'; he goes on to define the home in the following way:

Life at home follows an organised pattern of routine: it has its well-determined goals and well-proved means to bring them about, consisting of a set of traditions, habits, institutions, timetables for activities of all kinds, etc. Most of the problems of daily life can be mastered by following this pattern. There is no need to define or redefine situations which have occurred so many times or to look for new solutions . . . We not only may forecast what will happen tomorrow, but we also have a fair chance to plan correctly the more distant future. Things will in substance continue to be what they have been so far.

The intimate relationship in our society is the crucial element of the home. Children grow up within the home environment of their intimate relationship with one or more adults. The majority of adults go on to seek another home in a relationship with another adult (although of course not *all* homes involve other adults, nor necessarily adults having an intimate relationship).

The importance for the individual of the stability implied in the notion of 'the home' is often taken for granted in sociological studies. The reason for its existence is touched on by Berger and Luckmann (1966) when they say that the 'home world' of childhood 'is so constituted as to instil in the individual a nomic structure in which he may have confidence that "everything is all right" '. Another element of stability is 'habitualisation', and the need for this is again discussed by Berger and Luckmann. They state:

Habitualisation carries with it the important psychological gain that choices are narrowed . . . And by providing a stable background in which human activity may proceed with a minimum of decision-making most of the time, it frees energy for such decisions as may be necessary on certain occasions. In other words, the background of habitualised activity opens up a foreground of deliberation and innovation.

If the notion of home is most frequently embodied in the intimate other, and if 'home' implies stability, changelessness or habitualisation, then this intimate other must be seen to possess certain qualities. Those that appear most necessary are a strong and permanent commitment to one's partner; in other words he or she must show the qualities of acceptance, changelessness and permanence which are implied in the concept of 'home'. 'Changelessness' does not mean complete absence of change, but an absence of drastic or unstructured change which could disrupt the commitment to and acceptance of one's partner. If the individual leaves the home for any length of time, then his place in the home (and perhaps also the very existence of the home) is threatened. This does not of course mean that the home consists of 'a strictly continuous, primary face-to-face relationship but rather of a series of merely intermittent face-to-face relationships' (Schutz). It is impossible to answer the question of how much discontinuity of face-to-face interaction can take place without threatening the existence of the home. It is, however, suggested that the stability of the home can best be maintained when there is relatively little discontinuity.

After reflecting on these two concepts it was possible to draw up a list of what seemed to be the likely conditions for the fulfilment of each of these goals. Looking first at the development of a sense of identity, it appeared that the following factors would be required:

1 An intimate relationship with a 'significant other', where both can converse openly about aspects of their identity which would be private from others. As Berger and Luckmann say, 'to retain confidence that he is indeed who he thinks he is the individual requires not only the implicit confirmation of his identity that even casual everyday contacts will supply but the explicit and emotionally charged confirmation that his significant others bestow on him'.

2 An equal chance for both partners to develop or maintain their own sense of identity. Each requires that the other should not impose an identity upon him, nor severely constrain his identity development. (Of course, there may be situations in which one imposes an identity upon the other, but one which the latter is willing to have imposed.)

3 Periods of privacy (which may be construed by the individual as periods of freedom or independence) so that each may distance himself from the relationship in order to reflect on the interaction and on the other's interpretations of reality.

4 Since 'identity' is something which develops and changes with experience (which it must do if the individual is not to feel that his identity has become incongruent with changing situations or changing potential future goals) then the relationship with the significant other requires allowance for redefinitions of identity – in other words, it must be a developing relationship.

5 The relationship, as *publicly* defined, should not be perceived as constricting the roles of either person. Neither of them must be seen as having a given identity which constricts the ability to perceive and to perform other identities. For example, the role of 'husband' is widely expected to involve certain types of action and to preclude certain other types.

6 For the relationship to continue as an identity-building one for each person it must not constrain the opportunities of the individuals involved for new experiences. For in order to converse (i.e. to maintain the identity-building process) the individuals must feel that they have something to converse about. If perceived experiences do not change or develop then eventually the conversation will cease.

7 Finally, there should be the possibility for the individual to have a relationship with more than one significant other. He should at least have the chance to talk to a third person about his relationship with the main significant other. For we form our ideas of what another person is like by talking to others about him or her, as well as by talking to the person himself.

On the other hand, for a sense of stability to be maintained, any tendency perceived as likely to cause the relationship with the significant other to fragment must be inhibited. Consequently, the following types of condition looked likely to be required for the maintenance of stability:

1 Avoidance of conversation on many topics; areas in which it is felt that definitions of reality will differ and cannot be made to merge are likely to be avoided, so that dissension which is likely to threaten the relationship is minimised.

2 Avoidance or concealment of actions which one individual feels will either cause himself or his partner to experience a sense of instability because of their potential effect upon the other's commitment to and acceptance of him.

3 Encouragement of behaviour which is likely to make the relationship seem more solid or real (for example, a legal marriage ceremony, joint ownership of goods or property).

4 Discouragement of outsiders, who may interfere with the created stability of a relationship, from forming an intimate relationship with either of the partners.

5 Discouragement of development or change in definitions of identity,

for since the outcome of such developments cannot be known in advance then it is possible that, were they allowed, such developments would lead to loss of commitment and acceptance on the part of one or other of the partners.

6 Attempts to deny independence or privacy to one's partner, for in such periods he or she may redefine reality in such a way as to lose commitment to the other.

The above points, although not expounded in detail, are sufficient to show the apparently contradictory nature of the two activities of identity-maintenance and stability-maintenance. Thus, on the one hand, identity-maintenance seems to require open and wide-ranging conversation, a certain amount of privacy or independence, the possibility of new experiences for each individual, a minimum of imposed restrictions, and the chance for intimate interaction with third persons. On the other hand, stability-maintenance would seem to require the inhibition of all these factors.

Although recognising that these sets of conditions were an over-simplification, at this point it seemed plausible to suggest that if people were seeking to develop a sense both of identity and of stability in the intimate relationship of marriage they were likely to have a problem (unless of course the type of identity they sought was wholly congruent with the conditions which seemed necessary for the maintenance of stability). But were they seeking these two ends? And did they have ways of dealing with the apparent contradictions? A research project to examine these questions seemed an inevitable further step. But before that it was necessary to see whether previous research on marriage had touched on these questions, and how it could help in formulating the questions and method of enquiry for the proposed study.

2

‣‣

Ways of looking at marriage: an introduction to the study

Theoretical approaches to the study of marriage

The types of question raised in the previous chapter about the ends pursued in marriage do not fall neatly into either of the main theoretical approaches so far used in the study of marriage by sociologists. Leaving aside studies not explicitly tied to any theoretical framework (a situation far from uncommon in this field), there have been two major theoretical approaches: functionalist and conflict or exchange theory (the former waning, the latter still influential).

The functionalist approach is not without relevance to the study proposed here, but it must be largely rejected on account of its tendency to direct attention to the macro-social context rather than to interaction between individuals, and of the assumptions it makes about the relationship between the behaviour of individuals or small groups and the wider society. As far as marriage is concerned (as opposed to the family in general, or parent–child relations), functionalists have been most interested in sex-role divisions, and are well-known for their distinction between the instrumental role of the husband and the expressive role of the wife (Bell and Vogel 1960; Coser 1964; Parsons 1959; Parsons and Bales 1955). In so far as such an account of marriage merely directs one's attention to the likelihood that married people will be constrained in their adoption of marital roles by the expectations prevalent in their society, and that there might be a constellation of roles one could call 'instrumental' and another which one could call 'expressive', then it is of use to someone planning to study marriage relationships. But few would now take the functionalists' account of sex-role division as an accurate statement of marital roles today. Their view is criticised for being over-simplified and for failing to recognise

14

the possibility of change in role behaviour; in other words functionalists have failed to see how complex and multi-faceted are the patterns of sex-role division in marriage, and how social change of various kinds has helped to bring about change in the roles and relationships of husbands and wives. Parsons' failing, as Poster (1979) says, was to treat his own view of marital-role division as an 'inviolable principle'.

The second aspect of the functionalist approach relevant to marriage is its very emphasis upon the *functions* of marriage, both for the wider society and for the individual participants. Functionalists have, as is well known, viewed marriage as having a positive function for society and for the individuals involved, seeing it as providing society with relatively stable structures within which the necessary work of legitimating and socialising children can be carried out as well as stabilising the adult personalities and fostering their physical and mental health – this being both functional for them and for society at large (Parsons and Bales). Again, in so far as this viewpoint simply directs attention to the ends actually being pursued or achieved by married people, it is relevant to this study; 'stabilising the personalities' has a certain similarity to the concept of stability discussed in chapter 1. Yet again, however, the approach must be criticised for its readiness to assume functions, and particularly to assume that these are positive functions (see Morgan 1975). On statistical grounds alone, some of what the functionalists say about marriage can be discounted: for instance, the opinion that marriage is necessarily beneficial to people's mental health, since Bernard (1972) for example shows that the mental health of married women compares unfavourably with that of spinsters.

The opposing approach, which emphasises conflict and change in contrast to consensus and stability, is for different reasons also unsuitable for the proposed study. Although there are a variety of slightly differing schools of thought within this approach, they all recognise three fundamental concepts (even if their order of emphasis varies): conflict, bargaining and power. The basic assumption is that, without some means of avoidance or resolution, partners in a marriage will inevitably conflict with each other. Two types of reason are offered: first, the partners' differing and incompatible values, norms or goals (see Bernard 1964; Sprey 1979; Waller and Hill 1951); or second, the differential access of husbands and wives to, or control over, scarce and mutually valued resources (see Safilios-Rothschild 1976; Scanzoni and

Scanzoni 1976). Such a viewpoint is to some extent useful in the context of the proposed study, for it encourages one to recognise the possibility that husbands and wives may not think alike on the desirability of developing both the sense of stability and the sense of identity (that is, for example, one may wish to emphasise the former, the other the latter), or that even when their goals are the same one may achieve them for himself whilst the other does not, because one has greater power to impose his or her wishes on the marriage. However, as a basic tenet it is unhelpful, since the prime object of this study would not be to ask what husbands and wives conflict over, what causes conflict, and how conflict manifests itself. For the proposed study this approach over-emphasises conflict between marital partners. For in its concentration on the opposition between husband and wife it neglects not only the possibility of joint enterprises but also the possibility of conflicts or contradictions which do not involve conflict *between* the marital partners themselves. It is of course unfair to criticise an approach for what it does not purport to do, but it is fair to point out that it does not, and perhaps cannot, take into account other aspects of marriage such as the fact that men and women form relationships not only to engage in gaining rewards *from* each other but *with* each other, that is rewards which are seen as only, or best, achieved by two people operating together; or the possibility that there are mutually exclusive goals within marriage which do not necessarily involve conflict or negotiation between the partners; in such a situation, where contradictory ends are recognised, conflict between the partners is possible, but what is also possible is that each partner assists the other in recognition of the problem and in seeking an acceptable compromise. Clearly these two alternative viewpoints could be appropriate ways of seeing a couple's standpoint on stability and identity pursuits.

The second assumption of the conflict approach is that of bargaining: such analysts see couples negotiating with each other over the exchange of resources in order to achieve a satisfactory balance of rewards over costs. The marital bargaining situation is seen as a complex one, involving a wide variety of costs of varying severity and a wide range of benefits of varying degrees of desirability: for example, socio-economic status, income, material goods, sex, love, housework, amiability or companionship (Safilios-Rothschild 1970, 1976). Again, in so far as this viewpoint directs attention first to the fact that the quality or nature of a marriage is at least partly the result of the interaction between the partners, and second to the probability that many different ends will be sought by marriage partners and that some of them may only be achieved with resulting costs to oneself or one's partner, then it is relevant to the interests of this study. For the proposed investigation also assumes the importance of marital interaction; in addition it needs to bear in mind the fact that many other pursuits apart from the possibility of the development of identity and stability are engaged in within marriage. However, the conflict approach has been criticised for failing to examine and to test its assumptions fully by means of empirical research. There is still very little data either on the 'goods' couples actually bargain over or on the process of bargaining itself (see Scanzoni 1979). It is perhaps because of the lack of empirical research that the approach can be criticised for presenting an unrealistic picture of marital interaction. At a very fundamental level it is convincingly suggested that this approach presents an over-rational view of man: that it tends to use the economic model of man as an individual intent upon the maximisation of profit, and that it does this because it fails to recognise the importance of people's own perceptions and definitions of situations and is inclined to see costs and benefits as having an objective rather than a subjective value (see Burr, Leigh *et al.* 1979; Safilios-Rothschild 1976). It is also criticised for frequently failing to take into account the whole range of resources with which spouses may bargain; that is, for concentrating mainly upon economic factors such as socio-economic status and income rather than personal resources such as love (Safilios-Rothschild 1976). An empirical study which attempts to consider couples' own definitions and interpretations of marriage is therefore preferable to further unsubstantiated theorising.

The final major concept of the conflict approach is that of power. It is seen as an important classificatory and explanatory variable, with couples viewed as varying in the extent to which one partner dominates in the marriage, and with that partner who wields most power over desired resources seen as likely to achieve most power within the marriage. The complex nature of power is recognised, and the possibility of different types of power, under different circumstances, taken into account (see Safilios-Rothschild 1976; Scanzoni 1972; Sprey 1972, 1975). Both the benefits and drawbacks of this concept as far as the proposed study is concerned have already been covered: in exploring the possible existence of a search for identity and stability one should not ignore the notion of power and its impact on the search for a resolution of two contradictory goals (for example greater power over valued resources may enable one partner to impose an identity upon the other). On the other hand the concept encourages the definition of marriage as involving inequality, opposition and competition between the partners, and ignores the possibility of mutual goals and co-operation. The latter way of conceptualising marriage is equally appropriate in the exploration of a search for identity and stability.

An approach different from these two is therefore required for the examination of the existence of identity and stability pursuits. Its basic assumptions can be best described as falling into the symbolic–interactionist school. Although the school itself defies description and is, as Rock (1979) says, 'peculiarly resistant to summary', the four basic tenets of the approach to be used here can be outlined.

First, it holds that one cannot understand social behaviour without understanding an individual's own 'interpretation of objects, situations or the actions of others' (Blumer 1962). Marriage behaviour thus cannot be understood without an examination of how the participants themselves define and interpret its existence. One cannot, for example, assume from a knowledge of statistical facts about marriage in Britain the reasons why married people behave as they do or the goals they are seeking to achieve. Second, it holds that although the behaviour of husbands and wives is constrained by the norms or expectations of their group, community or society, it is not determined by them. It believes both that individuals interpret norms or expectations differently, and that all have the opportunity to make choices about their marital roles, goals and modes of operation. It is through the interaction between husband and wife that the special character or nature of each marriage emerges, as each person influences and reacts to the behaviour and attitudes of the other. Since they are the product of a very wide range of 'ingredients' marriages are extremely complex relationships, and since they are not externally determined they are likely to vary considerably from couple to couple. Third, and implicit in the above, it holds that marriage is a process, that it is a relationship which can develop or change as the couple continue to act and react to each other and to events and individuals in their external world (though the extent of change will vary from couple to couple depending upon the individuals involved and the kinds of external changes to which they have to react). In saying that the marriage relationship can change one is also saying that the values, norms, goals, habits of the participants may change, bringing with them changing ideas of 'self', which may in turn affect the way each spouse responds to or relates to his partner. The final element in this approach is the assumption that a married person is likely to experience contradictions between the roles or identities he or she wants or feels an expectation to fulfil either within marriage or between marriage and other spheres of life, or between his own roles and those of his spouse; that these contradictions do not necessarily, though they may do so, lead to conflict between husband and wife; and that they can be dealt with in a variety of ways: by attempting to change the situation either through unilateral action or through interaction between self and spouse, or self and others, so that both desires and expectations can be either fulfilled or abandoned; by an individual decision or a decision reached with others to emphasise one desire or expectation without any attempt to fulfil the other; by a decision to compromise and accept less than complete fulfilment of each desire; or by not resolving the contradiction at all but continuing to experience stress and strain. With these tenets in mind it is now possible to describe the design of the proposed study. But this will be preceded by an examination of previous research, without which it would not be clear to what extent the present study breaks new ground, covers old ground, or develops existing findings.

Previous research on marriage

The pursuit of identity and stability in marriage represents a virtually new and unresearched topic. Yet there are research findings on related topics which needed to be borne in mind when designing the present study. First, however, it should perhaps be re-emphasised that there is very little sociological research on marriage itself. This is not due to lack of interest in the subject, since it is one much discussed, but to the fact that marriage is such a private phenomenon (Morgan 1975) and therefore less easy of research access than other types of behaviour or relationships. Second, there is no previous empirical research taking as its theme the development of either a sense of identity or a sense of stability within marriage. However, by placing these themes within a rather wider context one can see some relevant findings. Thus the area of interest could be said to be the kinds of gratification people either find, or fail to find, in marriage. The proposed study suggested two possible factors, but it was necessary to know whether other researchers had identified similar or widely different factors.

An interesting preliminary point is that, given the suggestion (see chapter 1) that it is impossible to satisfy both identity and stability goals and therefore unlikely for couples trying to achieve both ends to attain complete satisfaction in marriage, yet studies of marital satisfaction show most people as very happy with their marriages. The figures vary slightly from study to study but the tendency is for between two-thirds and four-fifths of married people to report themselves as very happy, satisfied, etc; about one-fifth to one-third pretty happy, etc; and under one-tenth not too happy, or unhappy in their marriage. (See, for example, Bradburn 1969; Glenn 1975; Gurin, Veroff and Feld 1960; Orden and Bradburn 1968). This may mean that most people do not seek both stability and a sense of identity in their marriage, or that they do seek these goals and yet manage to reach what they see as a thoroughly satisfactory compromise, or that the answers they give to such questions do not adequately take factors such as identity and stability into account, or that the findings of such studies are of doubtful validity. Although each of these explanations may have some merit, the latter point about the validity of marital satisfaction studies is an important one. Such studies are often criticised on grounds of conceptual ambiguity, of the assumptions they make about the simplicity of the notion of marital happiness and about people's ability to make such value judgements at all, and of sample bias and inappropriate data gathering techniques (see Burr, Leigh *et al.* 1979; Hicks and Platt 1970; Lively 1969; Spanier and Cole 1974; Udry 1966; Williamson 1972). Marital satisfaction studies, therefore, need not be seen as providing strong counter-evidence to the hypothesis of the proposed study.

Turning then to aspects of marriage identified by others as sources of gratification it was possible to distinguish three types: first, factors which may accompany marriage but are not part of the marriage relationship itself; second, the purely emotional stance of each partner towards the other; and third, aspects of marital behaviour following quite closely those identified (see chapter 1) as involving the conditions necessary for the achievement of either identity or stability. The first set of factors are those such as income, property, status or children – matters which some studies have shown as a possible source of people's satisfaction or lack of satisfaction with marriage. For example, a decline in marital satisfaction over time can be shown as associated with the coming of children (Walker 1977), as can increasing marital conflict (Blood and Wolfe 1960); similarly poverty or financial problems have been seen as leading to marital disharmony (Gorer 1971) whilst secure financial circumstances can be one of its gratifications (Cuber and Harroff 1965).

No one however would assert that these are all, or even the major, sources of marital gratification. Thus emotional factors have also been seen as highly relevant. For example, the extent of regard or affection one has for one's spouse and perceives him or her as having for oneself have been associated with marital happiness (Bell 1971; Lewis and Spanier 1979) and jealousy and disregard with marital unhappiness (Gorer 1971). But the actual behaviour of the spouses has also been considered important, and it is here that previous studies come closest to the proposed investigation. Chapter 1 has described five areas of marital behaviour where a conflict between identity and stability needs might occur: in the extent of conversation between the spouses, in the extent of their shared activities, in the amount of change experienced within marriage, in the marital roles they assume and in the extent to which they allow outsiders to form relationships with them. Although not tied to ideas about identity and stability, other researchers have also touched upon these areas of activity.

With regard to communication between marital partners the most relevant question being investigated is whether discussion or avoidance of discussion is the most effective way of dealing with marital conflict. (The hypothesis of the proposed study would suggest a leaning in *both* directions.) There is some difference of opinion among researchers. Rausch *et al.* (1974) for instance stated that avoidance is a common pattern for dealing with conflict, and that 'avoidance couples' reported the same amount of marital satisfaction as did those who dealt more openly with conflicts. Other findings, however, point in the opposite direction, showing a positive association between frequency of communication and marital satisfaction (Bienvenu 1970; Lewis and Spanier 1979; Navran 1967). But research on marital communication is still in its infancy. It seems that both sets of findings might well be true in different situations, and with different meanings attached to 'communication' and to 'satisfaction'. One of the problems of studying marital communication, apart from methodological ones, is thought to be that there are now fewer rules imposed for family behaviour as a whole, and thus that communication is becoming more fluid, that there is more variation between couples and more blurring of the divisions between marital and non-marital communication (see Rausch *et al.* 1979). There is therefore a continuing need to examine marital communication, since previous research, even without other limitations, might well be obsolete.

Studies of the sharing of activity by spouses show, as one would expect, that this is certainly seen as one of the gratifications of marriage, and also that the greater the sharing the higher the satisfaction felt by the partners. For example two American studies (Marini 1976 and Miller 1976) associated the amount of time the couple spent together with marital happiness; in Britain Gorer (1971) found 'neglect', 'spouse going out', 'lack of common interests' among the five main factors thought likely to wreck a marriage; and Cuber and Harroff (1965), again in America, found that those marriages which they called 'vital' or 'total' involved a great deal of shared activity as well as a strong interest by each partner in the other. Again, however, there is a lack of any detailed study of the extent and nature of shared and separate activity within marriage which could lead to an accurate assessment of whether there really is a simple positive association between shared activity and feelings of marital gratification, or whether it may not be a considerably more complex matter, with satisfaction reaching a peak some way before a maximum of shared activity is attained, and being dependent on the kind of activity shared as well as on its extent.

As far as change within marriage is concerned, one has to rely again almost exclusively upon marital-satisfaction studies with all their drawbacks. These indicate that some changes produce a decrease and some an increase in marital satisfaction (for example lower income or declining opportunity to spend time together lead to a decrease, and higher income or status and more time together to an increase). They do not compare couples' overall experience of change, though by implication they seem to suggest that it is not the experience of change itself that matters but the nature of that change. Whilst not strictly comparable this seems to run counter to research on 'life-events' which shows that any change, even positively valued ones, can produce anxiety, illness or stress (see Dohrenwend and Dohrenwend 1974).

Research on the assumption of marital roles has been more extensive, and is more relevant to the proposed study, which is suggesting that the assumption of at least some of the marital roles might bring about either gratification or dissatisfaction, or both, depending upon whether the individual is trying to develop and maintain a sense both of identity and of stability within the marriage. Whilst not answering this question, previous research does provide some useful information about such roles. First, it outlines their nature and variety. It confirms the commonsense view that since marriage typically involves common residence, children, and the assumption of a certain amount of responsibility for one's spouse's physical and emotional well-being, the role dimensions of marriage would include care of the residence, care of the children, provision of income, provision of meals, warmth, clothes, etc. to support each other's physical well-being, and of counsel, companionship, etc. to support each other's emotional well-being; and in addition the organisation of these various activities and liaison with external persons or bodies (see Bott 1957; Tharp 1963).

Second, research in this field sheds light on the question of whether the roles of husband and wife are uniformly imposed or whether there is variation from couple to couple or from group to group (the implication for the proposed study being in the hypothesis that the more freedom individuals have to choose their pattern of roles or role division the less likely they are to feel that their marital roles clash with their preferred sense of identity, but the more likely they are to experience a sense of instability). The pioneer work in the field of conjugal role division is of course that of Elizabeth Bott (1957). She defined the conjugal-role relationship as 'the extent to which husband and wife carried out their activities and tasks separately and independently of each other'; distinguished between complementary, independent and joint organisation of activities; and labelled as a 'segregated conjugal role relationship' that where joint organisation predominated. Of the twenty couples in her sample she found only one with a clearly segregated role relationship, five with joint role relationship, nine intermediate and five who appeared to be in a transitional state between segregated and joint roles. Clearly, then, there could be considerable variation between couples (although one should not expect to find many with a segregated relationship). Further research also shows that even more variation could exist than Bott herself discovered; for example, that a conjugal role relationship could be joint in some respects and segregated in others (see Platt 1969), or joint up to a certain point and thereafter segregated (for example, in a study of managers and their wives, Pahl and Pahl (1971) found all their sixteen couples saying they would discuss together any important decision, but nine said the husband had the final responsibility for taking the decision). So in our society there is no uniformly imposed pattern of marital role division. Third, research shows that variation might be becoming even more prevalent. It is generally accepted that couples now have greater opportunity to choose the degree of 'jointness' or symmetry of their marriage (see for example Blood and Wolfe 1960; Fletcher 1962; Gavron 1966;

Young and Willmott 1962, 1973). Segregation is still possible but joint-ness, at least in some areas, is much more acceptable than it was twenty or thirty years ago – even though it is still true that by and large wives have the greater responsibility in their traditional areas of housecare and childcare.

Finally, there is a limited amount of research on the relationships of spouses with outsiders (the hypothesis of the proposed study suggests that such relationships would be both encouraged and discouraged). As is well known, Bott found an association between type of conjugal role relationship and type of external social networks of husband and wife (close-knit networks went along with a segregated role relationship and loose-knit ones with a joint relationship). This finding fits the proposed hypothesis to some extent. For Bott argued that the members of a close-knit network 'will get some emotional satisfaction from these external relationships and will be likely to demand correspondingly less of the spouse. Rigid segregation of conjugal roles will be possible because each spouse can get help from people outside.' Couples in loose-knit networks, however, 'must seek in each other some of the emotional satisfactions and help with familial tasks that couples in close-knit net-works can get from outsiders'. From this it is possible to argue that close, intimate relationships with outsiders can be maintained by some people because they do not seek identity and stability primarily within marriage (or that they do not have to seek identity and stability primarily within marriage if they have close, intimate relationships out-side it, such as Bott describes those with close-knit networks as having). Those with joint roles do not lack a network of friends, etc. outside marriage, according to Bott, but their relationships are less intimate and any friends they have tend to become friends of both husband and wife jointly. This analysis is useful in highlighting the impact of the type of external relationships upon the internal marital relationship (and possibly vice versa) and showing that outsiders can either be allowed into, or excluded from, positions of intimacy; but it still leaves open the question of the possibility of a leaning in both directions at once by the marriage partners. One or two other minor studies show that outsiders can be seen to affect the stability (e.g. Gorer 1971) and the happiness of a marriage (e.g. Spanier 1972), but again do not investigate the possibility of conflict between a desire both to admit and to exclude them.

In conclusion it seemed as though the proposed study would be investigating topics which up to now had received relatively little attention from empirical research. There was an absence of research (as distinct from discussion) about marriage and its consequences for the sense of personal identity. The same was true of research on understandings of, and desires for, security or stability within marriage. There had been a limited amount of research on other marital behaviour topics, but even so not a great deal relevant to the proposed study, especially perhaps in the areas of communication, companionship – 'perhaps the most prized aspect of marriage and one of the least studied' (Blood, 1976) – subjective perceptions of marital roles, and change within marriage.

The topics of the proposed study

Interest aroused and previous studies consulted, the next step was to design a study with the aim of providing evidence about whether or not married people experienced contradictory desires (or wants, preferences, requirements) in the five areas of marriage behaviour already outlined. This approach was chosen rather than any direct exploration of people's perceptions of identity and stability needs since it was not expected that people would think of their marriages extensively in these terms; the main focus therefore would have to be upon those specific areas of marriage behaviour which had emerged during consideration of the conditions for achievement of identity and stability. The five topics can be posed here as simple questions; their complex nature will be dealt with more fully in later chapters:

1 Conversation: is there a contradiction involving a desire to talk to one's partner about anything one does and thinks, in order to develop and maintain one's own sense of identity, and a converse desire not to talk about some subjects because they might undermine the stability of the relationship?
2 Privacy or separation: is there a contradiction involving a desire to have periods of privacy or independence from one's partner, in order to assist the development or maintenance of one's own sense of identity, and a converse desire to spend one's time with one's partner (and to deny privacy to him or her) in order to assist the development or maintenance of the sense of stability?
3 Conformity to expected behaviour patterns: is there a contradiction

involving a desire *not* to conform to behaviour patterns (roles) expected of one, in order that one may feel no constraint upon the development of one's own sense of identity, and a converse desire that one *should* conform to the expected behaviour patterns, in order to further and maintain the stability of one's relationship?

4 Change in oneself and in one's behaviour: is there a contradiction involving a desire for the opportunity to change one's self and one's activities, either as one's sense of identity changes or in order to permit a change or development of one's identity, and a converse desire not to seek or encourage change, in order that it may not be a threat to the stability of one's relationship?

5 Third persons: is there a contradiction involving a desire for relationships with other people, in order to develop one's sense of identity, and a converse desire not to seek or encourage other intimates in case they should be a threat to the stability of one's relationship?

For each of these topics the first aim was to gain information about the *behaviour* of married people. This would tell one, for example, whether they appeared to compromise between what has been called stability-maintaining and identity-maintaining behaviour, or whether they favoured the latter over the former, or vice versa. The questions to be asked, therefore, were what people saw as the nature of their behaviour in the five areas, and (where relevant) how much or with what frequency they did it. Thus, taking the area of 'conversation', one would preferably want to find out what kinds of activity people had in mind when they referred to talking to their spouse; what kinds of topic were raised, or rarely or never raised; how much people talked together, or thought they talked together; and how frequently they did so. In the area of 'privacy or separation', one would preferably want to know what was seen as separate activity; what kinds of activity people engaged in together and apart; how long they spent together or apart at any one time; and how frequently they did so. Whilst these first two areas are to some extent quantifiable, the remaining three are difficult to measure. 'Conformity to expected behaviour patterns' involved primarily an examination of the ways in which people are, or feel themselves to be, constrained to behave in certain ways as a result of marriage. To ask how much time is spent on such behaviour was obviously not feasible since these patterns of behaviour may have so permeated the person's time or his sense of identity that he saw himself as always constrained even when not actually performing any specific activity. With regard to 'change in oneself and in one's behaviour', one would want to examine people's perceptions of the kinds of change which had taken place since marriage and the things that had remained unchanged, and to make some crude assessment of the extent of change. Finally, in the area of 'third persons', one would want to discover what kinds of relationship married people had with outsiders; the number of relationships; how much time they spent with such people; what they did and talked about; and how such behaviour had changed since before marriage.

It was intended that the data just described would be used to answer various supplementary questions. First, one would want to know whether there were any clear patterns within the sample of marriages. Were there, for example, individuals whose behaviour in all or most areas suggested an overall emphasis upon stability rather than identity, or vice versa? Or is it the case that most people are characterised by behaviour which seems to lie somewhere between these more extreme situations, and to indicate a kind of compromise? If one did discover people whose behaviour was towards the extremes, what kind of people would they be? How did people account for the way they behaved, and would such accounts fit in with the hypothesis about identity and stability?

The other type of data required would be on people's *feelings* about their behaviour or situations. First it was necessary to ask whether people were content with their present behaviour and situations, and if so, how content they were; and what the association between contentment or dissatisfaction and actual behaviour was. For example, was dissatisfaction, as one would expect, most evident among those whose behaviour lay towards the suggested extremes (i.e. behaviour which indicated an emphasis on either the sense of stability or that of identity)? Second, it would be necessary to ask how people interpreted their contentment or lack of contentment. Did they, for instance, see their present situation as imposed (and, if so, by what or whom) or as chosen by themselves? Were the reasons they gave for feeling as they did in line with the hypotheses about identity and stability, or were their own interpretations quite different? Third, one would want to know what kind of situation would be preferred by the discontented. Did they want more of the suggested identity-maintaining behaviour (e.g. more opportunities for change, for independence, for outside friendships), or more of the suggested stability-maintaining behaviour (e.g. more prevention of change, more time spent with their spouse, fewer outside friends)? Or did they want a compromise? Finally, was there any awareness of contradiction, or did people think they could have the best of both worlds?

The method of investigation

The study chosen was an interview investigation of a small sample of married couples. This method is of course not without drawbacks, but for the purposes of this investigation it was preferable to other methods, such as the large-scale survey or an observational study. The large-scale survey was rejected since the use of a standardised questionnaire seemed inappropriate given the amount of complex, hitherto unexplored, qualitative material required. Observation would have been difficult partly because of the private, intimate nature of much of a marriage relationship (though for some purposes it has been successfully carried out: see Blood 1958; Henry 1972; Lewis 1962), and partly because some of the activities of interest would have been technically difficult or impossible to observe (such as what a husband and wife were doing when spending time apart). It was also unsuitable because of the interest in people's own perceptions of behaviour and their attitudes, feelings and preferences; these emerge most clearly in talk, and can be assessed most economically by interviews.

The semi-structured type of interview was chosen because of the wish to encourage people to talk in their own ways about each of the topics and yet to present all interviewees with an equal opportunity to talk on each topic. In semi-structured interviewing the way in which questions are phrased, and the point at which subjects are raised and closed are interactionally determined; since these are characteristics of 'normal' conversations it was hoped that they would encourage talk. On the other hand the interview is structured to the extent that a certain number of topics must ideally be covered to the same extent with all interviewees; this allows for comparisons within the sample. The danger with semi-structured interviewing is that one achieves neither aim very satisfactorily; to combat this danger therefore considerable effort is required from the interviewer throughout the talk; it is also a method in which one is likely to achieve interviews of varying quality (though this is true of all fieldwork methods). There are many well-known criticisms of interviewing as a method, stressing particularly the effects of the interview setting and its form upon the data produced, and asserting that what people say in interviews is not necessarily a reflection of the kind of reality one wishes to examine but merely a record of what people are prepared to say in that particular situation (see for example Becker and Geer 1970; Brenner 1978; Cicourel 1964). However, interviewing remains a useful method of data gathering, for since in everyday life we are prepared to accept reports of events and feelings as approximations to reality after we have carried out various measures for assessing meaning and validity (social life would otherwise be impossible), then we can reasonably do the same with research interviews. These measures involve such things as probing for fuller explanations, examining consistency of answers, rephrasing questions and so on (see Richardson *et al.* 1965; Lofland 1971).

The sample was a small one (twenty wives and their twenty husbands). As is commonly stated, large samples are primarily used for quantification and generalisation to whole populations, and small samples for exploration of the nature of complex events or feelings. Of course ideally one may wish to achieve both aims, but time and other resources usually make this impossible. The positive advantages of dealing only with a small sample in a study involving the collection of qualitative data are, first, that since such studies tend to generate fairly large volumes of data, the larger the sample the more unmanageable it is from the point of view of analysis; second, that for qualitative analysis there is an advantage in having one researcher carry out all the interviewing and all analysis, and of course it is easier for one researcher to manage a small rather than a large sample.

One of the dangers of a small sample is that it may be unrepresentative of its population. This is less likely to occur if one chooses a sample with basic characteristics known to belong to the centre rather than to the extremes of the population distribution. A quota sample of married people was selected which avoided, for example, those with large families, the previously divorced, those born or brought up abroad, unusual religious affiliations, etc. It comprised legally married couples, half of whom had been married for five years or less, and half for fifteen years or more; half had husbands in a manual occupation and half in a non-manual occupation. These divisions were made in order to allow some comparisons within the sample and yet to restrict the extent of that variation (See appendix 1 for further details of sample selection.) All lived in or near Aberdeen, a city in the north-east of Scotland whose population is not known to differ markedly from people living in other parts of provincial Britain. One might have expected a sample biased towards marriages seen as non-problematic by the participants. However, as will be seen in later chapters, three of the forty interviewees expressed serious reservations about the state of their marriages, and a further three some moderate reservations (as a proportion of the sample this is slightly above that provided in marital-satisfaction studies, which suggest that about 10% are 'not too happy' or 'unhappy' with their marriages). Some of the other characteristics of the achieved sample were: half the wives were between twenty-one and thirty years old, and half between thirty-one and sixty years old, while the husbands were slightly older; almost everyone (thirty-two out of the forty) had been brought up in or around Aberdeen; sixteen of the twenty marriages took place in a church; three-quarters of the couples had children under the age of sixteen (usually either one or two); half the wives were working but only five full-time. (See appendix 1 for further details.)

The fieldwork plan was to interview people in their own homes, to talk first to the husband and wife together, and on subsequent occasions to each separately. This was accomplished in almost all cases, although there were one or two in which the spouse was present at what was to have been a separate interview (this had to be borne in mind at the analysis stage). The joint interview acted as a preliminary setting of the scene in which accounts, mainly of factual, historical events, were obtained, around which it was possible to weave questions on the five areas of interest in the later separate interviews. The fieldwork took place in 1977.

As already stated, the interviews were semi-structured, that is the specific topics and many of the questions were set down on an interview guide; however they were not necessarily asked in the order in which they were listed on the guide but were allowed to follow the natural flow of the conversation; nor were they designed to be asked in a standardised way but to allow for the selection of words or phrases to match those used by interviewees, or to be altered so that they appeared to be understood in the desired way by the interviewees. (See appendix 2 for a copy of the interview guide.)

All the interviews were tape recorded and then transcribed before the process of coding, classification, assessments of range and distribution, matching of findings against hypotheses, and the search for, or ruling out of, alternative explanations could be accomplished. The following chapters present those findings, and show how the hypothesis was both supported and modified in the process.

3

Knowing and talking to each other

Before discussing the five areas of behaviour in which identity and stability needs are expected to conflict it seems sensible to provide some introductory information about the marriages of the twenty couples in this study. The introductory topic chosen is the extent to which the marital partners feel they know one another. This is not a purely arbitrary topic but one chosen partly because it should help to show whether the marriages studied are sufficiently significant or important to the participants to allow them to seek identity or stability goals within them. If by chance a couple had been selected who were virtually strangers to each other, sharing the same house merely as a matter of convenience, they would be unlikely to be interested in, or affected to any great extent by, the actions or attitudes of each other, and would be furthering their identity and stability ends solely in relationships with other people. What follows will show that the sample did not include any relationships of this kind, although there was of course a certain amount of variation in the extent to which people felt they knew their marriage partner, or were known by him or her.

Knowing each other

Most people when asked how well they knew their partner and how well he or she knew them said that they knew each other very well (and it was a question they appeared able to answer with ease). There was a range of answers but not of course covering the full spectrum. At one end were those who said they knew their partner (or were known) very, very well, so that there were no surprises: they knew what the other was thinking, what he would say next, how he would react in any situation, and so on. For example:

32

JA: How well do you feel you know Anne?

Mr A: Er . . . I think I know her very well . . . I think I knew her before I got married. I can tell you anything what she thinks before she says it. I can tell you what she's thinking /// As much as I know her I don't think she knows that much of me. I can tell when she's going to say anything, do anything . . . and without consulting her would know what would be the answer to that . . . before she says it.

Or:

Mrs D: I know him better than himself I think. Well, I . . . *think* that. I always tell him I can read him like a book. But mind you, I don't think *he* believes that maybe. He wouldn't want to. [L]

Or:

Mrs J: I think when you're married you know one another inside out, you know their every mood, you know what they're going to say next.

Or:

JA: Do you feel you know him very well by now, or do you think there are some sides you don't know about?

Mrs R: You ask him that question. [L] You ask him if he thinks his wife knows him well. It annoys him. He says: 'You know me *too* well – I canna hide anything from you.' Often he laughs about that, he really does.

Or:

JA: And you say you think you know one another very well nowadays?

Mr I: Oh aye, I know her now. I know her every move. Oh I know her every move now.

Knowing one's partner very well, and being known very well by him or her, was said to be the case by two-thirds of all those interviewed (although this figure can be divided into three-quarters of the longer married compared with half the younger respondents). The older working-class couples were particularly unlikely to express any reservations about knowledge of each other. After this group came those who said they were known or knew their partner well or pretty well but did express some slight reservations (about a quarter); and after them came those who expressed somewhat more considerable reservations in knowledge (about an eighth of the sample).

Reservations about knowledge were explained in various ways: time was one of the obvious ones. Some people said: 'It takes time to get to know someone', 'We're still learning about each other', 'I don't always know how she'll react' and so on. Another explanation was that there were 'sides' to a person which the partner did not see, and therefore he or she could not know the other completely. There was the husband's work 'side', and the wife's work or home 'side' when the husband was out, there was what they were like when they were with their friends, and so on. Perhaps it is surprising that such reservations were expressed comparatively rarely, for it was clear from the interviews that couples did spend quite considerable periods of time away from each other (see chapter 4). The infrequency of such answers may be because they had occasionally seen each other at work or with friends and therefore felt that they did know what their partner was like in such situations (or that their partner knew what they were like then), or it may be because they held a somewhat monolithic view of individual identity, believing that if they knew (or were known) well in one situation they would know (or be known) well in any other.

Another explanation given for lack of complete knowledge of each other was a personality one: some people, it was said, just happen to be easier or more difficult to know than others. For instance:

> Mrs E: I think he knows *me*. Yes I'm probably easier to know than he is. [L] Oh yes, I think so, 'cos he's deeper really. You don't always know what he's thinking whereas I tend to be more open and sorta . . . more free and open. He tends to hide his feelings more really.

Or:

> JA: And do you think you can read *him* like a book?
> Mrs K: No, he's queer – he's nae deep, but deep enough. He doesn't express his feelings or anything.

Or:

> JA: And how does he know you?
> Mrs R: Oh I think he knows me pretty well. I'm nae sae maybe obvious to read as he is – nae sae obvious.

With this kind of explanation it was implied that others could not know such a person completely: he or she just happened to be difficult to comprehend.

A further explanation, and one that unlike the others struck a blow at the marriage relationship, was that which implied that something had intervened between the partners to prevent the development or continuation of knowledge of each other. The other explanations were seen as normal or inevitable, but this one was abnormal. It was however a rare explanation; in fact one which was only substantially discussed by two wives, and with one of these it was not so much the case that she used to know her husband but now did not, as that she used to *think* she knew him, but since finding out certain things about him and his past which he had not told her, she realised that she did not know him very well. The other woman said that she no longer knew her husband as well as she used to because they had grown apart, had stopped communicating and had ceased doing things jointly, so that she no longer knew how he spent his time or what he thought about things.

Usually it was clear that extensive knowledge was highly valued; it was seen as a good thing, and less than complete knowledge was something that had to be excused, had to be accounted for. This however was not true for all. For whilst some of the younger couples might go out of their way to emphasise their extensive or growing knowledge of each other, there were some older couples (but only middle-class ones) who said that complete knowledge of each other was not a good thing:

> Mr D: I wouldn't like to feel, to be in a position to predict every move she's going to make. She's an individual in her own right you see. So . . . I wouldn't want just to know everything . . . life wouldn't be so . . .

One can only surmise why such views were expressed by some of these older couples, but it may well be that when two people have been living together for a long time and might begin to find little of interest left in their relationship they emphasise, or even try to foster, the unknown and the mysterious. As Komarovsky (1962) says, in talking about the couples in her sample who did not communicate fully, reserve can be compatible with a happy marriage because it retains interest and propounds fictions.

One can also ask how well matched were the spouses' expressions of knowledge of each other; that is whether the interviewees said they knew their spouse as well as he or she knew them; and whether what one partner said about the extent to which they knew each other matched what the other said. A relationship in which each partner knew the other equally well was the most common response. Thus two-thirds of the interviewees (twenty-six out of forty) said that they were known as well as they knew their partner; other replies were evenly divided between those who said they felt either they or their partner had the advantage in terms of knowledge. As for levels of agreement between the answers of husbands and wives, this is obviously something very difficult to assess since different individuals use different terms, mean different things by the same terms, have differential tendencies to exaggerate or understate, and so on. However it looked as though approximately half the individuals said they knew their spouses about as well as their spouses said they were known by them. The other half were more-or-less equally divided into those who said they knew their spouse better or less well than he or she admitted to being known. Those in agreement tended to involve extensive knowledge on either side; for example Mr and Mrs C:

> JA: How well do you feel you know your husband?
> Mrs C: Oh very well.
> JA: And how well does he know you?
> Mrs C: Oh very well.

When asked the same question Mr C replied:

> Mr C: Oh very well – and she knows me too.

Mr and Mrs I provide an example of a couple whose assessment differed:

> Mrs I: My husband *thinks* he knows me. There is a lot about me that he doesn't really know. You know you can't actually know a person a hundred per cent.

Mr I has already been quoted as saying:

> Mr I: I know her every move. Oh I know her every move now.

Of course several of the themes already touched upon (such as time, change, inevitability, agreement) will be taken up again later on. The present intention is only to show that these marriages were significant relationships as demonstrated by the expressed levels of knowledge which one spouse has for the other. One can also – as stated earlier – look at this question by asking how the level of knowledge of or by the spouse compares with knowledge of or by other people. This was sometimes clearly very difficult for respondents to answer: some people did not put spouses' knowledge of each other on the same continuum as that on which they placed friends' or other relatives' knowledge, and some said that you could know people in different ways so that it was difficult to compare them. For example, when asked whom they felt they knew best, they sometimes said: 'Do you mean out of family or out of friends?'; and on occasions they would answer in terms of a non-family member but then when asked whether their answer would be the same if they included family members, they would say: 'Oh you mean including family. Oh of course the wife's the person I know best.'

When interviewees were asked then whom they felt they knew best and who they felt knew them best, thinking about spouse, family and friends, very few specifically mentioned someone other than their husband or wife. In fact only four out of the forty mentioned someone else as the person they knew best (workmate, friend, brother, mother); and five said someone else knew them best (mother, sister and three friends). Out of these nine answers, seven were among those with the shorter duration of marriage, which is not surprising since among these would be found people whose spouses had known them for a shorter period of time than had relatives or friends and who might therefore feel that they had some way to go in knowing or understanding each other. For example:

JA: Would it make sense to ask you if there is one person – out of all the people you know – whom you feel you know better than anyone else?

Mr A: Oh well one guy . . . he works at the same place, the same place I work /// Oh we're more or less like brothers. If he's in difficulty he tells me /// We've known each other since we were little children in primary school . . . and we used to stay in a flat together until I got married.

This man also said (see earlier quote) that he knew his wife very well indeed, but his relationship with his friend seemed to involve more mutual knowledge (he said that his wife did not know him very well) and also more knowledge of each other's past. The answer of another of the younger people seemed to be based not only upon the length of time she had known someone but also upon similarity of personality:

JA: And who do you think knows you best of all?

Mrs L: Maybe my mother; she can read me like a book.

JA: Can she?

Mrs L: Oh yes, I think so. Leslie maybe knows me quite well but /// my mother seems to know what's ticking over in my mind quite often, she seems to sense things. We're very much alike.

As stated, not everyone could give an answer in which they chose one specific person (or in which they consistently chose the same person: there were four respondents whose replies were contradictory at different points in their interview); yet twenty-four did say that their spouse was the person who knew them best, and twenty-six that their spouse was the person they knew best; though in their comments some did try to take account of the complexities of their choice. For example:

> JA: And who do you think knows you best of all, out of all the people you know?
>
> Mr K: . . . oh, that's hard to say . . . I dinna think anybody kens me right.
>
> JA: Don't you?
>
> Mr K: No. I'm awful shy you see (L) . . . She [wife] kens me when I've been drinking – truth comes out in it. [L] So I suppose it's her.

Or:

> JA: Do you think he [husband] is the person you know best of all among all the people that you know?
>
> Mrs S: Oh I think so – though I think when you're very close to a person and they do something or behave in a way you don't quite understand it's harder to understand why *they're* behaving in that way than if it was someone outside.
>
> JA: Because you're too close to them?
>
> Mrs S: Uh-huh. Because it's affecting *you*. So then you say: 'I don't understand why he's behaving like that', whereas if some other woman came to me and said: 'My husband is behaving in such and such a way', I would immediately know why he was doing it, you know.

Others however saw no complexity in it. For example:

> JA: Is there anybody else whom you feel you know better than your wife?
>
> Mr B: Eh . . . oh *no*, I dinna think so.
>
> JA: You feel then that she is the person that you know best?
>
> Mr B: Oh yes – bound to be.

Or:

> JA: Do you feel you know your husband better or just as well, or not as well as you know those other friends you mentioned?
>
> Mrs C: Oh better. Definitely.

This section has described the ways in which interviewees talked about their knowledge of their marriage partner; most people said they knew the other very well and very many put their knowledge of each other above that of anyone else. No couple appeared virtual strangers to each other, although there was considerable variation within the sample. Assuming therefore that for all respondents the spouse was a significant other, the analysis of the areas suggested as likely to involve contradictory views can now begin.

Talking to each other

It has been suggested that in the search for a sense of identity all aspects of each other, each other's behaviour, and the behaviour of the rest of the world will be a topic for the continuing conversation of the participants in the intimate relationship; but that in the search for stability many topics will be avoided as threatening the relationship.

There were certainly people in the sample who appeared to come closer to either one or other of the two conceivable extremes, but to assume that these findings could be used as a thorough test of this study's hypothesis or of that of Berger and Kellner (1964) about 'conversation' within the intimate relationship may be unfounded. For what the hypotheses really refer to is not necessarily the amount of verbal discussion but any form of open and continuing communication whereby partners inform each other of their views on the world. Thus a certain kind of grunt in response to a statement by a television newscaster could be a very significant and comprehensible communication; yet it is difficult in an interview to ask a question about all forms of communicating. However the problem can be exaggerated: to a certain extent people must talk to communicate, and by hearing what they say in answer to a question about talking we can draw some conclusions about the perceived extent of communication between the pair.

First of all the interviewees were asked what they talked about when, for example, they were sitting down in the evening after work. This preliminary question was asked somewhat hesitantly at first, in case it should be seen as a foolish or impossible question, but since it was not derided and was generally answered it continued to be used.

Of course this topic did not take one far, though it was useful in leading some people to say that they did not talk much whilst others said they talked about 'anything and everything'. The subjects mentioned did not vary by duration of marriage, sex or social class (although sometimes different terms were used: 'current affairs' versus 'what's in the papers' or 'reminiscing' versus 'what we did in the past'). Seven subjects comprised the bulk of the answers; first were those which can be assumed to be to some extent shared responsibilities or possessions: the house, money and children (though not necessarily in that order); second there were the activities which either have been, or are seen as likely to be, shared: for example, 'what we've been watching on television', 'what we've been doing', 'what we'll do when we retire', 'where we're going for our holidays'; and finally there were two topics which do not necessarily directly involve both partners, but which may have some effect upon them both: these were the husband's or wife's work, and what was usually referred to merely as 'family' or 'the family'. This meant something wider than selves and children (though it could include them), and was usually taken to refer also to spouses' parents, brothers and sisters and other relatives. Perhaps the world outside the fairly narrow one of children, home and shared activities is for many people not one whose reality is confirmed primarily by conversation with one's spouse. For example subjects like politics, religion and current affairs were only mentioned seven times as general topics of conversation between the spouses. However, of course, such a question cannot be answered by reference to the findings just described. It might perhaps be, for instance, that such subjects do not require the frequency of communication which matters of more immediate day-to-day concern need but that they are discussed or have been discussed in the past. It might also be that in discussing more mundane matters one is also implicitly – or even explicitly – talking simultaneously about matters of wider concern; for example, the country's educational system when discussing the children, the economy when talking about budgeting, taste and fashion when discussing decorating the sitting-room.

In order to get a clearer idea of whether the spouses were people who did communicate with each other it was decided to ask more specifically whether they talked to each other about 'their day'; a subject that was not necessarily one that had to be talked about because it required joint decisions, and yet one that could well be assumed to have a great deal to do with personal identity. If what one spends one's day doing forms the material of a significant part of one's identity then, if a relationship is one in which an individual seeks the maintenance or development of his sense of identity, one would expect him or her to talk to the spouse about it. Of course the first premise may not hold; and there were some members of the sample for whom this appeared to be largely the case.

There was very little disparity between the answers of husbands and wives to this question (unlike the findings of Brown and Rutter (1966) who stated that agreement between husbands and wives when asked about amounts of everyday conversation was low). It thus appears that they are in agreement about whether or not they talk about their day and whether or not one is more inclined to talk than the other. The patterns of reported behaviour varied considerably within the sample, although of course the great majority fell somewhere between, rather than at, the two possible extremes. Only one couple said that they both tended to talk a lot about their day and only one that they hardly ever discussed each other's day. The former couple were from the older, middle-class group, and both described themselves as talkative people. They each had a job (the husband's of an administrative kind, the wife's in the social/medical services); and they said they liked to discuss interesting issues or problems which arose at work. Both of them, however, added some reservations about the extent of their discussions: Mrs S said she thought she talked less about her 'actual work' than she used to because there was much which her husband did not understand and was not interested in; Mr S said they did not talk about their day beyond the point where the other was 'switching off'. Nonetheless the way they described the extent of their talk put them above other members of the sample. The couple closest to the other extreme were in the younger, middle-class group; the wife, Mrs A, has already been mentioned as someone who said she did not know her husband well although *he* said he knew her very well. Mr A worked in the social/ medical services, and Mrs A did not work but looked after their young daughter. She said in her separate interview that she would like to talk to her husband but that he was unwilling to hear about her day or to talk about his own. In his interview Mr A said he liked to keep his work separate from home and would not talk about it. He also said they did not talk very much in general, and only when there was something that had to be discussed. It looked as though one of the husband's reasons for not talking about some aspects of his work was that he thought his wife would react unfavourably (and perhaps that this might then disturb their relationship):

JA: Are there any other things that you would talk about with him [friend] that you don't think you'd talk about with Anne?

Mr A: Um . . . like if you work in [names place of work] there's a lot of gossip or at times some people happen to get involved in minor scandals . . . you know. Well I wouldn't like to discuss it with my wife you know /// I'm married now, I'm finished with . . . uh . . . teenage life, you know. But we still comment on things. Things like that we [Mr A and his friend] might discuss . . . seeing you can't discuss it with your wife, you know. She might have a different opinion, or might say you might be carrying on with somebody out there.

The feeling that work and home should be kept separate was, however, not unique to Mr A, nor need it be seen as motivated by a desire to prevent any marital disagreement. In fact the most frequent type of answer to the question whether the couple talked about their day was for both partners to state that the wife talked about her day (whether at home or at work) but that the husband talked less or not at all about his. Of course the husband's reason was not necessarily that he felt (or that they both felt) he wanted to keep home and work separate though some did say this. For example:

Mr R: I'm maybe not very communicative about my work /// She used to ask a lot about it and then she used to say: 'You know I get more information about the work when I meet somebody's wife.' [L] But I want just to turn it off when I come home. I never was one of these types who took home his work, you know.

JA: Why do you think you like to turn it off?

Mr R: Well I think you've got . . . ten hours a day is long enough without that . . .

Others said that work was boring, the same thing happened every day and it was just routine and therefore they would only discuss their day when something unusual happened or if they had something to say about colleagues or work-mates:

JA: Do you and your wife talk about your day when you come home, do you discuss what you've been doing at work?

Mr G: Oh no, nae very much. It is the same thing every day so there is nothing much to talk about, just the same thing every day.

A very different kind of explanation (though one not often made fully explicit) was that although the man found his work interesting he did not think his wife would, nor that she would understand it, and therefore he was unable to talk to her about it. Mr W, for example, was a research worker, whose wife's job was in a very different field; he said he did not discuss his research (which was 'what I'm almost exclusively interested in') because Mrs W did not know anything about it.

A little more common was the simple explanation that the husband just was not 'a talker' or not as much of a talker as his wife. Mr K. for example, clearly fell into this category:

JA: When he gets in in the evenings does he talk about his day?

Mrs K: No.

JA: So it's not something you discuss?

Mrs K: No. If you *ask* him he'll maybe say . . . but he doesna really tell you much about *anything*. He might say: 'Oh I met so and so in the town', and I ask him: 'What were you saying?' – 'Och, just . . . you ken.' And you have got to sort of drag it out of him what they were saying, y'ken.

Mr K confirmed this:

Mr K: She speaks a lot – I dinna. [L] I just come haim, sit down and watch this [points to television]. We hardly ever speak about things – she just tells me what's been happening to her – and I don't speak ///

JA: Yes. Is that because nothing very much is happening or because . . .?

Mr K: Just because I'm . . . I'm nae very talkative.

These statements were supported by the fact that Mr K frequently told me during the interview that he was not a talker, and it was indeed impossible to get him to talk at any length (although he was very co-operative).

Finally, a further explanation was offered by one husband who said he talked little about his day; this was that he and his wife had 'grown apart'. Mr E said he felt he could no longer talk to his wife, that he could not 'get through to her', that their interests were no longer the same, and that he was not interested in what she said and did. (His wife has been mentioned in the previous section of this chapter as saying that she no longer knew her husband.)

Although this pattern (of the husband being said to talk less about his day than the wife) was found in all groups, it was a particularly working-class response, with eight out of ten working-class couples saying that they behaved in such a way compared with only four of the middle-class couples.

The other two patterns were less common. There was the intermediate one, when both partners said they talked to some extent (but not a great deal) about their respective days; and there were two cases (one middle-class and one working-class) when the husband was said to talk more about his day than did his wife. One of these concerned an admittedly very talkative husband and a young non-working wife who said she did not talk about her day because 'housework and babies quite bores me'; she said she was trying to get a job partly in order that she would have something interesting to talk to her husband about. The other case also involved an admittedly – and in the interview apparently – talkative husband and a less talkative wife; similarly the wife said that her day was mainly routine and therefore not worth discussing, unless she went visiting or anything unusual happened. However, by the time of the second interview with Mr C, his wife had started a new evening job, and he said she was talking 'quite a lot' about that.

The main thing to be noted in these comments on talking about one's day is the great variety (a similar finding was made by Komarovsky 1962.) Although interpretation is difficult it appears that lack of talk is not necessarily, though it may be sometimes, due to a desire to prevent marital discord or disturbance by avoiding threatening topics or identities. Such an interpretation may well be appropriate, first to those marriages which are not felt to be working satisfactorily, where talk may lead to disruption whereas silence may hold the relationship together longer, and second to some of those marriages in which work is said to be something which should not be 'brought home' or those in which it is thought that the partner would not understand the work. (Without further information, however, one cannot be certain at this stage.) Lack of talk may also be due to the fact that the workday is a very insignificant part of an individual's identity: it is boring, it is merely something one does for a wage, and one does not begin to be oneself until one comes home. Alternatively, although the workday may be an important part of a person's sense of identity, it may be a part which is created, developed or confirmed not in interaction with a spouse but in conversation with others. For example, some people talked about the work conversations they could have with friends or workmates which they could not have with their marriage partners. In addition it could be that although an important part of the sense of identity, it is nevertheless a part which has been well developed and confirmed in previous conversations with the spouse, and because it changes little needs very little continuing conversation for it to be maintained. Finally, one must not forget a previously mentioned point, that talk and communication can be different things: people may describe themselves as non-talkers but still be able to communicate as much as is needed for the maintenance of their own sense of identity without the subtleties of complex verbal utterances. One also has to be careful in interpreting those who say they do talk about their day, for although it may mean that they discuss some things in detail others could still be avoided as topics of conversation with the spouse.

Thus though we have little idea of levels of communication, we do now have some rough notion of the stated perceptions of the extent of talking between the husbands and wives in this sample. To help clarify this picture, people were also asked whether in general they felt that as a couple they talked a lot or a little compared with others. (Here the topics of conversation were not stipulated; nor were they asked who was doing the talking: thus people could say that they 'talked a lot' when what they meant was that the partner did most of the talking and they did most of the listening.) It was an interesting if unsatisfactory question in that the interviewees obviously found it difficult to compare themselves with other couples: they did not know how much other people talked. They also made comparisons – which they obviously found easier – between themselves now and themselves in the past. In addition their answers were apparently often influenced by a belief that 'talking' was a good thing in marriage, and that not talking could have detrimental results. For example they said such things as:

JA: What would you think about a couple that didn't talk to one another a lot?

Mr J: It's usually the marriage that doesn't work.

Or:

Mr B: I think you've *got* to be able to talk to a wife about everything.

JA: Why?

Mr B: Well, anything at all. I mean, I dinna think you should speak about every small detail of the day's routine, or anything like that, but I feel you should be able to discuss with your wife anything that she feels like talkin' about.

Thus when people said they did talk it might mean that they thought one ought to say so rather than that they did in fact talk a lot. As Benson (1971) says, 'couples are supposed to talk to each other about the things that are of interest to either and to listen to what the other has to say'.

Almost all the answers fell somewhere between the two extremes (again with little disparity between the answers of wives and husbands as given in separate interviews) with both wives and husbands saying that they talked 'a fair bit', 'quite a lot', and so on. For example:

> Mr M: [We talk about] Just general family matters. Aye, I mean sometimes there's quite a lot, the next night there's nae so much to talk about.

However three couples admitted to talking a little, and four to talking a great deal. Of the three non-talkative ones, two were couples who have been mentioned before as including partners who did not know the other well and did not talk about their day (Mr and Mrs A and Mr and Mrs E). These people expressed dissatisfaction with the situation, but the third couple was quite different, being a working-class marriage of long standing in which not talking appeared quite unproblematic to both partners (Mr and Mrs G). In fact the wife said such things as 'we just live for one another'; she also said: 'Sometimes we don't speak for hours – when we're together we often have nothing to discuss.' It might be that this reticence (which Mr G also mentioned) was due partly to a desire to avoid threatening topics of conversation. For example Mrs G said that she spent a lot of time with her parents and would use their services and advice as much as those of her husband; she said that sometimes if she were short of money she would be given help by her father, which she would not tell her husband as it would only upset him. Further examples of things she had 'kept from' her husband were also given by Mrs G; though it should be added that Mr G seemed in the interviews a very quiet man, and was said to be so by both husband and wife. This might be a partial explanation of the untalkativeness of the pair, although of course one may still be able to interpret Mr G's quietness in terms of the nature of his marital relationship rather than in terms of a psychological trait.

Of the four most talkative couples one has been mentioned before (Mr and Mrs S) as an older, middle-class pair who both talked considerably about their day. Two of the others were young couples, one middle-class and one working-class (mentioned before as pairs whose husbands talked more about their day than the wives: Mr and Mrs C and Mr and Mrs L); the fourth was a middle-aged, middle-class couple: Mr and Mrs D. They all said such things as: 'We like a good natter', 'We enjoy a good argument', 'We've always plenty to talk about.'

If it is true, however, that most of the interviewees fell somewhere below the extreme position of talking to each other a very great deal, were they aware of topics of conversation which they avoided discussing? It has been suggested above that certain topics are probably avoided in order to avoid threatening the relationship, but we have not yet examined whether interviewees were prepared to say that this was the case. In fact they did on the whole agree with this. They were asked (in their separate interviews) whether there were any occasions when they avoided mentioning things to their partners, and what kind of things they were. Of the forty members of the sample only eight said (and at no other point said anything to the contrary) that there was nothing they were ever aware of avoiding saying to their spouse. Interestingly six out of these eight were working-class respondents and six were men. Perhaps this is accounted for by a difference between the acceptable image of a wife and that of a husband: wives may be expected to be tactful and sensitive to the feelings of others whereas husbands may be allowed to be more blunt and forthright. If this is the case such images may affect both their actual behaviour and the way they answer interview questions about behaviour. As the following quotations show, those who said that nothing was ever avoided appeared to be expressing either approval of a relationship in which nothing need be hidden, or pride in themselves or their husbands for being forthright people:

> Mrs J: If you do tell each other everything, well you know each other . . . I would say you get to know each other better.

Or:

> JA: Do you think you ever avoid saying things to your husband because you think they would lead to rows or because you think they might make him feel upset, or sad, or something?
>
> Mrs D: Och, he's got a hide like a rhinoceros . . . I would say he's pretty thick skinned . . . it doesn't matter . . . he takes more-or-less everything I like to give him without too much . . . he doesna harbour any grudges. *I'm* usually, I would say, hurt when *he* . . . you know, I tend to be a bit – maybe take things a bit too seriously. He just – doesna bother, you know. [L] Oh I'm maybe a bit harder on him because he is inclined this way. You know, I have to really put it home to him.

The men said such things as:

> JA: Are there ever any subjects that you feel you wouldn't want to talk about? Or you wouldn't mention in case it would lead to a row or make your wife feel upset or sad?
>
> Mr B: I don't think so, no. If I was going to tell her anything that was going

to lead up to that I'd probably prepare her for such a shock or something beforehand. I think you've got to be honest with one another. It
doesna matter what it's about. I think you've got to be told.

Or:

> Mr F: Oh I dinna think I'd hide anything frae her . . . no.

Or:

> JA: Do you ever find that you avoid saying things because it might lead to
> a row, or might make your wife feel upset or sad, or does that not
> really . . .?
>
> Mr I: Oh no, I call her all the stupid old so-and-so's and everything, but it
> doesn't . . . we haven't had a row for . . . I don't know how
> long . . .

Since it could well be that such respondents were demonstrating
something about themselves or their relationships in these answers not a
great deal of reliance should be placed on them as a guide to behaviour.
Much more common (thirty-two out of the forty interviewees) was the
expression of opinion that some topics were avoided on some occasions.
The subjects were of course of various kinds, as were the reasons given
for avoidance. Some of these reasons have already been mentioned; for
instance there was the desire to keep home and work separate: sometimes it was said that work had nothing to do with 'the family' and
therefore should not be discussed, sometimes that it was nice to get
away from it and forget all about it. Some topics were said to be avoided
because it was felt that the spouse was uninterested and therefore either
would not attend or would not have any relevant or helpful response to
make. For example there were the subjects Mr and Mrs O
avoided:

> JA: Is there anything that you don't think you would talk to one another
> about – things that you wouldn't discuss?
>
> Mrs O: Gossip. [L]
>
> JA: He won't listen to that?
>
> Mrs O: Well not really. If I happen to come out with something, you know,
> some sort of bit of gossip, he's not really that interested, you
> know.

Or:

> Mr O: I suppose we talk about almost everything but I suppose there are
> some things we don't talk a great deal about. You know, some things

I am interested in she wouldn't share.

JA: Yes. What kind of things?

Mr O: Just general sort of topics. It is the same in politics. Er . . . she knows my views. She doesn't necessarily come out against me with my views, in fact possibly more and more she is coming round to my way of thinking, but she has not any great views on the subject /// So that is one thing we never talk a great deal about.

Other topics were said to be avoided because the *speaker* was uninterested and did not want to bore himself or herself with them. Things could be avoided in order not to worry the spouse, especially if he or she were ill or in a particularly worried frame of mind; or if the partners felt they were growing apart and could no longer communicate; or in order not to hurt the spouse's feelings or to encourage rows or differences of opinion. These reasons look more like the avoidance of conversation in order not to disturb the stability of a relationship. It was very common for interviewees to mention such avoidances. For example one man said he would avoid criticising his wife's cooking so as to prevent 'things coming to a head'; another said he had not told his wife about his feeling for his former girlfriend, and a wife that she would not tell her husband if she happened to meet her ex-boyfriend in town, because he might 'feel a bit jealous'. Her husband said he did not talk to her about his irritation with his father-in-law (who lived with them) because 'it might lead to a barney'. Another husband would not say anything hurtful to his wife, for example about her figure; and one said he could not tell his wife about occasional feelings of boredom with his marriage relationship. Such matters, and others like them, are all potentially threatening; though it should be added that people said they felt that *not* talking could also be threatening or counter-productive if 'carried too far'. For example it was said that there were occasions when if you keep something to yourself resentment builds up in you, or your spouse becomes aware that you are concealing something, so you have to speak out and 'clear the air'. This looks very much like a conflict between identity and stability. Almost everyone acknowledged that they did not always avoid rows, barneys, tiffs, or whatever label they used. Only four people (all women) said they never had rows or disagreements of any sort, and three of these said they had done so in the past but did not now. (In fact it was common for the longer-married couples to say that disagreements had declined 'over the years'.)

Finally, this subject cannot be left without asking whether the kind of talk spouses said they had with one another differed from the kind of talk they had with other people. To this end the interviewees were asked whether there were any things they and their spouses talked about which they would not discuss with others. All except one man (Mr E, who admitted he no longer had any 'real' conversation with his wife) and one woman (Mrs G, who maintained very strong links with her parents) agreed that this was so; that they and their partner had a 'private life', 'private concerns', 'personal matters' which they would not consider it appropriate to discuss with others. Among these, as one might expect, sex and money featured strongly. In fact they and the couple's own worries or disagreements were the only three categories of subject specifically mentioned.

In summary, therefore, these couples said that they talked a good deal to one another, sometimes about things which caused rows or disagreements, and sometimes about things which they would not discuss with others; but they also avoided certain matters on some occasions, and did not on the whole describe their marriages as ones in which they both did a vast amount of talking.

Implicit in this chapter has been the wish to find out whether there is any evidence that married couples either reach some compromise between a desire to talk to their partner and a desire not to talk, or experience difficulty or uncertainty in deciding which course of action to take when they desire both. One can therefore end by asking whether at any point in their interviews the respondents expressed the wish either to talk or to be talked to more, or to talk or to be talked to less. Most people expressed no dissatisfaction with the middle way they appeared to have found between the two extremes of extensive talk and talk avoidance; and it therefore looks as though for them some satisfactory compromise had been reached. In fact what struck one most in listening to these couples was the apparently skilful way they had learned when to speak and when to be silent. There was, however, some evidence of uncertainty and dissatisfaction but only from among that minority of couples or individuals whose expressed behaviour was at the extremes compared with the majority of the sample.

Using the findings of the previous sections it is possible to pick out three couples who, compared with others, said they talked very little, avoided some subjects and of whom one or both partners talked rarely or never about their day (the As, Es, and Gs). Neither Mr nor Mrs G expressed any desire for more communication with each other; Mrs A, however, appeared very anxious to be able to talk more to her husband and for him to talk more to her. The avoidance of discussion perhaps maintained a precarious stability for the relationship, but she appeared to want more companionship and the chance to share experiences. For example:

> Mrs A: There's a lot of things . . . that I can't talk to him about. A lot of things that I would like to say . . . I'm a bit frightened of him at times, you know.

Or:

> Mrs A: I think that I would get to know him better if he maybe did tell me a little more.

Or:

> Mrs A: He doesn't want to hear . . . when he comes home from work he doesn't like to hear what's happened during the day. Things like that. He likes to think more about workin' to a budget and . . . what he's going to buy, things like that. But I like to talk about . . . well, when I was here all day I like to say what happens during the day. He doesn't talk about his work.

Mrs E was apparently in a very similar position, and so was her husband, except that he stated that his wife did talk to him but it was no longer 'real conversation' but 'all pretence and sham'. Mrs E said such things as:

> Mrs E: He's out more often really than he is in, so I really don't have the same companionship . . . the companionship went away. Well, I've found the children are the most important part of our marriage really.

Mrs E therefore appeared to be placing more emphasis on her relationship with her children. There were indications that other interviewees might well at one time have wanted to talk more to their spouse than they did, but by the time of interview had found an alternative significant other to whom they could talk; however it is obviously not possible fully to explore such a suggestion except in a longitudinal study. (Relationships with third persons will be discussed in chapter 7.)

One further couple described their wish for more conversation of a certain type (Mr and Mrs S). This was somewhat unexpected in that they both said they talked to each other a great deal. However they also said they avoided certain subjects (their feelings about their relationship, reactions to each other's behaviour, their own wishes or preferences) in order to prevent disagreements. Both (in their separate interviews) said they had never been able to 'fight' or 'row' with each other and that this was a bad thing. Mrs S said she thought 'one of the big mistakes' in their marriage was that 'I haven't fought with Sam more than I have.' She also said:

> Mrs S: We talk about all sorts of things, but sometimes important things I get all up-tight about, and if I get annoyed and think Sam doesn't understand how I'm feeling about it, instead of having either an argument or a fight over it, I just say: 'Well he doesn't understand, so I can't be bothered discussing it with him', and resentment builds up /// We discuss all sorts of things, about politics, and religion and bringing up children, and things like that, but when it comes to our own personal lives I tend to think: 'It's going so well just now – let's not discuss it . . .'

Mr S also said: 'I can't lose my temper with her, and she has difficulty doing this with me. This isn't a good thing.' He admitted, however, that he thought it a good or 'healthy' thing to avoid some topics, the reasons he gave being a desire not to hurt his partner and the belief that one should not speak out about some things unless one was certain one was right. This couple therefore showed signs of considerable ambivalence: on the one hand not talking about some things meant that the situation went on 'going well' and prevented disturbance or distress, but on the other hand might lead to resentment or annoyance.

Only one couple stood out from the rest as saying they talked a great deal and did not avoid topics (Mr and Mrs D). The husband expressed no desire for less talk, but Mrs D did say that she sometimes got annoyed with her husband for his tactlessness, and that he could say something hurtful without realising it. In addition, two more wives who said that their husbands spoke out and failed to avoid certain topics complained about this trait: Mrs K said she found that her husband's openness in making adverse comments about her or about their relationship led to rows; and Mrs T said that, unlike her, Mr T did not avoid mentioning things which could be hurtful or lead to disagreements, and that – partly because of this trait – she had been the one who had had to learn tact, diplomacy and 'wily' behaviour in order to 'keep things running smoothly'.

It was expected that one would find dissatisfaction largely among the two groups of those with both low levels of talk and reported talk avoidance, and those with both high levels of talk and no talk avoidance; the fact that such predictions were not wholly fulfilled gives one an opportunity for commenting upon some of the findings, which may help to explain this situation. A preliminary point is one already made, that one cannot equate talk with communication (so that, for example Mr and Mrs G who said they talked very little may have been communicating quite extensively). Second, quantity of talk cannot be measured absolutely; when interviewees made assessments about the extent to which they talked with their spouse it was often clear that they were making comparisons either with their general expectations, with other people, or with themselves at other times. Thus one cannot compare one couple with another because their estimates of what constituted high or low levels of talk might vary considerably (for example, Mr and Mrs G might in fact talk rather a lot compared with Mr and Mrs E and for this reason express less dissatisfaction than the latter couple). On the other hand, if expectations vary, and if satisfaction is to some extent dependent upon expectations (as one would anticipate) then one might find dissatisfaction amongst couples who on somewhat more objective criteria appeared to belong to a category of interviewees from whom one was not expecting dissatisfaction (for example, Mr and Mrs S, who appeared from their accounts to talk a considerable amount, might have expressed dissatisfaction partly because they had expected to be able to talk to each other more than they did).

Third, there is the fact that the extremes identified in the analysis are identified not by reference to the general population or to any absolute criteria, but by reference to the rest of this sample. This sample is however a small one and may not have picked up any couples whose behaviour is particularly extreme. It is only at particularly extreme positions that one would expect to find a *clear* association between reported behaviour and dissatisfaction, since at other points expectations would intervene to cause differential attitudes towards similar levels of reported behaviour (or vice versa).

Fourth, it is evident that one should not equate quantity of talk too closely with quality; people may need to talk in order to assist the development and maintenance of their sense of identity, but a greater volume of talk does not necessarily mean that this end is more effectively achieved than with a lesser volume; all they would require is opportunity to talk about the relevant matters. Similarly people may need to avoid talking in order to assist the development and maintenance of a sense of stability, but it is not how much they avoid talking that is important but whether they avoid stability-threatening topics when necessary. Thus, for example, Mr and Mrs S may have talked a great deal but perhaps still avoided discussing topics of relevance to each other's sense of identity.

Fifth, one must, of course, beware of equating actual behaviour with reported behaviour. It has been stated that talking to one's spouse seemed to be normatively reinforced, and therefore people may have reported that they talked a good deal whereas they did not in fact do so. Thus one could possibly get reports of dissatisfaction in couples from whom, according to their reported levels of talk, one did not expect it. Finally it has to be remembered that one cannot necessarily assume that all felt a need to confirm or maintain aspects of their identity within their marital relationship; it may well be that, as has been suggested earlier, some people have alternative significant others with whom to talk and can thus be content with relatively low levels of talk within marriage. Conversely it cannot be assumed that everyone has aspects of identity which if talked about with his spouse would be threatening to the stability of the marital relationship; in some cases there may be a congruence between identity and stability needs so that there is no perceived necessity to avoid topics of conversation.

Having made these reservations, however, it can be stated that, as expected, most people expressed the view that they talked to their spouses a good deal but avoided certain topics, that this situation was satisfactory to them, and that it was a good thing both to talk to one's spouse and to avoid talk on some occasions. There was, however, no clear evidence that people saw this situation as a compromise between contradictory *ideal* preferences both for more talk and less talk – but some of them did discuss, and encourage more attention to be paid to, the complexity of the situation; for example, sometimes talk avoidance was recognised as a bad thing not just for the individual involved but also for the relationship (i.e. a bad thing not just for identity but also for stability reasons); sometimes rows (non-avoidance) were seen as good not just for the individual but also for the relationship.

4

‣‣‣

Separate and joint activity

The answers reported in the previous chapter suggest that most couples perceive themselves as talking to each other a good deal but also as avoiding some topics on some occasions. Such a situation appeared satisfactory to them; but on the other hand *dis*satisfaction was not always expressed when there appeared either relatively little talk or an absence of topic avoidance (that is, some of the people whose answers placed them at the extremes said they were unhappy about the situation but some did not). This chapter examines whether a similar 'middle way' was reported in another area of marital behaviour, and whether dissatisfaction always accompanied interviewees' reports which placed them at the extremes. The subject of the chapter is the perceived extent to which husband and wife engage in separate activities, or spend time apart or together; the causes of separation, and also people's stated attitudes towards their situation, will be examined. Again it was anticipated that most people would report compromise situations and would say they found them acceptable; and that those particularly high or low on separation would voice discontent. It will be shown that the former appeared to be the case and that the latter hypothesis to some extent also held true.

Amount and type of separate and joint activity

The working lives of married couples tend to separate them from each other for longer periods than any other activity, except in those rare cases where one partner works at home and the other does not work, or where both work in the same establishment. There was one dual-worker couple of this kind (Rapoport *et al.* 1978) in the sample. Couples' work situations did vary, and it would be of course incorrect merely to see a dichotomy between couples who are separated from each other for eight hours or so per day and those who are together during the daytime. All the husbands in the sample worked in some way, but there were differences in the amount of time spent away from the wife as a consequence of work. Some were separated by considerably more than the 'normal' forty hours a week: one, for example, said he had a great deal of seasonal overtime and worked until eight o'clock on most weekdays at certain times of the year; another worked on Saturdays and Sundays most of the time because, as he said, they needed the money for household goods (both these men were in the recently married, working-class group). A third was in full-time training for a professional job and spent far more than forty hours out of the house, either in studying or in training on the job; a fourth was in a professional job which took him away from his home city at frequent but intermittent intervals. Others had a lower than average separation through work; for example one man left for work at 5 a.m., when his wife was still asleep, and was back home by 4 p.m.; another was a farmer and spent a good deal of his time around or near the farmhouse where he could see and talk to his wife; a third at the time of interview was away from work with an injury incurred through his job. He had been at home for several weeks, and since his wife did not have a job they were in each other's company far more than when he was in work. Of the wives in the sample, nine did not have paid employment, six worked part-time, and five full-time (with no clear divisions by class or length of marriage). Two of these jobs led to higher than average separation and one to lower; the lower was the farmer's wife who worked part-time around the farm, and the higher were a wife whose job involved Saturday working and another whose job was in the evenings, at both of which times the husbands were at home. The other wives' jobs did not either increase or decrease separation since they took the wives out of the home at times when the husband was also at work.

However, even though work separates couples for varying and not easily quantifiable periods of time, other activities are even more difficult to assess in terms of the amount of separation they involve. All the couples were asked to talk about the kind of things they did independently, and at times when they could be together, that is, mainly in the evenings or at weekends (i.e. the concern here was not with what the wife might do with her time while her husband was at work, or vice versa). Of course this is very difficult to assess in any objective sense without, for example, getting respondents to fill in diaries of activity over a period of time. Yet since the main interest was in how people perceived their activities (and one has to equate this with 'expressed') then getting them to talk about what they thought they did was useful. It should also be said that it is difficult to define an independent activity; for example, people can be doing separate things in the home and yet be communicating and having a sense of being together; on the other hand they can be sitting in the same room and yet feel very separate. Naturally such complex situations could not be explored, nor did the interviewees interpret the questions in this way: they almost invariably took independent activities to refer to situations in which one partner was in the house and the other out of it, or in which both were away from the home.

There was, as one would expect, great variation between couples in the amount of 'spare' time they claimed to spend independently. The women's main independent activity was visiting friends or relations (mentioned more by the relatively recently married than by the older women); this was followed by meetings largely for women, such as the Women's Institute, Tupperware parties, dressmaking classes; and then by what was often referred to as 'girls' night out', when a group of women would get together for a visit to a public house or club, usually to celebrate some event such as Christmas or someone's engagement (again this was a younger woman's activity). Perhaps such activities help to confirm people's identities as women – identities which can only be confirmed in a limited way in conversation with the spouse. Most of the older women either said they had no separate activities outside the home (two women), or mentioned organised activities such as evening classes, political meetings, helping to run organisations for young people (four women), or referred to spending time helping to care for elderly relatives (two women). Incidentally, most of the wives' separate associates were either relatives or other women (further discussion of this point occurs in chapter 7); it seems likely that one of the reasons for limitations on independent activity is the public recognition of the husband and wife as a couple, so that when activity involves an invitation from other people they will be invited as a couple – except for those occasions which are defined as men-only or women-only activities. Unless they can educate their friends to treat them independently (as Mr and Mrs W, described below, appeared to have done), then the pair must either go together or refuse invitations if they do not wish to be together.

The main male activity was going for a drink at the public house or club (mentioned by thirteen of the twenty men, nine of whom were in the more recently married group, but evenly split between social classes). Unlike the women, only one mentioned independent visiting at the homes of friends or relatives. Sport was the second most popular activity (either as participant or spectator); and all other things were mentioned only once or twice; for example, 'pottering with the car', political or union meetings, evening classes, going to the pictures, going to church.

Variation between couples in amount of leisure-time separation

Although, as one would expect, almost everyone seemed to place himself some way away from the two extreme positions, three groups could be distinguished: those whose comments indicated particularly high leisure-time separation (three couples); those indicating particularly low separation (six couples); and those in between (eleven couples).

Two couples will be described to show the middle of the spectrum: the Ds and the Ls. The 'middle' should not be taken to imply that these were people who spent approximately 50% of their leisure time together and 50% apart; in this particular sample, as will be shown below, the people in the middle were those who said they did things independently 'on occasions' or 'now and again', but nonetheless spent most of their spare time together. This fits in with the findings of others. For example, Marini (1976) found that when married couples were asked how much time they spent doing things with their spouse 48% said a lot, 32% a moderate amount, and 19% said a little time.

Mr and Mrs D were in the older, middle-class group, and described their independent activities of Women's Institute, evening classes, visiting and pub-going as follows:

> JA: What would you say you tended to do mainly in your spare time?
> Mrs D: Well, I've my WI . . . What else? I've been to evening classes – dressmaking . . . I'm afraid we're rather home-birds.

And:

> Mrs D: Oh I don't go out much at all really . . . you know, I go to the WI, I'm secretary of the WI you know, the local branch . . . Well there's quite a lot of activities concerned with it one way or another . . . you know, we go on different things . . . I haven't much in the way of

hobbies, I don't have any sporting activities /// Och, I go up to mother maybe once a fortnight, and have a run maybe up in the afternoon. Other than that I don't really go out much.

After the question about what they tended to do in their spare time, Mr D said:

Mr D: Well, we'd probably watch something . . . or read. Sometimes go out, sometimes I go for a pint . . . sometimes we go out together at the weekend – sometimes meet some friends and go out – that's about it.

And in his separate interview he was asked:

JA: Are there many things, apart obviously from work, are there many things that you and your wife do independently of one another?

Mr D: No . . . I shouldn't think so. Recreational sort of things you mean? She would read a lot more than I do, I suppose . . . she reads this women's books and that I suppose . . . that would probably occupy her time quite a bit. Independently . . .

JA: When you go out do you tend to go out together?

Mr D: Oh . . .

JA: If you're walking down to the pub she wouldn't necessarily come with you?

Mr D: No. Probably, as I say, on a Saturday night we'd go down together – when we could get away. We're goin' to a dance this Friday . . . a dinner dance, and we were at a party last Saturday night ///

JA: You don't ever feel the need to get away on your own?

Mr D: No. Don't get me wrong here . . . yes, well, I go out alone, but not for the sake of being alone, just to be . . . well, just as I say, pop down to the pub maybe once, or maybe twice a week, knowing I'll meet three or four of my friends and have a couple of drinks and come home . . . But . . . 50% of the time I take somebody back here with me, or him and his wife back . . . something like this. I don't live an independent life at all, in no respect.

It is interesting to note how the emphasis made by this couple is upon joint rather than separate activity, and indeed how it took some time to get Mr D to discuss his separate visits to the public house. If it is seen as non-normative (see below) to spend much leisure time apart or to enjoy much separate activity, then the likelihood that couples will underemphasise or underestimate such activities has to be borne in mind.

The second example of couples whose leisure-time separation was neither particularly high nor particularly low is Mr and Mrs L, a younger, but also middle-class couple. They talked of occasional separate outings with their friends:

> Mrs L: I'm quite free to go out with my friends for a night out myself if I want to /// I also go to Bingo occasionally /// I like to – if I just feel like going out I say to Leslie: 'I'm off to the Bingo', and he says: 'Oh well, bring me back something from the chipper on your way back.'

And later:

> JA: When you said earlier that you were quite free to go out on your own with girlfriends or whatever, whenever you want to, *do* you often do this?
>
> Mrs L: No, not often, but I do get . . . Now, I could stay in for maybe three months, then one Wednesday I would say: 'Right, I just want to get all dressed up and go out with females . . .'

Mr L said:

> Mr L: We [Mr L and his work friend] often go out for a drink – it's usually before I come home for my tea.

And he was asked:

> JA: If you ever feel like getting out on your own, do you feel you can do that without difficulty?
>
> Mr L: I do, most nights [L] . . . Oh no, I mean, Laura's the same – we go out socially together, but if there's anything on, you know; I've been to a couple of nights out recently. Laura's been to . . . she's probably been to one or two more actually . . . she's got a pal she often goes with.

Thus these people in the 'middle' are those who say that they do not go out separately very often but that they do have some regular or occasional separate outings; most of their leisure time however they see as being spent at home with, or sometimes going out with, their spouse.

Some couples indicated rather higher levels of leisure-time separation, and three in particular stood out from the others. The first of these were Mr and Mrs E, shown in the previous chapter to have described themselves as talking to each other relatively little. They also seemed to spend relatively little spare time together. This was partly because Mr E said he spent much of the evenings as well as the daytime away from home studying or working; but this was not all. Mrs E also worked, but in the evenings she was said to visit her mother (who lived nearby) very often:

> Mr E: And she's down there [at her mother's] . . . if there's one day in a week passes that she doesna go there . . . then there must be something wrong.

Mr E added that his wife used to force him to visit her parents as well, but that he did not get on well with them and eventually 'just didna bother going'. Mrs E also said she went out to local community activities and to visit people, neither of which activities her husband liked. She compared this situation with a previous time when they used to do things together:

> JA: Do you tend to go out together most of the time when you go out, or do you sometimes go out . . .
>
> Mrs E: No, I think that . . . well, we've the problem of baby-sitters . . . we've tended to go out sort of separately really. Aye there are the things I go to here . . . and I would maybe go visiting, say, and he doesn't like doing that. He likes going to boxing . . . he's going to that sort of thing whereas I might go visiting /// He likes taking [names her son] swimming . . . and I canna really be bothered. But mostly we used to just go to dancing really when we *were* going out. We haven't been to one for a long time. And now we never go to the theatre, and I used to quite enjoy going to a play.

Mr E summed up the situation when he was asked in his separate interview whether there was anything they now did together:

> Mr E: Well, we've pulled away. We dinna really do anything. I occasionally ask her to come swimming. She won't do it very often /// It's a simple thing we could share but we just don't. No . . . no . . . no, we're basically getting to be strangers really as far as socialising's concerned.

Thus this couple appear to do quite a number of things outside the home, but they do not do them together, and one can see that this situation is regretted. The second couple was very different in that they expressed no regret, nor did the situation appear to have changed during the time they had been married. Mrs W said she went out less than her husband, but that he often did not come home until 'late' in the evening if he was working or seeing his friends. She also, however, talked of her separate friends whom she went out to visit at least once a week. They stressed this matter of separate friends in their joint interview:

Mrs W: We're hardly ever out together.

Mr W: No, we have quite separate groups of friends, though we know each other's friends a little. They are quite distinct, aren't they?

JA: You don't always get invited out together and things like that?

Mrs W: Well if we do you hardly ever go out with me. If I'm going up to see [names two friends] for instance.

Mr W: Yes, I don't know why that is.

Mrs W: You just never come. When he's invited he phones up and says he can't come.

Interestingly Mrs W, like Mrs E, explained the separation in terms of the difficulty of getting baby-sitters and added:

Mrs W: If we didn't have her [names her daughter] we'd probably go out more together.

Mr W: Yes, I think so – for a while anyway.

Mrs W: Till we got bored.

The third couple, Mr and Mrs F, was different again in that it appeared to be mainly the husband who went out, while the wife seldom went out with him; however she said that he did sometimes bring people home with him afterwards, so that she was not totally cut off from his leisure pursuits. In addition she helped to run a Sunday School and a Boy Scout troop in which her husband was not involved. Mr F said he went out for a drink most nights, and this was confirmed in the joint interview when they were asked:

JA: What do you tend to do in the evenings or at weekends?

Mrs F: You've got a better hobby than I have. [L] He likes to go for a pint . . . yes, quite a few evenings ///

JA: Do you ever go out together in an evening or at weekends, or is there not much opportunity for that?

Mrs F: No opportunity. The last time we were out was in July [it is now November] /// On the other hand I'm quite happy . . . the same doesna apply for Frank . . . he's nae so keen on sittin' at the fireside. He has a game o' dominoes at the local . . . Ah well.

Attitudes towards these different situations will be discussed in more detail later on. The point to be emphasised here is that these three couples describe more frequent separation than the middle-range couples; they do not say they spend most of their time together; and they do not say that when they go out they often go together.

A larger number of couples stood out as having a particularly low level of leisure-time separation (two in the younger working-class group, one in the younger middle-class group, and three in the older working-class group). This appeared therefore to be a mainly working-class phenomenon, which is interesting given the number of studies which assert that companionship in marriage is higher among middle-class than working-class couples (see Blood and Wolfe 1960; Cunningham and Johannis 1960; Gavron 1966; Levinger 1968; Palisi 1977). There was no length-of-marriage difference, and this may be due to the nature of the sample which is confined to couples at earlier and later, rather than middle, stages of marriage. For as Orthner (1975) says, the importance attached to joint leisure varies over the marital career, and is seen as particularly important in early marriage and again when the stage of having young children is passed. For this group separate leisure-time activities were said to be few or rare. For example one of the younger couples was Mr and Mrs C. They made the following kind of comments:

JA: Are there some things you do on your own without him, and are there some things that he does on his own?

Mrs C: No, not really. He doesn't really have any hobbies or anything much, no. We usually do things together, yes.

For herself she added later:

Mrs C: You know, sometimes there's Tupperware parties, things like this, but that's about all really. He doesn't go to stag nights and things like that.

JA: No, so most of the things you do you do together?

Mrs C: Yes. I did used to go out quite often with the girls in my work, you know. Sometimes on a Saturday night . . . about twice a year or something, you know.

Mr C confirmed these sorts of perceptions in his separate interview:

Mr C: I'll ging oot every Saturday night for a couple of pints, that's all. I'm nae oot drinking sort of thing. I'm off maybe for an hour or so every Saturday night except when we're out together like. But apart frae that . . . och I'll maybe spend a few evenings pottering about wi' the car now and again /// I dinna hae any clubs or anythin' myself /// Just a pint on a Saturday night – that's the only time I'm oot myself. As for her she's never oot . . . och, she gings to Tupperware parties or oot wi' the girls she worked with – once in six months or somethin' ///

> But apart frae that we stay together – it's nae a case of 'You go oot one night and I'll go oot the next' sorta thing.

The Hs were an older couple with a similar story, and with a strong negative evaluation of separate activity and a positive evaluation of being together. In their separate interviews they made the following kind of comments:

> Mr H: I don't think any two marriages can be the same, but I would say that mine is different from most I know inasmuch that I prefer that if *I* go out, I go out with the wife. I am not a great lover of going out with the boys ///
>
> JA: What kind of things do you do separately?
>
> Mr H: I have my evening class – and I used to play football when I was younger but not now. I would say most of the things . . . you see most of your life is tied up with the house, the garden and the car – there's not much time for much else.

These couples have been placed in a group separate from the majority of the sample, and it can be seen from the above comments that Mr H too saw his marriage as different from others in respect of separate versus joint activity. His wife also made comparisons with some other types of couple, and said that she felt sorry for wives whose husbands were always out while they were always in with the children. She went on:

> Mrs H: And I think: 'Well, he's wrong' – but yet somehow she's wrong and all. But yet maybe he's not the kind of man who says: 'Well, get a baby-sitter and we're going out', you know. I mean Harry would never ever go out without me – except to something like his evening classes – for him to go out on his own, he has never ever done it. If I couldn't go out with him he wouldn't go.

The seven couples mentioned above illustrate the range of leisure-time separation described in the sample. If one combines the estimates of high, medium and low leisure-time separation with similar estimates for work separation one finds only one couple (the Es) with very high levels of both work and leisure separation, and none with very low levels in the two areas. Three appeared to compensate for a high level in one area with a low level in the other (the Cs, Fs and Ns); three remained high in one area but medium in the other; and six were low in one area but medium in the other.

Couples' support for some degree of separate activity

Only one person (Mr E) said that, because they had grown so far apart, he did not enjoy doing things with his wife; all the others said they liked joint activities. Respondents were also asked whether they 'ever felt like doing things on their own'. Given that it might be seen as non-normative or as implying criticism of the spouse or of their marriage to say that they *did* want to do things on their own, perhaps it is surprising that twenty-five out of the forty gave an affirmative answer.

There was no difference in the numbers of men and women saying they liked to get out on their own; but the impetus behind their desire appeared somewhat different. For women the impetus was often given as a desire to get away from something, i.e. the house:

> Mrs B: I like to get out of the house for a few hours and meet other people . . .

And

> Mrs F: Occasionally I'll say: 'I'm fed up with this', and I'll maybe just go into town for the forenoon – that's usually enough. It gets you out of the house.

Perhaps it is the negative evaluation of the identity of housewife (see next chapter) which motivates such people rather than a positive evaluation of an identity to be sought outside the home. The women could also give more positive replies; Mrs L for example said: 'I just feel all of a sudden that I want to get dressed up specially to go out', and talked of her enjoyment in finding out what other women were thinking, about fashions, jobs, boyfriends. The positive answer was even more common amongst the men in the sample. They of course differed from the women on the whole in that since they spent less time at home anyway, they could not give the desire to get out of the house as a justification for being away from their spouse; they therefore had to talk about their positive enjoyment of 'men-only' activities. For example, in talking of going to the public house, Mr D said:

> Mr D: I like company. I always did like company. Yeah, even such company that you could argue with, you would differ with . . .

Or:

> JA: Why do you like going to the club?
> Mr F: I've met a lot of people there, like. Aye, good people, like . . .

Or, after Mr J had mentioned going out to play football:

> JA: You wouldn't give that up?
> Mr J: Oh no.
> Mrs J: Oh no – you'd have to cut his legs off first. [L]
> Mr J: I think I look forward to the weekend for that.

Or Mr E:

> Mr E: I'm no culture vulture by any means, but now and again I like to go
> and listen to music, go to a concert.

The men could also give the more negative replies, but this was not typical. For example:

> Mr P: I've been able to get away once or twice for a complete break . . .
> into the car and you drive south . . . and just the fact that you're driving
> a car and there's nobody relying on you for anything, you're not
> expected to get home and get the kids ready for bed . . . it's just a
> break . . . and it's great, and you have a few days away and you come
> back . . . and you wish you had a few more days away. [L] But you do
> come back refreshed, and after half an hour back to your normal state
> . . . But I think it is good to get away on your own occasionally.

Or:

> Mr F: I do really like goin' away for a couple of days, like. Just . . . I don't
> know, something different. I dinna like digs either, mind – it's just
> . . . I don't know, just a change I suppose.

The fifteen who said they never felt like getting out on their own were again of course evenly divided into men and women. It should be added that this kind of answer did not necessarily mean that they never did go out on their own; at other points in the interviews they often revealed that they did have occasional separate outings. For example Mr A, who said that he went for the occasional drink after work, also said that he never felt like going out on his own and only wanted to go out with his wife. Other answers tended to be along the following lines:

> Mr D: No, I prefer going out with her than without her. There's a case in
> point: we had a wedding, we were all set to go to this wedding the
> week before she went into hospital. Well, she wanted me to go. I
> said: 'No, I wouldn't go.' I'd no desire to go myself. We tend to do
> things in a family sort of manner.

In the previous section it has been described how Mr D went on to say: 'Don't get me wrong here . . . I go out alone, but not for the sake of being alone.' These comments help to explain the apparent discrepancy between on the one hand saying that one does have separate activities and on the other that one never feels like going out on one's own. For in his answers Mr D appeared to be saying that he never felt like going out for the negative reason of being apart from his wife, but only for the positive reasons (in his case, of enjoying the company and arguments to be found at the public house), and that he never felt like going out alone to activities which people are expected to attend as couples but only to those which they are expected or permitted to attend as singles. It seems likely that others with a medium amount of separate activity meant the same thing if they too said they never felt like going out on their own. Those with comparatively low levels of leisure-time separation may however be rather different; and it looked as though they rejected separate activity even when there could be positive reasons for it and when one could be permitted to go on one's own. For example:

> Mr B: I think that a good husband should share quite a deal of his leisure time with his wife. I don't know if I do or not. I don't play golf, and I would think that people . . . men, who play golf, are golf fanatics and never at home is just a bit out of the question. I think if I went to play golf I'd probably take my wife along with me.

In the previous section Mr and Mrs H have been mentioned as a couple with a low level of leisure-time separation. They both said they never felt like getting away on their own, and Mrs H said she thought it was 'wrong' for a husband to go out frequently and leave his wife on her own; Mr H's reasons for rejecting separate activity were partly lack of time ('most of your life is tied up with the house, the garden and the car – there's not much time for much else') and partly dislike of 'men-only' gatherings. For example he said:

> Mr H: We have had a few down at the works who say: 'Oh we'll all have a night out.' And the whole object of the exercise is – it seems to be that you drink as much as you can in the shortest time as possible, and you wake up in the morning with a head like Birkenhead. It just seems an awful waste of time. I'm not a lover of it.

Others more briefly said that going out separately was just something they never thought of doing. The reasons for rejecting separate activity, therefore, were that it was morally wrong, the activities one could engage in separately were not enjoyable, there was no time for it, or one never thought about the possibility of doing it. As shown, however, the majority of the sample did have a preference for a certain amount of separate leisure activity, either seeing it as an occasional 'break' or 'change' or means of 'getting out of the house', or expressing their enjoyment of non-couple activities like football, drinks at the pub, a night out with the girls, and so on. By and large these were described as 'occasional' activities, absorbing far less leisure time than was spent with the spouse. It appears that, on the whole, couples prefer some separate but more joint leisure-time activity.

Satisfaction or dissatisfaction with amount of separate and joint activity experienced

Having looked at how couples tend to support a limited amount of separate activity, the next step is to see how satisfied they are with their own ratio of separate to joint activity. For example, do those with relatively high levels of separation wish for less, and those with relatively low separation for more? (Although the hypothesis is of a different kind, in that personal satisfaction is being examined here rather than specifically marital satisfaction, it should be noted that the view of this study is not in line with that of those who suggest that the greater the interaction between spouses (i.e. joint activity) the greater the marital satisfaction – see for example Lewis and Spanier 1979; Marini 1976; Orthner 1975.)

Interviewees were asked to talk first about whether or not they could get out or away as often as they wanted, or whether they experienced too much separation from their spouse. With three exceptions the respondents said that the extent of separation and independence was satisfactory to them. It has been said that only two individuals (Mr and Mrs E) could be classified as having particularly high levels of both work and leisure separation, and that none had particularly low levels of both work and leisure separation. Dissatisfaction was therefore expected, and found, in the comments of the E's; the other dissatisfied person was Mr K, who had a low level of work separation and a medium level of leisure separation. His dissatisfaction was in the expected direction; that is he said he wished for more independence. These respondents will be discussed below, but first one can look at the kind of comments made in expressing satisfaction. For example, Mr and Mrs L said that they did not think they were out of each other's company to an unacceptable extent; on the other hand they said they felt they could be apart whenever they wished, they could go out separately as much as they wanted:

> Mr L: But I've been out a few times and she always sort of jokes about it, but I don't . . . she's got no real objections. She knows I'm pretty safe. Apart from that too many people know me [L] /// Now, eh . . . if there's anything on, neither of us have much objection to the other person going out, if it's an all-male or an all-female night. So straightaway no problem.

Mrs L said very much the same:

> Mrs L: I'm quite free to go out with my friends for a night out myself if I want to. I mean Leslie doesn't mind that, and vice versa he can go out any night with his friends; I mean I never say to him: 'You're not going' or anything; and he doesn't do that to me. So I am quite free to go out and enjoy myself if I want to – though I don't go out a lot.

In other words there appeared to be no problems (such as partner's objections) inhibiting their going out separately as long as they stayed within the limitations (such as not going out too often and not going out with a member of the opposite sex). Others summed up the situation in a similar way; for example Mr R said his wife did not mind him going out and he did not mind her going out, adding:

> Mr R: I don't take advantage of it, and neither does she.

And

> Mr R: We've had our own little interests – but not too much.

Mr O made particularly clear this notion of satisfaction accompanied by recognition of limitations:

> Mr O: I can get out, as much as I want. If I wanted, you know, I could get out every night but, er, let's face it, it's not on.
>
> JA: Because you don't want to, or because you think you ought not to?
>
> Mr O: Both ways, both ways. I get out of course. She lets me out after work, but I never go out otherwise on my own /// I never go out more than three times a week on my own. But I'm not tied down.

Some, when talking of acceptance of the situation, said that it had changed since the earlier days of marriage, that is it had improved. For example Mr P said:

> Mr P: Well, we found that as our marriage progresses we actually see less of each other /// There certainly was a time when I occasionally wanted to go out . . . but knew that if our relationship was to remain fairly good for the next day or two . . . I'd better not.

Mr P's wife therefore was said to have become more tolerant of separate activity; for Mr I the reverse change was said to have occurred: he had become more tolerant of joint activity. For instance he said:

> Mr I: I found that if you want to go out and have a good drink, take your wife with you, because if you go out and have a good drink and she's with you she won't say nothing. But if you go out and have a good drink and she's not with you, there will be a row the next morning. So . . .
>
> JA: Yes, yes. So now she comes out with you. Do you ever go out on your own at all nowadays?
>
> Mr I: No, no. I haven't been out on my own for . . . not since my accident. Oh I've been down to the pub for a pint, but back again . . .

Mrs B also expressed satisfaction in an increase in joint activity; this had been prevented earlier in their marriage because her husband was working away from home, and she said she had disliked the lack of opportunity to do things together as a couple. For instance she said:

> Mrs B: It's lonely for the wives [when husbands work away from home]. I remember I used to get invitations to weddings and everything, and I went to one or two myself and the rest I just used to refuse. It's horrible goin' yourself, it's terrible.

Mrs S was different again. She said that she had not had as much separate activity as she wanted when the children were young and she had felt tied to the home:

> Mrs S: What it was was jealousy of Sam being able to say: 'I'm running down to the library' or 'I'm going to such and such', and he could *do* it without even considering anything else.

As with the Ps and the Ss, there appeared to have been an increase in separate activity for the Es; but for them the separation seemed to have become too extensive, so that they expressed *dis*satisfaction. In the previous chapter Mrs E has been quoted as saying that the companionship had 'gone away' and that the children had become the most important part of her marriage. Mr E has been quoted above as saying that they were 'getting to be strangers'; they no longer spent time together enjoying each other's company. For instance he commented:

Mr E: I mean she goes to work, she comes home, she does a bit of housework, she's got the kiddies, and she's dog tired and goes to her bed. Well that's it, that's what the life becomes. And there's no place in that for any sorta . . . 'let's get somebody to watch the kids and we'll away and do something different' – that's gone, right out of the window.

With Mrs P and Mrs I an excess of separation was said to have led to jealousy and annoyance or to anxiety about what the spouse might be doing during the separation. It is as though their dissatisfaction is over the *potential* detrimental effect of separation on the marriage. For Mr and Mrs E there appears to be no jealousy nor anxiety about possible effects, only a recognition of an *actual* detrimental effect. If one could carry out a longitudinal study of changes in degrees of separate activity within marriage one could examine in more detail what appear to be stages (e.g. anxiety stage, acceptance, or recognition of an undesired situation) in marital life.

Mr K, one of the more recently married men, was dissatisfied because he said he could not go out on his own as often as he wished. Being an untalkative person he offered little analysis of this sentiment, although he did say that it was a question of 'freedom':

JA: What, on the other hand, do you think are the worst things about being married?

Mr K: It just comes back to that same thing really – nae getting out.

JA: And what is it about not getting out that's such a burden? I mean is it that it's more boring because you don't get out so much, or what?

Mr K: No, it's more or less your freedom. You get out when you like – you don't have to be home at a special time, or . . . you can just please yourself [when you are single]. I don't like having to be in at a special time.

It is interesting to speculate about how the situation in this marriage will develop. Will this couple for example become more like the Ps and develop a tolerance of separate activity, or will they become like the Is and accept joint activity, or will Mr K rebel to the extent of going out separately as much as he wants and thus risk a recognition of a serious detrimental effect upon the marriage?

It has been said that the marriage of Mr and Mrs K was not one categorised as having very low levels of both work and leisure separation; but it was in the next most extreme position in which there was a low level of separation in one area coupled with intermediate separation in another. Mr K's dissatisfaction was therefore not wholly unexpected. Yet if this is so, one ought to expect dissatisfaction amongst other couples in a similar position. There were in fact five other couples in such a position, but none of them expressed dissatisfaction with their relatively low levels of separation. These five however had all been married for the longer period of time, and it may be that in this period they had been able to adjust to, and accept, a compromise situation which Mr K had not yet reached.

Recognition of restrictions

With the exception of Mr and Mrs E and Mr K, the respondents appeared satisfied with the amount of separate and joint activity they experienced. There were indications, however, that people recognised limitations on the amount of separate activity they could engage in. The notion of limitation was thus examined again in discussions about whether marriage restricts one or ties one down, as far as separate activities are concerned. (Wider examination of the perceived constraints of marriage will be given in the following chapter.) Of course this kind of question can only be sensibly discussed in relative terms by a comparison either between marriage and the situation one previously experienced (e.g. living with one's parents) or the envisaged alternatives (e.g. living on one's own). Most of the respondents made such comparisons in their discussion of this topic. The commonest opinions were either that marriage did restrict one's activities, or that it neither restricted nor facilitated them. The latter view was particularly likely to be expressed by the couples who had been married longer (half of whom gave that type of answer). The younger people divided more evenly into three groups: those who said marriage restricted one, those who said it made one more independent, and those who said it did both or neither.

The kind of comments made by those classified as seeing marriage as restriction supported the comments or implications made earlier about limitations on independent activity (that is, that one is restricted by one's spouse's reactions or attitudes, by the inability to be apart from one's spouse because of the presence of children, and by norms which involve disapproval of extensive separate activity and of activities which might involve being with members of the opposite sex). Mrs N, for example, said that marriage tied one down (adding that if one had children – which she did not – one would be even more tied):

> JA: When you go out nowadays would you go out with your husband? Or do you occasionally go out on your own?
> Mrs N: No, we usually just go out together. Sometimes I'll go out to see my mate.
> JA: That's all is it? [Yes.] You wouldn't have a night out with the girls or . . .?
> Mrs N: Maybe – I've been invited, but I haven't been. But I went before, when I was just engaged.

And:

> JA: Some people say marriage makes you more independent and freer, some say it ties you down. What do you think is true for you?
> Mrs N: Ever since . . . well since we got engaged he . . . never sort of let me go out much on my own, and he now doesn't really either, so I think for me it sort of ties me down. Because whereas before, when I was single and that I used to do what I wanted, but not now.
> JA: Do you find that irksome?
> Mrs N: Well I did at first, when I was younger and that – but not now – I suppose I've got used to it.

Mr P, although he had said earlier that the situation had improved so that he could go out apart from his wife, also said he saw marriage as restriction. For example:

> JA: Are there any disadvantages in being married? ///
> Mr P: Oh yes. I can't think . . . well, the worst is . . . occasionally lack of freedom. Not that I want to get away from you [to wife], just that should I want to go somewhere . . . I always have to limit it to a reasonable length of time . . .

Similarly Mrs S who had expressed the opinion that the situation had improved and that she and her husband now had more separate activity, recognised that restriction still remained:

> JA: Nowadays do you feel tied down still, or does the fact that you go out to work and the children are fairly independent – does that mean that you don't feel tied down?

Mrs S: I'm not *so* tied down. You're tied down having a house, you're tied down at mealtimes /// But I'm free to say: 'Well, there'll just be salad for dinner tonight because I want to go and visit somebody.' I'm free to that extent, and I think a lot of the limitations in my life are my own fault. I think I got into the habit of not having very many interests outside, and not going anywhere /// It's time that I found something else to do. I think a lot of married women are like this because they have been tied to a family for a long time and got out of the way of thinking for themselves.

This woman is making two rather different points: that being married and having children inevitably restricts the opportunity for separate activity, but also that some independent activity is a good thing and can be achieved if one has the will to do it. Thus we return to the notion of a balance between separation and jointness, and the importance of getting the balance right. Mr I appeared to be saying that he had at last got the balance right: he now spent much less time apart from his wife, and his acceptance of the restriction had made his marriage much happier:

Mr I: I think it takes about two years to bring the man into, you know . . . I can't explain it really – to take him down to everyday life, as you would say. If you get them to marry, now they are still leading a single life, you know, and he expects to . . .

JA: Carry on doing that?

Mr I: It takes about two years. Well it took me a lot longer than that. But oh now, I'm quite happy now. Not a happier man in this world than I am . . . I come home every night, and we never ever fight.

Although it has been suggested in this chapter that dissatisfaction is most likely to occur when there are particularly low levels of separation between husband and wife, the above quotations are a reminder that perceptions of what is an acceptable compromise will differ, depending upon such things as people's expectations and norms about marriage, the extent of previous independence or what they see as the likely alternative living arrangement to their marriage, and their perceptions of what they or their spouse would be doing while engaged in separate activity. It is likely, for example, that if before marriage they felt accountable to no one in their leisure activities, if they expected to be able to continue like this after marriage, and if they thought such activities would go on being enjoyable and would not be disapproved of by their spouse, they would set their acceptable compromise at a higher ratio of separate to joint activity than someone who, for example, had had his separate activity strongly restricted by his parents before marriage. Differences in expectations, etc. will affect not only what people see as an acceptable compromise position, but also the ease or difficulty with which a compromise acceptable to both partners can be reached. For if a husband and wife start marriage with different expectations, then there is likely to be more conflict than if they start from similar points. However it is *not* being argued that satisfaction is entirely a matter of expectations; it is still suggested that if identity and stability needs are to some extent to be met within marriage, then some compromise must be achieved. Thus, for example, one would suggest that a husband and wife who both began marriage with expectations of high levels of separation would eventually abandon these views to some extent and would modify their behaviour accordingly in order to maintain the stability of their relationship. The influence of expectations lies not at the extremes but in the middle ground, where one sees different but equally acceptable levels of separate and joint activity between different couples.

So far in this section it has been argued that although most of the respondents said they accepted their combinations of some separate and some joint activity, they nonetheless recognised that they were restricted, that there were limitations on what they could do independently. Some confirmed this by saying that marriage does tie one down. Some others confirmed it by saying that even though, compared with a previous way of life, one was in some ways more independent, one was nonetheless still restricted or limited in what one could do. All these people mentioned previous parental restrictions now lifted, but accompanied by the imposition of other restrictions such as those mentioned by Mrs N, Mr P, Mrs S and Mr I. For example there was Mr L who said that he was now independent from 'parental control' but was nevertheless tied down as far as 'getting out' and as far as 'going with other women' were concerned. This sounds contradictory, but Mr L (and others like him) may have been implying that restrictions, although still present, were altogether less rigorous, or that restrictions in some areas of activity were less rigorous but as tight or tighter in other areas, or even that restrictions in general remained but were different in that they were self-imposed rather than imposed from without. Mrs W for example – who also talked of restriction *and* independence – appeared to be saying that restrictions remained but were imposed by having a house and child rather than by the external authority of her parents.

JA: What changes did it make in your life, being married?

Mrs W: Well in some ways it made me far more independent because William doesn't mind if I go out as long as he's not going out that night. And *he* doesn't mind what time I come home /// But you do feel more restricted having a baby. It makes – it makes *me* feel that I don't really want to go out too often.

When one turns to those who said that marriage neither restricts nor makes one more independent, or merely that it makes one more independent, one is ostensibly faced with the problem of reconciling those answers with the hypothesis that people do recognise and accept a restriction on independence of action. However the characteristics of these respondents and the nature of their answers make reconciliation quite easy. Only five of the forty interviewees said that on the whole marriage makes one freer or more independent. It was a sentiment expressed with one exception by younger people, and with one exception by women. They all appeared to be making a strong comparison between their present situation and that before marriage, when they were living with parents and were subject to parental wishes and rules. For example:

Mrs D: No, I felt more independent really. I think . . . because, well, as I said, I was an only girl in the family . . . my father had been . . . well, he was dead for quite a number of years before I married and I think my mother tended to depend too much on my company. I mean I got to the stage before I was married when I used to say, well . . . I think, you know, if I wanted to go maybe to the pictures or something with some of the girls . . . I felt I had to come home and sort of tell her, or ask her if I could go.

Mrs J's mother had also been a widow, and she said:

Mrs J: No I wouldn't say that [that marriage ties you down]. I would say it's fine to get peace and quiet. [L] A place of your own just to please yourself – if you're used to someone being there all the time telling you what to do.

Similarly Mrs O said:

Mrs O: No, I think it makes you more independent . . . because when you were at home, if you were going out you had to be back at a certain time, you know, sort of 'don't be late'. They sort of kept awake listening for you coming in and things like that. Whereas now you can please yourself you know . . .

Comments such as these suggest particularly forceful restriction but do not imply that marriage has meant the disappearance of all restriction.

More men than women said they felt neither restricted nor more independent in marriage (and as stated earlier it was a more common opinion among the older group). The kind of things they said were for example:

> JA: Do you feel tied down . . .?
>
> Mr B: Not really, 'cos I can adjust myself pretty well. It disnae matter what the situation is.

Or:

> JA: Some people say it ties you down, and some people say: 'No, it makes you more independent, it makes you freer.'
>
> Mr S: Well I wouldn't say it ever tied me down because this would be a hellish selfish thing to say, and it's not in my nature to be selfish about it. No, I think as I said before, that marriage would be to me the normal sequence of events, that I would get married and would be a father, and have a wife and have a house to consider, so that I wouldn't feel it ties me down.
>
> JA: Yes, I see. You just wouldn't consider . . .
>
> Mr S: No, no. I would say that it projected me into another phase of life which was necessary to go into, and no more than that, but as important as each stage in life is.
>
> JA: So really these two things don't have much meaning for you?
>
> Mr S: No.

Or:

> Mrs F: I didna feel more tied down . . . I dinna suppose I feel freer either. Felt quite secure, you know, I felt quite the big cheese I suppose, because you were now married. But I dinna think it made much difference – as we said Frank was away, working at the time, so it made so little difference . . .

A few minutes later she added:

> Mrs F: Obviously you are tied down I think – but it is a matter of choice – I'm happier tied down as you put it than I would have been.

Or:

> JA: Do you feel at all tied down by being married do you think?
>
> Mr A: No, it doesn't feel much different for me. I feel like . . . it's part of

> myself . . . where I am now . . . why should I escape from it? Just
> carry on. What's the use of bucking and getting away from it, you
> know? That's my way . . . my place here . . . why should I run away
> from it?

These comments are very interesting, but again they do not lead one
to conclude that the respondents perceived no restriction or felt they
were not tied down within marriage. Several kinds of answer are given
in the above quotes, and all of them seem to imply some sense of restriction in marriage. There is one which mentions the ease of adjustment
(but for that to take place there must be some change to have to adjust
to); there is the unwillingness to agree that there is restriction because it
sounds selfish to do so (but this does not mean that no such restriction is
actually felt); there is the statement that one should not say one is restricted when the marital state is what one expected or chose or when it
is what exists (but again it does not follow that there is no sense of constraint); and finally there is the wife who said that restriction was not
felt at first because her husband worked away from home (but one
could argue that her marital relationship did not fully begin until her
husband ceased working away). It seems reasonable to conclude that
there is a general awareness of restriction in independent activity within
marriage and that it exists alongside the equally common acceptance of
this restriction.

Acceptance of partner's separate activity

As a final examination of the notion of the acceptable compromise one
can look at what the interviewees said when directly asked how they
felt about their spouse going out on his or her own. One would expect
them to say that some separation was tolerable (or even desirable) but
that it should not be excessive; though one would also expect the point
where the line is drawn to vary somewhat. If people wish to help maintain a sense of identity and stability they might really prefer a situation
in which they themselves could engage in separate outside activity (to
help maintain their identity) but in which their spouse could not (to
help maintain stability). This would, however, be a difficult situation to
justify, and one might therefore anticipate a certain amount of
ambivalence in what people say about their spouse's separate
activities.

Only one person said she objected to her husband going out at all on his own, but when she began to discuss her opinion she did in fact sound very ambivalent. This was Mrs K, and she talked about her views at some length. Part of the discussion was as follows:

> JA: Do you go out together much?
>
> Mrs K: Well, nae really all that much now, but I don't like him going out himself ///
>
> JA: You don't like him going out on his own?
>
> Mrs K: No, I don't trust him . . . it's not that I don't trust him . . . I dinna ken – it's just putting temptation I suppose. And yet I dinna mind . . . when I say . . . well I could go out myself and I don't suppose I would go wi' anybody /// But I just dinna like it, I dinna think it is right him going out himself.

It is significant that Mrs K was the wife of the one man in the sample who expressed the view that he had too little opportunity for separate activity in his marriage.

Everyone else endorsed the 'some, but not too much' point of view when discussing their spouse's separate activity in general terms. For example:

> Mr R: This I've to say – don't try to govern your other partner's life – you'll never make a go of it.

In his own interview Mr R amplified this point when talking about his wife going out to meetings:

> Mr R: Why should I stop her? She has a life of her own. I knew what she was carrying out. I wasn't suffering. She was enjoying it, and the children wasnae suffering, and they were getting everything, so there was nobody losing. And she was still having a life of her own, which I think a lot of men just think she's a wife and she's there for one thing, and that's it . . .

This quote brings out the point that it is not just the amount of separate activity in itself which concerns people but also what the spouse is doing while out, and how other members of the family are affected by the activity.

People not only think it is good for their spouse to have some separate activity; they may also see it as good for their relationship. Mrs T indicated this when she talked about her acceptance of Mr T's occasional absence on business:

> JA: Does the fact that he's away quite often make for any difficulties, or does it have any disadvantages?

Mrs T: In some ways I think it's an *ad*vantage. You know I think there is something in this 'absence makes the heart grow fonder'. Oh there are some very small disadvantages [like having to take a decision about the children while the husband is away] /// But as I say, in some ways it's an advantage, because I think, you know, when he comes back it's super to hear all *his* news, and we bring him up to date here, and I think he appreciates home more, having been away.

The remarks of Mr R and Mrs T were *post hoc* justifications of an existing situation, and can be seen as amplifications of a generalised point of view. This generalised view was made more explicitly by some. For example:

Mr O: You've got to allow each other a bit of freedom, you know, but not *too* much of course – as long as there's a line that's drawn you see /// I think you need a certain amount of freedom.

Or:

Mrs E: I think they should have a certain amount of freedom, and should be able to go out at least one night a week themselves if they want to.

Such general statements provide of course little guide to action. They can be used to justify an existing situation (as we have seen above), but if one wants to complain about one's spouse's activities it can be very hard to argue that he has crossed 'the line'. Almost everyone in this sample was, as stated earlier, satisfied on the whole with the amount of joint and separate activity in their marriage, and perhaps this was partly *because* the line was so difficult to draw. There were occasional indications that people wanted to complain but did not know on what grounds they could do so, and therefore summed up by saying that they had no complaint. For example there was Mrs F:

Mrs F: I often niggle him about his – 'Oh, you're never in' or something. And then I say: 'Oh well' – especially just now, he has got nothing else to do [husband is off work].

JA: Yes, that's true. What sort of things irritate you about him going out? Is it the fact that he isn't here to talk to, or that he's been spending money . . .?

Mrs F: Just the fact that he is going out – no, not the money, because I get my wages, you know – I never have to go short. The day I have to go short I might niggle him about that I expect. No, I never – if I had to go short he wouldna go out for his pint, I must say that. No, I suppose it is a jealousy, you know, nae a deep-seated jealousy, but you just think that's him awa oot again. I have nothing to object to – I know where he is goin', I can get in touch with him at any time, and when I say jealousy it's nae 'cos of other women or anything like that. It is just a general sort of a jealousy – 'Why should he get oot all the time when I canna?' – and then if I got the chance I widna go oot anyway, you know, so it's just unreasonable.

Conclusions

Thus in concluding that most interviewees perceived themselves and their spouses to have found an acceptable compromise, one must make the reservation that some people might wish to complain (either in their everyday lives or in the interviews) but find themselves unable to because of an absence of grounds on which to do it. However, as expected, people tended to recognise restrictions even when they said they accepted them, and they tended to see some separation, both for themselves and for their partners, as a good or reasonable thing as long as it did not pass certain limits. Also as expected, the one couple with a very high level of perceived separation was dissatisfied with their situation. None had very low levels of separation (when work and leisure time were combined) and therefore no evidence to support the proposition that such couples would also be dissatisfied could be examined.

The reasons people gave for agreeing with a mixture of joint and separate activities varied both in type and in depth of analysis. Separate activity was endorsed partly because the activities engaged in were seen as enjoyable (e.g. playing football, talking to friends in the public house), or for the sake of getting away from the routines or boredom of being at home, or because a 'break' or a 'change' was seen as a good thing, or because some freedom or a life of one's own was seen as good for one, or finally because the separation was seen as good for one's marital relationship in leading one to appreciate or put up with one's home or spouse more (in this they match writers on privacy, such as Schwartz (1968) who argues that withdrawal helps to make possible life with an unbearable, or sporadically unbearable, person). Joint activity was endorsed because, apart from work, separate activity was not thought of, or because there was little time for separation, or because being with the spouse and doing things together was enjoyed, or conversely because doing things separately was on the whole disliked, or because it was thought that one *ought* to spend most of one's non-work time with one's spouse, or that separate activity would lead to the spouse's anxiety, jealousy or disapproval and thence to marital disagreement. These comments show very little theorising about the impact of joint and separate activity upon individual identity and marital stability, except where marital discord is seen as likely to follow excessive separation, whilst a certain amount is seen as good for the relationship, and where some separation is seen as a good thing for the individual.

The findings of this chapter are similar to those of the previous one, in that most couples seemed to adopt a 'middle way' and to be content or resigned to it. As with the previous chapter however, there were a few people in more extreme positions. It is interesting to see whether these are the same individuals who reported either a lack of talk with their spouses, or an absence of talk avoidance. One would not necessarily expect them to be the same, since for instance it might be that an identity-threatening or stability-threatening pattern of behaviour in one area was compensated for by a different and more conventional pattern in another area. In fact there was some overlap. Of the seven extreme or dissatisfied couples in chapter 3, only the As, and the Ss failed to appear in this category in the present chapter. Three of the remaining five couples (the Es, Ks and Ds) seemed to have stability-maintaining behaviour in one area and identity-maintaining behaviour in another. Only for the Ds, however, did this appear a satisfactory situation: they both said they enjoyed their relatively low level of separation, and that they liked to talk openly (although Mrs D complained a little of her husband's openness, saying that he could be hurtful). With the Ks the wife disliked the lack of talk avoidance, feeling that they said hurtful things to each other which led to rows, and her husband disliked the lack of opportunity for separate activity. It seemed with this couple that the wife wished to emphasise stability-maintaining behaviour and the husband to emphasise identity-maintaining behaviour. Thus neither was satisfied. The Es were even more dissatisfied: both disliked the fact that they could no longer talk to each other, and both bemoaned the lack of companionship intimated by their high level of separation. Perhaps their lack of talk helped to preserve a precarious stability, but the high level of separation seemed virtually to cancel this out.

The fourth couple – the Gs – appeared to have identity-threatening behaviour in both areas: they spent a great deal of time together, and yet communicated little. Neither of them, however, said they felt dissatisfied nor gave any indication that they felt personally 'squashed' or 'inhibited' from doing and being otherwise. It looked as though in their case identity could be fulfilled within the types of behaviour being called stability-maintaining.

The final couple – the Ts – were rather more complicated: Mr T was said not to avoid topics of conversation; he was also away from home a good deal. Yet this emphasis on identity-maintaining behaviour for him did not appear to be seen either by him or his wife as a risk to the stability of their marriage. Perhaps the evidence of later chapters will help to explain this couple's satisfaction. In the following chapter the perceived constraints of marriage and the associated interpretations given will be examined in more detail.

5

‣‣‣

Constraints on behaviour within marriage

This chapter takes a different starting point from the two preceding ones, in which the specific topics for discussion were imposed in advance and the interviewees were then asked – among other things – whether they felt constrained in any way in these areas of behaviour. In this chapter the topics will not be imposed. The aim is to address those initial hypotheses which posited that married people will wish to impose upon their partners particular types of behaviour, modes of being, or constellations of behaviour and being (which one may call identities) and that they will each feel constrained by the other's wishes and expectations; and that married people will be constrained by the fact that marriage is a publicly recognised institution involving certain typical expectations and pressures towards conformity to certain types of behaviour, modes of being, or constellations of behaviour and being.

Of course it is quite possible that individuals may find their partners' expectations and the expectations (as they perceive them) of the wider society thoroughly in line with their own preferred identities. But there are other possibilities; for example, some may find their partners' expectations problematic because they are *not* in line with publicly recognised expectations (or vice versa); and some may find both sets of expectations in some ways constraining. If individuals do feel constrained by their partners they may be content to accept this constraint because it enhances their sense of security; that is, they may feel that by doing and being what their partner wants them to do and be they are thereby ensuring, or increasing the chances of, his or her continued attachment and commitment to them. Similarly by accepting what they see as the publicly recognised and expected ways of behaving as a married person they may feel – even though constrained – that they are increasing the chances of public recognition of, and support for, their marriage. They may feel that such a marriage has become more objectively real and thus more secure than it would be if it did not conform to these public expectations.

This chapter therefore starts by looking at the ways in which people see themselves as being constrained (if at all) to behave in certain ways in their marriages. For with the sparseness of previous research in this area (see chapter 2) it would not be appropriate to assume knowledge of the likely constraints (of course the fact that decisions were taken in advance about what sort of questions to ask and what areas of behaviour to ask about means that certain underlying assumptions were made). The chapter will also ask whether it is possible to distinguish between constraints arising from the partner's expectations or wishes and those which arise from doing and being what is seen as normal or conventional for married people. It will examine the reasons people give for feeling constrained or wanting to constrain (if they do) as well as any reasons they give for finding constraints acceptable or bearable.

The constraints

The data were drawn first from direct questioning about constraints ('In your marriage / since you've been married do you think there are any things you do that you used not to do / don't enjoy or don't always enjoy doing?'; 'In your marriage / since you've been married do you think there are any things you don't do / can't easily do, which you used to do / you'd like or sometimes like to do?'), and second from any other comments in the interviews which indicated an experience of constraint (for example, in discussion of working, leisure time, ways in which the partner irritated one, grounds for separation, whether one felt different or was treated differently after marriage). Sometimes people's comments referred only to their own marriages, and sometimes to marriage in general; frequently they were a mixture of both, since people seemed prone to generalise about marriages even when asked specifically about their own. Of course there was a wide variety of answers, but it was found that the expressed constraints could be placed loosely into five categories, each of which will be discussed in turn.

Lack of freedom
This area of constraint overlaps considerably with perceptions about restriction on independent or separate activity discussed in the previous chapter. For men it was the most commonly discussed type of con-

straint, being cited by all but two; but there was a strong sex difference, with only six of the women mentioning it. There were no social-class nor duration-of-marriage differences. Most of the men said that marriage meant settling down, it meant not being able to act as a free and independent agent nor doing things one could have done before or would still be able to do if one had remained single (for a similar finding see Komarovsky 1962). They did not necessarily mean that they *had* done these things before they were married but that the opportunity had been there, or that if the opportunity had presented itself they would have been able to take advantage of it. It was thus largely a negative concept, in the sense of being a loss of something. The kind of things they mentioned as being prohibited in the settled-down state of marriage were opportunities to go out with other women, or to go drinking with their male friends when they felt like it. For example:

> Mr C: I wouldna like to go back to the situation as it was ten years ago. Mind, you think for a couple of minutes: 'I wish I was single again' . . . but I suppose every man thinks that now and again . . . and every woman as well I suppose.
>
> JA: What sort of things are you thinking of when you think back to being single again?
>
> Mr C: Well, I think I would like . . . if I'd been single I'd have travelled aboot . . . rather than stayed in one place. I'd like to see a bit o' the . . . well if I'd stayed single . . . to see a bit o' the world . . . if you stay single you've nae ties an' you can just up and away, sorta style. You just throw your case in the boot o' the car an' you're off . . .

Or Mr K who was quoted in the previous chapter as saying:

> Mr K: No, it's more or less your freedom. You get out when you like – you don't have to be home at a special time, or . . . you can just please yourself [when you are single]. I don't like having to be in at a special time.

In talking of other women they said such things as 'because I'm married some women I've fancied haven't responded to me', or 'other women – that's gone right out of the window', or 'you can look but you can't touch'.

In other words marriage meant a closing down of options, a loss of mobility, a loss of ability to do just what you feel like when you feel like it, a restriction on choice of action. As Bernard (1964) put it, ' "helling around" which might have been acceptable in the bachelor is viewed with disfavour in the married man'. When seen in terms of the future it also meant that life had become more predictable, it had a set pattern: one knew that one was not going to be able to take off and move to Australia, or take up with the blonde next door, or give up one's job and try for something better down in London. It meant one knew that what one was doing this week was likely to be what one would be doing a year from now, the woman one slept with tonight was the person one would be sleeping with in five, ten, fifteen years' time, and so on. Their remarks show some sense of regret, even if accompanied by acceptance.

The six women made comments similar to the men's, although only one mentioned the closure of opportunities to 'go with other men' (and it was impossible to tell whether she was expressing any notable sense of personal regret). In talking of other kinds of loss of independence they said, for example, that they would like to have travelled, to have done something exciting, to be able to go out just whenever they felt like it. For instance:

> Mrs N: Ever since . . . well since we got engaged he . . . never sort of let me go out much on my own, so . . . and he now doesn't really either, so I think for me it sort of ties me down, because whereas before, when I was single and that, I used just to do what I wanted, but not now.

Of course it can be seen – and was seen by respondents – that settling down and loss of freedom was not a result of marriage alone, but of having children. Most people however saw the two as so inextricably linked that whenever they talked of marriage they were implying motherhood and fatherhood also. 'Settling down' therefore was a constraint in that it meant not being able to do things one could otherwise have been able to choose to do.

Give and take

This was the most frequently mentioned group of constraints; and this phrase is used to stand for comments which indicated that in the relationship with the spouse people felt that they could not or should not force or demand their own way but must put up with the sharing or loss of preferred decisions, opinions, goods, activities, and so on. In other words, if the previous constraint referred to lack of freedom to do things *outside* the marriage relationship, this one refers to a lack of freedom to get one's own way *within* it. It was mentioned again by three-quarters of the sample, slightly more often by men than women, but equally by the two social-class and duration-of-marriage groups.

The sort of things interviewees said were either general comments about not being able to get their own way or having to take their spouse's views and wishes into account; or more specific comments such as that they could not determine the amount of money they had nor spend it as they would prefer, that they could not do the kind of things they liked doing because their spouse's behaviour, abilities or preferences did not fit in with theirs (for example to work abroad, to go skiing or walking, to play chess, to go to dances or to go to bed late); that they had to endure some of the things their spouse did or the kind of person he or she was (for example the partner's work, or their not working, their nagging, their attitude to the children, their choice of friends, their attitude towards money, their impulsiveness, moodiness, dogmatism, and so on). In other words give and take involves some loss of one's own preferences together with some acceptance of one's partner's. Sometimes this situation was said to involve a compromise and sometimes a total loss of an individual preference. Two examples can be seen in the comments of Mrs A and Mr E:

> JA: And what about taking decisions? Do you think you take decisions together, or that one of you tends to take decisions over some things, and the other over other things, or . . .?
>
> Mrs A: Well, sometimes we agree about things, but at other times if Alan has got something fixed in his mind, some thing that he wants, he gets it no matter what I say. It's the opposite way if . . . if there's something that I want, he just won't let me have it /// Now there's one thing that I do need in the house; I do need a new carpet sweeper, and he says we don't need one . . . and I'm frightened to buy one in case he says . . . I don't like to go against any decision that he makes.

Or:

> Mr E: [Says that he would love to go abroad to work but that his wife would hate it] . . . and while I want to do these things, like to go to these places . . . if she's no' goin' to be happy then the thing's still a disaster whether I'm makin' money or no. So that . . . you just have to consider her a wee bit . . . as I say, a compromise maybe, gettin' a job up north, somethin' like this . . . and six months away would be fine an' it'll no break her heart for that, because she knows we'll be gettin' home . . .

Often people mentioned that they divided up the areas of autonomy, so that for example one would take all the decisions concerning the house and children whilst the other took all those concerning the car, garden, financial matters. This would probably cut down the conflict but not necessarily the feelings of constraint, since one area tends to overlap with others:

> Mrs T: We had a row once when we were changing cars. This is one thing that is very much his department; and I don't think I was awfully keen on the new car – because I think it was going to be using far more petrol – you see the canny Scot in me – and I think we were a bittie shirty towards one another for a day or two until I accepted the fact that he uses the car a great deal. But I think it's me that usually gives in you see.

Responsibility

The third type of constraint is one which can be called responsibility and refers to certain of the things people say they positively have to do within marriage. It was mentioned by over half of all the interviewees, but whereas it was only discussed by half of the women, the middle-class and the young, it was mentioned by three-quarters of the men, the working-class and the older couples (Komarovsky (1962) also found the responsibilities of marriage mentioned more often as a male than as a female constraint.) The responsibilities of marriage were usually mentioned in a taken-for-granted fashion; that is, it was assumed both that marriage incurred responsibilities and that the meaning of such a term would be understood without any further description. Additional comments however indicated that what people meant by responsibilities were duties towards their spouse and towards their children; the duty to provide an income in order to give them a home, food, clothes, etc., the duty to manage money efficiently; the duty not just to provide for the present but for the future; the obligation directly to feed and clothe members of one's family; and also – less tangibly – to provide for and ensure their emotional and moral welfare. Often of course these duties were seen differently by husbands and wives: women were usually more concerned about the management of money, about feeding and clothing, and about the less tangible duties; men were particularly concerned about the provision of an adequate and stable income. For example:

Mrs A: You just had more responsibility [after marriage]. Living with parents you're totally dependent on your parents for everything. And then you get married and you just find yourself, suddenly, you're the one that has to find the money, you know, who's going to pay the rent, where this is coming from. I haven't actually been able really to face up to my responsibilities properly. I think if I'd been given more advice by my parents . . . I mean my mother . . . when like an insurance man or anyone came to the door or something, I would ask my mother who it was. I was always asking questions. I was just told, you know, to mind my own business. And I just didn't know anything about . . . well anything about marriage . . . all the things behind marriage.

Or:

JA: Does it change you at all?

Mr K: Oh I think it does. Um . . . you tend to worry a bit mair. You've got to get wages – get a wage – make sure it's coming in or the bairn will suffer.

Or:

Mrs F: I get the heavy end: he sees to his car, his petrol and all the car expenses and that, and that is really it. I have to pay rent, electric, you know, everything, and I know that any week I'm really short – and it does happen – that I can get extra if I really need it, but it is very, very seldom that I would ask. I usually manage to make do from week to week. I suppose I have the responsibility.

Or:

Mrs H: I think once you're married you have sort of responsibilities; and if you have no children I mean you can still go your own ways, and do things and that; but once you have children it's a case of . . . well I mean the evenings it's bedtime so you have to stop going out so much.

In a way the notion of responsibilities and the constraints implied in people's statements are the same as those in 'settling down'; responsibilities are a constraint in that they prevent you doing other things (like going out or giving up your job). They are also a constraint in a more positive way: they require you to learn certain things, to hold certain attitudes, to behave in certain ways – you must learn how to manage money, how to look after a house, how to cook, how to bring up children, how to help or comfort your partner. A whole body of knowledge has to be acquired and the appropriate frame of mind to go with it. They involve, therefore, not just a loss of identities, but the assumption of new ones.

Tasks

For women, in particular, being married means having to perform various tasks, jobs or chores which one did not have to do before, or at least not to the same extent. Eighteen of the twenty women mentioned such things in ways that suggested that they were at least sometimes seen as a constraint upon behaviour, whereas only four men mentioned tasks which followed marriage and were seen as constraining. (There were no differences by social class or duration of marriage.) This is undoubtedly due to the fact that marriage meant more of a change in tasks for women than for men (see Bernard 1973; Skolnick 1973; Komarovsky 1962). Men carried on going to work and perhaps helping with the washing-up at weekends or in the evenings. But for many women it meant having a house to clean, shopping to be responsible for, washing, mending or ironing to do, cooking or childcare to learn. Not surprisingly most of them had some complaints to make, either about tasks they disliked, or about having too many to do, or about being prohibited from doing other things because housework was so time-consuming. For example:

> Mrs M: I think most marriages are like that today. You just at times, you feel they're after you for several things, maybe: 'Have you got my trousers ready?' And the next thing ready, and I say: 'Oh here we go again', and then you'll explode . . . well this last week somehow I've been – aye – somewhat under pressure, and this is the reaction this week – I'm just tired this week and I feel it's just been too much . . . There is times when you get too tired. You can over do it.

Or:

> Mrs E: I used to go to quite a lot of dances, quite a lot . . . but the routine of havin' to get a baby up in the morning, feed her, change her, away to work, and then pick her up at night, and then come home and do washing and housework [meant that we stopped going to dances] . . .

Or:

> Mrs N: My mother, she was . . . she never used to make me do a lot in the house, you know. She used to say: 'Well, you'll have plenty to do once you're married.' She was quite right – as I've found out [L] . . . I

didn't mind it so much at first, you know. I used to come home and clean and things like that, but well, it's just that . . . after a couple of months I got awfully fed up of it. But once . . . now I'm getting used to it again. I ken it's got to be done, and this is it . . .

Of course it would not be fair to say that men were not involved in household and childcare tasks; some seemed to share in them considerably. But it was never to the same extent as their wives; and since they or the wives often spoke about them being 'good' by 'helping' with housework it was more often a source of self-satisfaction to them than it was to women who felt they were merely doing something they had to do (see Oakley 1974).

Sharing space

Finally there was a constraint, mentioned by just over half of all those interviewed (somewhat less by middle-class than by working-class people, and less by the older than by the younger couples – in fact everyone in the younger working-class group mentioned it). Like give and take it refers to things which people say they cannot do within marriage or which they have to endure in their partners. It can be distinguished from give and take, however, partly in that it is confined solely to matters involving the senses (sights, sounds, smells, etc.) and things which occur in shared space (see Smith 1971), and partly in that it involves matters usually referred to as trivial (thus involving a difference of degree compared with some of the matters discussed under give and take). Before marriage people often have bedrooms or even flats of their own; almost everyone will have had a bed to himself. But after marriage, although one may have rid oneself of many of the people who used to share a sitting-room, kitchen, garden, etc., the number of places which can be seen as totally one's own, as totally private, are probably diminished too. Now one does not even have a bed to oneself:

Mr P: After you've lived with each other for a week, well you realise you canna stretch out in bed without meeting . . . I spent about the first three months of our marriage sleeping right on the edge of the bed . . . I couldn't bear to touch anybody when we'd actually gone to sleep . . . it was alright before we went to sleep . . . I didn't like . . . of course you get over that . . .

Mrs P: Yes, I lay there with him sweating and snoring beside me, and I thought: 'Have I got to live with this always?'

It was in connection with the bed and bedroom that many such intrusions upon personal space were mentioned, particularly (but by no means exclusively) by the more recently married. It might be the partner's cold feet, or the fact that he smoked or ate cornflakes in bed, or that he littered the floor with his clothes. But behaviour in other parts of the shared domain, and in later years too, also led to tales of irritation. There could be sights, sounds, smells or even tastes which people felt they had to share but disliked or, less strongly, said they found mildly irritating. For example here is a bathroom irritation:

Mr S: I'm basically a person who keeps things in order and tidy. In my office the doors are always leaded properly and I've one file on my desk and everything has to be tidy. Now I've to put on a different hat when I come home because it can't possibly be tidy. But when people leave the top off the toothpaste it drives me up the wall – oh aye. They get ragings about it. And soap left in a wet place on the sink; you see . . . One thing that does annoy me – now there you are, this is one thing – she smokes in the bathroom when she's putting powder on, or whatever it is, on her face, and she leaves the cigarette on the porcelain . . . you know, the basin thing, so there's a burn on it. Now that annoys me.

The interesting thing about these constraints is that they were typically said to be very unimportant or trivial (there are some intrusions upon private space which could be seen as neither right or inevitable nor as trivial: for example, invasions of body space involved in such things as physical violence or excessive sexual demands). It is as though one is allowed to complain about them but not to take them seriously. Mr S, for example, went on to say:

Mr S: I mean I wouldn't . . . it would have to be important before I would consider that it was necessary to have a wing-ding over it. No, I think if people complain about things like that there would be hell to pay.

This presumably is because the behaviour complained about breaks no generally held and important rule of conduct. It may break some internally constructed rule, but not one that all would uphold or from which all would consider deviance a serious matter. So a person might say: 'In my parents' house we never smoked in the bathroom', but he could not easily say 'I think it is immoral for anyone to smoke in the bathroom.' What one has to do in marriage, however, is accept one's partner's 'little idiosyncracies' or annoying habits and curb one's own, since this is seen as an inevitable part of marriage. So on the one hand one has a right to complain (mildly) about annoying habits, but no right to complain seriously because in so doing one becomes the person at fault. Thus one's partner's habits, or the habits one wants to engage in oneself but cannot, are one of the constraints of marriage. Although they are said to be trivial they may be important to the individual's sense of identity, for – as Goffman (1971) says – it is often through quite minor acts that the individual exudes assumptions about himself.

Having identified the types of constraint mentioned by the inter-viewees (and it should be added that none of the forty failed to mention a constraint; indeed only a quarter mentioned fewer than three types, and all but one of these mentioned two) one may ask whether, when people *talk* about constraints, one is justified in assuming that they do in fact *feel* constrained. At first sight it might appear that there are some reasons for not considering the statements entirely at face value: for instance, people almost always qualified their negative statements (see section below). It is also hard to avoid the impression that there are some things about which, or occasions on which, one is expected to complain about marriage. One gets the impression that 'real men' are expected to say they regret being tied down, 'real women' are expected to reject the image of the housewife–drudge, and both are supposed to hanker for the carefree irresponsible days when they only had them-selves to please, and to acknowledge each other's individuality by finding some things about each other difficult to live with. This feeling is strengthened by the fact that people often commented that the way they felt was common to all or most married people: 'I suppose every man feels like that sometimes', 'I suppose we all have our funny little ways', 'We wouldn't be human if we didn't want our own way some of the time', and so on; and similarly that the comments themselves were sometimes stereotyped or stock responses: 'a woman's work is never done', 'you've got to learn to give and take', 'marriage ties you down', 'oh for the good old bachelor days', etc. When asked why they felt as they did people often found it difficult to explain, as one would expect after they had uttered a conventional wisdom rather than something that had been deeply felt. In other words, in some cases people did not appear to have theorised about their complaints, they merely said: 'Oh well, that's marriage', 'It's just something that happens', 'I just *do* find it irritating', 'I'm not the domestic type', and so on. However these characteristics do not necessarily confirm that people feel no real constraint; the qualification of their remarks may merely mean that they feel constrained at some times but not at others; the fact that they universalise or speak in stereotypes may mean that they really do feel what they acknowledge others to have felt and to have provided a vocabulary for; and the fact that they often do not theorise does not imply that they do not experience the feeling, merely that they cannot or do not wish to explain it in detail. In addition one can feel some confidence in the proposition that they do feel constrained by marriage by the fact that some comments occur so regularly and with such certainty, and that they are always able to give such clear examples of what they mean. For instance men gave detailed plans of what they would have done had they not settled down in marriage, where they would have travelled, how many times a week they would have gone out; people described the things they found difficult to manage or irksome among the responsibilities of marriage, many of the little things they found irritating in the sharing of rooms or houses, precisely how they felt about specific household tasks, and about many particular occasions on which they had felt a lack of individual autonomy. Therefore, although of course marriages vary greatly, and some individuals undoubtedly find it easier to cope with the constraints than others, what have been shown here are some features which are typically found in marriage; indeed not only were they exposed by the research as common features, they were also frequently stated by the interviewees to be so.

Perceived sources of constraint

The question of who or what is perceived as the source of the constraint now needs to be examined. As stated above, people frequently remarked that these constraints were common to married people, implying perhaps that they are seen as societal or as community rules or customs. However it is necessary (since it has been postulated that in some ways people will be constrained by their husbands or wives) to ask whether such is the explanation in all cases or with all constraints, and whether the interviewees expanded at all on the subject of the sources of constraint.

The sort of constraints which limit freedom seemed to be very largely taken for granted; that is, most people did not or could not explain their source. This very taken-for-grantedness however implies that they saw the constraints as generally expected or as right and proper, and therefore not in need of explanation. In other words they could not, for example, go out or go off when they wanted, nor go with another woman/man, because married people are not expected to do so. As one man said:

> Mr F: We canna run aboot the same like. [L]
> Mrs F: What do you mean you can't?
> Mr F: Well, you're nae supposed to. [L]

Some however did attempt further explanation. Mrs H for instance talked about a hypothetical wife who was both a 'good-time girl' (not obeying the lack of freedom constraint) and a bad housekeeper (not obeying the task constraint). Part of the discussion went as follows:

> JA: What about a husband leaving his wife, what do you think are good grounds then?
> Mrs H: Well some wives, I mean . . . I don't know, a good-time girl . . . to me I would say, well I mean if she carries on like that, and that way. And I think a wife who sort of . . . who would never do nothing in the house, if she was a filthy woman, didna look after him, didna cook for him and look after him, and things like that, you know, I mean . . .
> JA: Are those the things you would say make a good wife?
> Mrs H: . . . A warm house, a comparatively tidy house – he wants a good meal, he wants looking after you know. If a man is not going to *get* that he maybe winna leave her, but he'll find it somewhere else you know, he'll find it somewhere else.

She implied in this that if a woman wanted to keep her marriage then it was in her interests to put up with the lack of freedom (and with the tasks). Other explanations referred to further negative sanctions imposed by the spouse: 'It annoys her slightly at times – she always wants to know where I've been till half-past eight at night' (Mr L); 'They all say I'm under her thumb and I am, aye – I thought I'd be getting oot mair, oot drinking' (Mr K); 'He never sort of let me go out much on my own' (Mrs N); 'There's a row if I go down to the boozer, like, an' overstay my leave' (Mr F). Alternatively the explanation could be phrased in terms indicating the wish not to hurt or upset the spouse. This was shown by an interchange between Mr and Mrs P, though their remarks also showed that the particular type of lack of freedom they were discussing (having extra-marital sex) was a rather complex matter:

Mr P: I don't think there's anything wrong having sex within marriage or extra-marital sex as long as your partner agrees to it.

Mrs P: And even supposing it's just for one night, as long as you're both happy . . .

Mr P: I could understand . . . you'd better not – but if you went to [names place wife is about to visit for a meeting] and you came back and said you'd slept with a bloke out of sheer madness for one night /// I doubt if I'd lose any sleep over it. I'd be a bit huffed I suppose.

Mrs P: Oh that's not true, you would certainly lose sleep over it.

Mr P: Not if you came back and gave me a decent reason . . .

Mrs P: Like what now? Rape?

Mr P: I don't know . . . I mean, I would be shattered and completely dumbfounded . . . but . . . I mean it could possibly happen, but . . .

They begin by saying that constraint in this area is an internally imposed rule (i.e. something both partners have agreed to); Mr P then tries to say that he personally, under certain conditions, would be happy to waive such a rule as far as Mrs P's behaviour is concerned. She however appears unwilling to accept the sincerity of her husband's attitude, at which point he changes it; so that having started by saying that he would not 'lose sleep' over it, he ends by saying that he would be 'shattered and completely dumbfounded'. Although this interchange does not provide the reason for his change of reaction, one can speculate that it occurred because, in order to show his attachment to Mrs P, he has to say he would be hurt by her having extra-marital intercourse. In other words, by emphasising her individual freedom (identity needs) he ran the risk of undermining her need to feel his attachment or commitment to her (stability needs). We shall return to the question of acceptance or rejection of constraints in a later section; the point to be emphasised at the moment is the difficulty sometimes found in describing the sources of constraint, the desire to see them in some cases as internally imposed rules, and sometimes as springing from a wish not to hurt one's spouse.

Mr S also saw the lack of freedom constraint as associated with the desire not to hurt the spouse, and tried to explain what it was about deviation which would cause distress:

Mr S: We [Mr and Mrs S] did talk about infidelities, about what would happen. And this is an interesting point – I don't know whether anyone else talked to you about this – we both . . . I think we agreed that it would not be the physical act of sex with someone else that would be the thing that would hurt me and hurt Sheila. It would be the

break of trust /// because there is a tremendous element of trust between us. No, it would be something which would be so foreign to
my concept of marriage that it couldn't be done.

It looks as though he is saying that he and his wife have an agreement (a
rule) and it would be the breaking of the rule which would hurt and not
the deviant act itself. There also seems to be a mixture of the internal
and external rule here: on the one hand Mr S and his wife seem to have
come to their own agreement (internal rule), but on the other hand
breaking trust with someone seems to be seen as the breaking of an
external rule.

However, sometimes people could see the deviant act itself as problematic, for example the danger of venereal disease for one's spouse if
one has extra-marital relations, or the dangers of neglect for one's
children and home if one spends time away from one's family. For
example:

> JA: You say that you came [home] when your boy was born, or soon
> after? Was this one of the reasons for . . .?
> Mr B: Yes, this was one of the reasons, yes.
> Mrs B: [Working away is] Nae much life for a married man.
> Mr B: It's alright for the married *man*, it's the wife and children.

So far, therefore, there have been four types of answer about the
sources of constraint: a taken-for-granted general rule, spouse's
annoyance (without further analysis of the source of the spouse's
annoyance), an internal rule whose breaking would hurt the spouse, and
an awareness that going against the constraint (i.e. the act itself) could
hurt spouse or children.

Some of the give and take constraints were talked of in a very similar
way. For example, a third of those in this category were either spoken
of in a taken-for-granted fashion implying that they are generally
expected behaviour, or were explicitly described as right and proper
conduct (without further interpretation). For instance:

> Mrs L: I mean . . . you've got to see their point of view, you can't always be
> in the right. You've got to think of them a lot, you've got to try and
> work out *between* you what you want to do and things like that.

Or Mr R, who said he put up with his wife's friends:

> Mr R: My wife's got some friends over here, the Women's Party. I'm pleasant
> to them, but they are not my cup of tea – they annoy me sometimes. I
> wouldn't say that to my wife because it's not fair . . .

On some occasions the constraint was said to be endured because otherwise the spouse might be annoyed, or impose negative sanctions (for example, the wife who said she could not always do housework when *she* pleased because her husband would 'give her a row' if it were not done when he came home from work). Sometimes it was spoken of as endured in order not to cause hurt, or in order to promote happiness or welfare, or even specifically so as not to jeopardise the continued existence of the marriage. For example there was the man who said he had to be lenient with his wife because she was often ill, and if he had 'started anything she would have been really ill – headaches would start off' (Mr G); or the husband mentioned earlier who said he could not get a job abroad because it would make his wife unhappy to leave her home area (Mr E); or Mr S who said:

Mr S: I've got a theory about marriage too, that it's . . . er . . . you adapt yourself, each other adapts oneself to being able to live . . . with all sorts of mutual aggressions.

JA: Yes, yes.

Mr S: And if you don't adapt it doesn't work, and if you do adapt it does work.

In addition to these factors there were two others which had not been mentioned in connection with the lack of freedom constraint. One of these was the implication that some constraint on preferred activities was imposed by the fact that it was not possible to alter the spouse's personality or interests so that they were in line with one's own preferences; one therefore had to 'adjust' because it was not possible to do otherwise. Mrs T, for instance, thought, though she was not quite sure, that she had had to change to fit in with her husband's impulsiveness:

Mrs T: In some ways it's [Mrs T's personality] been maybe dictated by circumstances /// Tom you see is very impulsive and impatient, and very moody really. He's either on top of the world or down in the dumps /// whereas I like to think that myself I'm more or less always the same. I'm not quite sure if I've been forced into that or if I was always like this or not, but I mean I tend to steer very much a middle course . . . especially mainly with regard to the children. You see, this is what I mean, circumstances do tend to change you, you know.

Another example was the husband (Mr W) who said he could not have discussions about his work interests with his wife because she did not understand them and was thus not interested. Finally there were a few instances in which the constraint on preferred activity was seen as due to either temporary or external special circumstances; for example one wife said she had to work even though she thought she would prefer to be at home looking after the children, because her husband did not have a job at the moment and the household needed her income.

As already mentioned, the area of responsibility was one which was so taken for granted that people did not generally spontaneously say very much about it. Further questioning did reveal some of the specific areas of responsibility they had in mind, but very little was said about the sources of these constraints. Just occasionally people would add that, for example, you have to be responsible towards your children because their welfare demands it. But in the main what the interviewees appeared to be saying was that 'when you are married you have responsibilities, they belong to you, no one else is going to see to them and it would not be right for them to do so; so you have got to be responsible'. Thus in so far as people recognised the possibility of deviating from responsible behaviour (for one cannot call something a rule if people think it inconceivable to behave otherwise) these constraints appeared to be governed by perceptions of a general rule about responsible marital behaviour.

The same was true of tasks. As mentioned earlier, housework and childcare were very much talked of as activities which had to be carried out, and had to be carried out mainly by the wives in a marriage. People used phrases (as the earlier quotations show) such as 'it's got to be done', 'having to do it', and they rarely expanded on these remarks. It was not seen as something imposed by the partner (either in the sense that concern for his welfare or happiness demanded it, or that he would be angry and the marriage would be jeopardised if one did not do it), though it could be seen as something unquestionably expected of wives not only by themselves but also by their husbands (and indeed by their children). It could be rationalised of course; and occasionally people talked of women being better at childcare than men, or of men being primarily responsible for income provision; but such comments were not made unless questions were specifically framed to elicit them.

Although the women appeared to accept tasks as part of the expected job of a wife, this did not of course mean that they saw housework as entirely their task and did not think there were some jobs the husband should do, or some occasions when he should do them or help to do them. There was certainly some variation of opinion here, and some apparent difficulty in formulating rules of conduct, but there were people who saw the constraint as alleviated with the husband's help, whilst on the other hand there were a few wives who saw the source of the particularly burdensome nature of their task constraint as their husband's unwillingness to help. For example:

> Mrs J: He just doesna want to learn. Some couples the man *likes* to know how to do things – he'll say: 'Well, seeings as you're not home I'll go and start the tea.' *He* wouldn't even know how to set the table.

Or:

> JA: What about household tasks? Can you tell me something about who does what in the house?
> Mrs E: Well. [L] I think if he was here for this particular one . . . well, when we were first married he used to quite often do hoovering and things like that /// I think deterioration has set in . . . I really must say, that apart from peeling potatoes, he doesn't really do . . . and he certainly never changes nappies! And he never takes in washing, and he certainly would never put out washing.

Finally there were the sharing space constraints. In one sense these were directly imposed by the spouse, since it was what one could not do because one's spouse objected, or what one had to endure in one's spouse's behaviour, that constituted the constraint. In addition, however, and as implied in the earlier section, they are things that are seen as having to be endured not because one's partner forces one to endure them but because one is expected to endure them. As one man said, when complaining of some of his wife's irritating habits: 'Well, you can't say anything about that – I suppose we all have our funny little ways.' Rather like responsibilities and tasks, the constraints of sharing space were very much taken for granted.

To sum up, therefore, it appears that it is not on the whole particular spouses who are seen to impose the constraints which people talk about; it is marriage itself and the expectations people themselves have of what marriage involves and what they can and cannot do within it. Having said that, it must be added that there was a small minority of the sample who did appear to feel more constrained by their spouses (and all were dissatisfied by it) than the rest of the sample. The comments of four indicated some considerable present spouse-imposed constraints, and those of one some considerable past spouse-imposed constraints.

The four were all in the more recently married group (two middle-class wives and one working-class couple). Thus Mrs A (already quoted) talked of how she could not get her own way, nor even an equal share in decisions, because her husband was 'the boss' and she was frightened to go against him. A further example of her comments was as follows:

> JA: You said that Alan likes to think of himself as master of the house. Do you think that he *is* the master of the house?
>
> Mrs A: I think that he is, but it makes me angry as well that he is – a bit angry that he won't listen to some things that I say . . . if I ask him to do something, if he doesn't feel like doing it he just won't do it, but if there's something that he wants done, sometimes I'm so frightened of him I just go and run and do it. And then I get so annoyed that he *can* do that and I come running.

Her husband would even, she said, do things without either consulting or informing her (such as when he drew money out of their joint savings account); she also said she felt that there was less 'fun' in life than when she lived in her parental home, because her husband did not enjoy fun and she could not try to change him. Incidentally it is interesting, and in line with what one would expect if Mrs A's comments were an accurate description of the situation, that Mr A appeared to be among those enduring the least amount of marital constraint.

Mrs E was somewhat different in that she did not appear to be constrained by fear of her husband and his negative sanctions, but by his lack of participation and interest in their marriage; thus like Mrs A she saw herself as having to 'give' more than she 'took' because her husband was not prepared to involve himself. For example she said she had too much housework and childcare to do because her husband had ceased to give her more than very occasional help; he did not have a job so she had to provide most of the family income; he would not participate with her in the kind of leisure pursuits she would have liked; and he did not try to compromise so that his spending habits (careless) became more like hers (which were careful). She did have various excuses for his behaviour, but she said:

> Mrs E: I think you both really have to work in a marriage. I don't think that one person can keep a marriage going. You both have to give, and I think in most marriages one tends to give more than the other. And one tends to see that things are done more than the other. And I suppose I tend to get things done more really. Eddie says they're to be done, but I'll probably go and do them. Like, he'd say that some-

thing's needing to be done, well, he himself probably won't go and do it . . .

Mr and Mrs K both appeared to feel constrained by the other. Mr K said he could not go out as often as he wanted because 'she won't let me', that he lacked freedom and was 'under her thumb', and that his wife took decisions without consulting him:

> JA: Who do you think takes most of the decisions? Do you think you take them together, or does she take some and you take some, or what?
>
> Mr K: Let's see – she takes maist of them. If she wants something she'll just go out and buy it without us both goin' out. I've nae say in it. If she thinks she's wantin' something she'll go out and buy it.
>
> JA: I see. And that's all right with you?
>
> Mr K: No.
>
> JA: No?
>
> Mr K: No – it'd be alright if she had the money . . . But she hasna got the money . . .

Mrs K said she felt that in order to avoid rows with her husband she had to put up with his behaviour and preferences, for example his untidiness, his switching off the radio and switching on the television when he came in, his occasionally coming home drunk, and his occasional unwillingness to take part in the leisure pursuits which she wanted.

The final person with spouse-imposed constraints was Mrs I, who talked at many points about the changes in her relationship with her husband since a very bad accident which had made him change many of his previous habits (this couple will be discussed again in Chapter 6). Before this, she said, he used to constrain her through her fear of his annoyance (temper and violence) if she went against him or tried to change him, so that she had sole responsibility for housework and childcare:

> Mrs I: Well, before, when he was making what you would say a wage to support a wife, then he wanted you to be there at mealtimes, it had to be put down for him, you know, and cleared away . . .

And:

> Mrs I: When they [the children] were younger he . . . I don't know, he was out too much and home too late, that *I* had the kids. If there's mistakes in them they are mine. I made them, they're all mine . . .

She said she had very little say in decision-making:

> Mrs I: My husband's the dominant partner – he tells you /// he tells you, and that is it, there's no argument about it. If he says that's it, that's it finished.

She had had no control over the amount of housekeeping money she received:

> Mrs I: You know how men are – well my husband, anyway, used to put your housekeeping up on the mantelpiece and that was your lot, and don't you dare get into debt, and you had better manage on it and that's it.
>
> JA: Did you know how much he earned or did he just . . .?
>
> Mrs I: No, no. The first time I knew what he earned was three years ago.

And she had had, so she said, to put up with her husband coming home having been drinking:

> Mrs I: Afore, he used to go out with the boys, you know, and there is nothing more irritating than someone stumbling home with maybe one or two boys, and they expect me to be in a good humour, and give them tea, and be nice, ugh . . .

These therefore were obviously described as spouse-imposed constraints, and they were resented. Most people however did not see constraints in this way and one would therefore expect their opinions about them to be different. The next section thus examines attitudes.

Attitudes towards constraints

The next question is to what extent people accept or dislike these constraints, and for what reasons. Some of the points to be made here have already been implied or referred to: this section therefore serves to draw them together as well as to emphasise or make new ones.

Lack of freedom

Three types of reason were given for disliking this type of constraint (one-third could give no reason, they merely said they disliked it). The first, and most common reason, was that it prevented one, or curtailed the opportunity for, doing more exciting, interesting things. For instance:

Mr C: [In discussing how if he had been single he could have got a job with an international firm] You could be in Canada one year, South Africa the next, Australia the next . . . however long the contract lasts. Now I'd have enjoyed that life.

Or:

Mr O: I'm pretty boring and sort of settled, you know. [L]

Or:

Mrs R: A wee bittie spark in your life – I think you really need a wee bit of spark /// I think women just . . . they're married, and their homes are their prison and their heaven, and that's it. To me I think there's more in life . . .

The second reason was somewhat less tangible, but appeared to involve the valuing of freedom for its own sake, the desire to be autonomous (outside the marriage relationship), and to do what one likes spontaneously. People said such things as:

Mr J: Well, when you're single you can go out any time you like, where you like. Things like that. You miss that.

The third reason (only mentioned by two interviewees) was the curtailment of contact with other people as a result of one's lack of freedom. For instance:

Mr A: Now that I'm married, I still have some friends, but some friends say: 'Well, what about going such and such a place?' I say: 'I'm sorry, I couldn't come today' . . . or such and such. And you feel like, at times . . . well, you gain *some* friends and you say . . . but the next friend will say you're a bit anti-social eh . . .

Since lack of freedom seemed to be preventing people doing and being what they would have liked to do and be, it is interesting to look at whether, and if so why, they found this curtailment acceptable. First it should be said that only two people made it clear that they did *not* accept the constraint (both more recently married men; one working-class and one middle-class). Mr K said there was nothing nice about marriage since it meant the loss of his freedom:

Mr K: I don't know why I got married, to tell you the truth. I haven't a clue. I wish I hadn't done it.

He said he would rather be single, but he did add that he would not want to be a bachelor all his life because it would be lonely. Mr W said he did not wish to accept the constraints and would really like to set up a communal living arrangement with additional people so that greater opportunities would be available. He spoke of his dislike of marriage in the following way:

> Mr W: I dislike it partly because nearly everybody does it, I think. I also think it's unnatural in a funny sort of way – which is very odd . . . er, though things seem to be what I call improving – people are getting freer – though people are getting married more often. So many people I've seen who are married, and so many people I've talked to who are, seem to have curious ideas about marriage: it is for a lifetime, or should be. Whereas if people are changing – as they should – then by definition almost it can't be very long that you can have a good relationship /// And also there's all the social pressure attached to . . . married people behave in certain ways . . .

Everyone else appeared to accept the constraint, as was almost invariably indicated before or soon after the complaint had been voiced. Their comments can be grouped to give six types of reason for acceptance. Among the most common were those which cited norms (seven people) or adaptation/adjustment (seven people). By these are meant comments such as 'you have to', or 'it's your duty to (to accept the loss of freedom)', or 'you get used to it', 'you adjust to the situation'. For example:

> Mrs E: When I'm home at night I've been away from the children all day, so I really shouldn't *be* going out at night.

And

> Mr S: It would be wrong [to have sex with someone else] . . . Now it's not fear of impregnating the girl or fear of getting a disease from her, or any other of the social ailments that come along, it's just a fact that I would have the most hellish job for a long, long time facing not just Sheila but the household.

Some examples of comments invoking adaptation were:

> Mr C: Well now I never think about being tied down really. No, you seem to get adjusted to the situation.

Or:

> JA: Do you find that [not being able to go out] irksome in some ways?
>
> Mrs N: Well, I did at first when I was younger and that, but not now – I suppose I got used to it.

Or:

> Mr M: You learn to accept things that comes along I suppose . . . you might nae have accepted them when you were younger I suppose /// when you're younger you widna accept the things you're doin' now I suppose.

A further group of reasons (mentioned by seven people) indicated that settling down had its compensations, or that there were some pleasurable things resulting from one's loss of freedom through marriage. For example it gave one freedom from one's parents (see previous chapter), one had the satisfaction of building a relationship, it gave one 'a broader outlook on life', and two people even mentioned specifically the security which came through marriage. The following are some examples:

> Mr N: I tend to have a broader outlook on life.
> JA: What do you mean by a broader outlook on life?
> Mr N: Well, like I say, I have to think about the future. Before I was married I was just living from day to day so to speak /// But now I'm working not just for myself but also for my wife, for the future.

Mr O having complained about the loss of freedom, went on to say that none the less he felt sorry for elderly single people, and added:

> Mr O: I think I'd have worried about it if by a certain time I hadn't got married /// I know it's something to do with security and that.

Or:

> Mr L: I was always one for . . . I was one for settling down /// You know, I'm just this type. I just . . . maybe I need to build a relationship or something.

Or:

> Mr P: When I was younger I always imagined that no woman would ever . . . stay with me . . . When I started going with girls I realised that possibly this wasn't true, but . . . I do, I find some security in marriage.

Three less common reasons were that one still had *some* freedom, or that one had had all the freedom one needed or was entitled to before marriage, or that one would not really want it because freedom has drawbacks or disadvantages. Thus one person said: 'I still can get out occasionally' (Mr L); another said: 'When we got married we'd had our fling, or a good bit of it anyway' (Mrs D); and another that: 'It was a pretty rotten existence really' (Mr N).

So, although these comments show that people on the whole do not theorise to any great extent about their loss of freedom (at least not to the extent of being able to give detailed comments in an interview), what they appear to be saying is: 'Although I cannot do or be what I enjoyed or would have enjoyed, none the less you get used to it or you have to get used to it; I still can do and be those things to some extent; or I want to do and be other things as well now.'

Give and take

This area of constraint was similarly accepted as well as disliked by most of those who mentioned it. There were in this case rather more reasons for disliking the constraints than in the case of loss of freedom. First, the main reason given (and again some people of course gave more than one) was that the constraint went against either a general preference for getting one's own way (five people) or a preference for getting one's own way over specific things (twenty-one people). Thus Mrs L said: 'I just like everything to go my way'; Mrs K said she would like to get her own way about staying up late:

> Mrs K: The thing that annoys me is that I used to like, some nights I used to like staying up late, and the next night I didn't, but he always goes to his bed about ten o'clock now, and I don't like sitting in here by myself so I just have to go to bed as well. I don't *have* to go , but I go, and I get annoyed because he won't stay up. I think if I had my life to live over again I wouldn't get married at my age.

Similarly others complained about things they used to do, or thought they would like to do, but could not do because of the spouse's attitudes or actions (for example, some people regretted that they could not go skiing, move house, avoid their spouse's friends, or be the family's sole breadwinner).

Second, and slightly different, were the dislikes based not on preferences but on normative stances: these were things one disliked having to do or endure because one thought they should not be so (eight people). In two cases they were phrased generally, indicating that the individual did not think he ought to do quite so much giving in; in others they referred to specific disapprovals, such as: 'I just think we ought to be more careful with money' (Mrs E), 'I think he ought to discipline the boys more' (Mrs D), 'I think a wife ought to get a little job when she hasn't children to look after' (Mr G), 'I don't think the wife should be working while the children are young' (Mr E).

Two further reasons were, for example, that giving in had either been bad for the respondent personally (seven cases) or had caused problems for the marriage or the family (seven cases). Instances of the former type were, for example, that giving in had sapped the individual's confidence, had meant that he or she took unwarranted blame for something, was squashed, had become bored or boring, was in a rut or vegetating. Instances of the latter type were, for example, that giving in to the other had caused money worries, difficulties with the children, social inconveniences, or had led to necessary decisions not being taken. The final reason was that the constraint was disliked because of a dislike of being dominated or ruled by the spouse. Mrs A and Mrs I have already been mentioned in this context. They said such things as:

> Mrs A: As soon as we were married . . . he made it quite clear that he was the master of the household, and I didn't think he was like that. I thought he'd be the type of person to work alongside – instead of rather telling me what to do.

Or:

> Mrs I: Well we dinna usually hae discussions or anything really /// He does like to be the boss you know – and it is irritating.

One can therefore see that constraints in the area of give and take were said to be disliked because they struck at preferred identities or modes of behaviour. Were they accepted as well, and if so was it because they allowed new identities to emerge, or because there were other compensations?

Only three out of the twenty-nine who mentioned give and take constraints gave no counterbalancing reasons for accepting the constraint: Mrs A did not find her husband's domination acceptable; Mr K could not accept putting up with his wife taking most of the decisions – he thought it caused problems; and Mr E did not feel that any good had been done to him or his marriage relationship by the fact that he had had to put up with his wife 'holding the reins'. For example, he said:

> Mr E: I think the thing that really bothers me most at the present time is /// the fact that I had plenty of confidence before I got married. I got married and still had, and then this situation of my wife sorta doing

all the earning, you know, bit into me really because . . . personally, for me, the way I was brought up makes this wrong, you know. I suppose intellectually you can say 'Ah well . . .', but you can't really emotionally accept it.

These three people, however, were commenting on situations which had been disliked either for normative reasons or because they caused problems of a fairly acute kind. When things were disliked because they went against personal preferences for getting one's own way, or when they had not caused severe problems, then acceptance as well as dislike was much more common. As with loss of freedom, two common reasons for acceptance were the normative (eight cases) and the adaptational (eight cases). For example:

> Mrs O: You've got to learn to forgive when you're married. You know, when you're not married you tend to . . . well, I know *me* anyway before I was married, it was awfully difficult for me to say 'sorry', you know. But now . . . I think er . . . I can say it easy. [L] But er . . . I think my pride wouldn't let me before. I think you've got to er . . . you know, not have pride . . . really when you're married . . . well not much anyway.

Or:

> Mrs L: Everything you do is in . . . well most things you do is in connection with them [husbands]. Like, you know . . . I couldn't just go out and spend all his pay and things like that, you've got to think . . . I found you've got to think of him when you are doing things . . .

Examples of adaptational reasons are:

> Mrs D: I think I've maybe learned a wee bit to sort of calm myself down a wee bit, probably through him [husband] /// That's one thing, I think. I do tend to take things a bit easier now. Och, it's maybe my age, I don't know, the older you get . . . But he takes things very much in his stride . . .

Or:

> Mr F: You learn to take things in your stride and this sort of thing . . . if you remembered every little thing you'd be off your nut in a couple of years I think . . . [L]

Similarly, as with freedom, some people said they accepted some loss of autonomy precisely because they felt they still remained autonomous to some degree. One woman said she probably did often get her own way eventually, two people said they accepted loss of autonomy in some areas because they had agreed to allow each other autonomy in others, and two said the constraint was endurable because it would not last for ever. In addition these people said that the constraint was acceptable because their spouse was also constrained, and thus it was 'fair'.

Again, like loss of freedom, the final set of reasons for acceptance referred to the compensations which came from giving and taking. Ten of these referred to the belief that accepting constraints made for a continuing or better marriage relationship, with less conflict or fewer rows; for example:

> Mrs J: Unless you can stick it out and learn to give and take, I don't think it ever works. There's an awful lot of people, once they get to that stage, just say: 'Right, that's it', and just break it off. But I think if you just say: 'Well, that's the way they are, and they're not going to change their habits . . .'
>
> Mr J: If one person can't accept the other partner's faults it'll never work, because everybody's got faults.

Or:

> Mrs S: And so you've got to learn to give and take and adjust to each other. And I suppose in our adjustments we must both have changed, otherwise we couldn't live together. So I'm sure every marriage must see a change, otherwise . . . you know, the people must change, otherwise life would be impossible, wouldn't it?

Or:

> Mr L: I think if anything's going to cause any trouble I'll shut up, which I think is the best way /// on the whole – a quiet life – that's the best way.

In talking of compensations five people merely said, after complaining of the constraint, 'but I'm quite happy' or 'happy enough' (with no further comment); four said that having the children compensated for any loss of autonomy they might have to endure; two that to some extent they also quite enjoyed the things they had to do (working, having children) for their partner's sake; two that it was good for their partner that they should give in, and two that it was good for *them* to have to give in (e.g. 'It wouldn't be good for me to get everything I wanted because then there'd be nothing left to look forward to'). Finally two people said they accepted the constraint within marriage because of the compensations outside (i.e. 'But I've got my work, I've got other things on my mind'; 'I can always go to my friends if I want to get things off my chest'). It is impossible to summarise this great variety of reasons for accepting loss of autonomy, but it does appear that this constraint was borne not on the whole because of specific new identities or modes of behaviour which it gave people, but more because of the feeling that if they wanted their marriages to continue, and to continue in a conflict-free state, they had to accept it (i.e. their answers pointed towards the satisfaction of stability rather than identity needs).

Responsibility

This was disliked for three fairly simple reasons. The first (mentioned by half of those describing the constraint) was that responsibilities were a worry or a burden. For example:

> Mr H: You start worrying about responsibility, and things like this [about whether one would have enough money, whether one could afford to buy a house] /// I wanted to be sort of . . . shall we say, reasonably comfortable, then the responsibilities are that much less, because if you can say: 'Yes I can do this' and 'I can do that', I mean that's half the problem.

Or:

> JA: What about becoming parents, do you think that changed you?
> Mrs L: It is difficult really . . . well personally I didn't imagine it would be so difficult.
> JA: Didn't you?
> Mrs L: No, now when [names her son] was younger I never thought anything of it, but now he is getting older you tend to look into the future now – when he goes to school and that. Now, how are we going to cope with him? Will there be any problems and that? We do sort of think of this. Well I worry about it a bit. Will I be a good sort of parent when he is older, or will he turn into a hooligan?

Second, a third of the people said that the responsibilities of marriage prevented one doing other things. For instance, one man compared present financial responsibilities with what one could do with one's money if one were not married:

> Mr J: When you were single you could go out and spend your money, things like that, and not worry about it really. Because you always

had somewhere to go – you were never in at weekends – things like that. And you didn't have to spend your money on a house, and things to run it. You could go out at weekends and spend your money.

Children also prevented some forms of activity, such as the husband and wife going out together in the evenings; or a husband studying. For example:

MR E: Certainly having children . . . obviously leads to difficulties I think.

JA: In what way?

MR E: Well . . . it's not possible to be as selfish with time as you need to be . . . you should be spending time with family, and then you don't want to as well.

A further third gave their reason for dislike as the fact that responsibilities can be difficult to carry out, or hard to learn; for example Mrs K said she found it hard to learn how to budget and look after the money. She said: 'Sometimes I'm nae bad, but the next time I dinna ken where it goes half the time.' Mrs I said she found it hard to learn to take the responsibilities of marriage because she had been spoiled by her father and had married for someone to lean on; it had been difficult for her when she found that she could not lean on her husband, and that he needed *her*, and that she had to run the household.

Yet everyone found some mitigating factor. As before, two very common reasons for acceptance were the normative (eight people) and the adaptational (seven people). For example:

MR J: You've got more responsibility – but you've got to take it at some time in your life.

Or:

MR B: Children stop you going out so much – but you've got to think about the children.

Or:

MR D: The adjustment to me wasn't so bad /// But surely for one to get married, accepts the change, knows that the change is inevitable . . . you see, this is my attitude to it.

Two rather similar reasons were that one accepts responsibilities if one has had a period of irresponsibility before marriage (two people), or that one does not think about them, merely taking every day as it comes without worrying (two people). Then came a wide variety of reasons citing the compensations arising from responsibilities: that they provide enjoyment or pleasure (seven people); that they give one control over areas of activity (three); that they provide a purpose, something to work for (three); that being responsible gives one a sense of achievement (one); that they make one less selfish (one), more confident (one), a better person, or that they are good for one's marriage (three). For example one man, having talked of the responsibilities of house and children mentioned the satisfaction of having one's own home and of seeing the children happy and well cared for:

JA: And what do you think are the nicest things about being married and having a family?

Mr C: Oh well . . . you get great satisfaction out o' seeing . . . like sitting here in an evening, the two kids playing awa' in front of the fire – an' playing wi' their toys . . . and newsing awa' to theirselves . . . it gives satisfaction really. To see them . . . what would you say . . . they seem to be happy . . . playing awa' wi' what you provide them wi' /// Apart frae that . . . it's fine to hae yer ain hoose – och, it's fine.

JA: What are the nice things about having your own house?

Mr C: Well . . . well . . . it means you've got a hoose and everything to yourself . . . it's aye something you've achieved you ken. It aye gives you satisfaction.

Or:

JA: Do you think that children are important in a marriage?

Mr D: Very /// It would not be such a happy marriage without them. I think they tend to give you something to think about, something to work for. Takes you out of a rut I should imagine and . . . you become less selfish /// Someone's got to have them so why not us? /// Oh, I think its a great fulfilment in life. It's the ultimate in life isn't it; to be able to reproduce? /// And we accepted them because they were there – and we wanted them in the first instance.

Or Mrs A, who had complained a great deal about the difficulty of learning the responsibility of running a home, but who liked the control it gave her over her own time:

JA: Are there any things that you're glad that you *can* do now, that you couldn't do before, before you were married?

Mrs A: Things that I . . . things that I can do now that I couldn't do before? [pause] Well, before . . . well, when I'm in the house myself I can please myself when I can sit down, when I go out to the shops, and I've still got time to myself, that I can do things in my own time . . . But before, at my mother's you know, you had your tea at a certain time every day, you had your own particular job that you had to do immediately, do as mother said . . . that's what I do like, about being in the house by myself, pleasing myself when I do things and that.

There are several reasons, among this variety of compensations, which specifically indicated enjoyment in new activities or modes of being, and only a minority that specifically showed acceptance for the sake of the security of the marriage. However, as before, many answers were not extended, and many showed little detailed theorising about the marriage constraints.

Tasks

These were also accepted as well as disliked by the twenty-two people (mostly women) who complained about them. Again no one found them totally unacceptable. But they were disliked for several reasons. First, because they prevented one doing other things: going out, working, being on one's own, earning money (eleven people). Second, because the actual performance of them was not enjoyable (eight people): it was boring, tiring, worrying, an effort. Third, they were complained of because of the amount of such work (five people): there was too much to do, not enough time to do it properly, it was never finished. Fourth because of a dislike of the way tasks made people feel about themselves (four people): 'I feel a bit of a drudge' or 'a menial', 'I'm not the domesticated type', 'I'm not me':

Mrs P: Small children are very demanding.
Mr P: Yes, but you feel you're completely wasted don't you?
Mrs P: Well I'm not me. I'm mother . . . or consumer in a shop, and that's all I am . . . I'm not *me* any more . . . I'm not me until they're in their beds.
JA: Did you feel you were you before you had children?
Mrs P: I don't think I knew what I was before I had them. I didn't discover myself until afterwards . . . and by that time it was too late.

Finally there were complaints explained in terms of the fact that the results of housework are not lasting, or that the interviewee had to do more of them than she considered her fair share.

The tasks were accepted for a variety of reasons, again starting with norms and adaptation (six and three people respectively). Beyond that, reasons were scattered; from people taking comfort from the thought that it could be worse, that spouses and children do help, and that the situation will change or can be changed; through expression of the feeling that there was really nothing else one would rather do, or that one would be bored without the tasks; to positive expressions of enjoyment to be gained from doing them: for example, that they are an area of activity over which one has control, that they give a sense of satisfaction or achievement, that it is nice to see things looking clean, and that it is pleasant to serve or give pleasure to others. For instance:

> JA: What do you think are the things that give you the greatest pleasure? It's probably a difficult question . . .
>
> Mrs F: I see. Well . . . let's say, even to me, if you spend . . . this is typically family you know. If you spend a good while preparing a meal even, the kids sit down [and say]: 'That's fine Mum', or however they put it, or even if they clear all their plates, to me this is a sign of fulfilment. Mind you, my lot, even my husband, are nae the kind to say: 'It was a lovely meal that', they just clean their plates and you think 'Oh well', you know, 'they've enjoyed it', this sort of thing.

Shared space

The category shared space comprised things people obviously either found hard to explain or saw as so self-evidently irritating that there was no need to explain them further. The most common comment was that they just *were* irritating, though one could also see that some were disliked because they prevented the individual from doing something or from being in a situation which he would have preferred. Disliked sounds, for example, prevented one either doing things which required peace and quiet (such as sleeping or reading), or doing things involving different sounds (such as watching television or listening to the radio).

Reasons for acceptance were again varied, but were along the same lines as those for other constraints: one has to put up with it, one gets used to it, one's partner has things to put up with too, the situation may or will change, one's marriage relationship may be harmed or become less congenial if one does not accept it. Such constraints were also accepted – as stated earlier – in that they were said to be very minor, trivial things; things therefore relatively easy to endure, and not worth making a fuss about.

Further discussion of reported attitudes

So far the emphasis of discussion has been upon constraints rather than individuals, and upon constraints said to involve at least some sense of personal regret. Before making some general points about these findings, the topics discussed can perhaps be clarified by shifting the emphasis somewhat, in order to see, first, whether there were any perceived marital constraints not accompanied by an element of personal regret, and second, how individuals can be described and distinguished according to the mixtures of constraint, dislike, and acceptance they said they experienced.

Obviously the constraints described in this chapter are not the sum total of all the ways in which married people feel their behaviour to be restricted. There are, in addition, the activities which people said they could not engage in but had no wish to do, or the activities which they said married people in general should not engage in (and again had no wish to do themselves). One thing which all members of the sample had done was to enter into a legal, monogamous marriage. What they said in trying to generalise about such norms showed a certain amount of ambivalence – about whether living together, for example, was wholly wrong or wrong in all circumstances – but all except two people said that the arrangement had been right for them, and that they personally would not have wished either to cohabit or to live in a marital arrangement of more than two people. One exception was Mr K, who has already been quoted as saying that he wished he were not married. He also said he thought it was a good idea to live together without being legally married, because 'if you didn't suit you could just part'. Mr W has also been cited as disliking what he saw as the fact that there is pressure on everyone to get legally married, and has been mentioned as describing his preference for a communal living arrangement. No one else described legal marriage as a personally regretted constraint. The kind of things they said about their own legal marriages were: 'Don't you just sorta take it for granted that you'll be married one day?'; 'We just never thought of not getting legally married'; 'I don't think I'd have considered living together. I wouldn't have felt secure'; 'I was brought up as a church-goer so it [living together] was completely foreign to me'; 'Legal marriage is essential if there's children'; 'It's better to be legally married, because you make more effort to patch things up when they go wrong'; 'Maybe I'd have been frightened to cohabit, in case my wife upped and went – because marriage does tie you up together'; 'I've nothing against it [living together] for those who want to, but it wouldn't have seemed right for me.' To summarise, there were four main reasons for favouring legal marriage: it was taken for granted, seen as right, thought to make the relationship more secure, and thought to be preferable where there were children.

Other restrictions not personally regretted came out in discussion of the factors thought to justify someone separating from his or her spouse. Some of the things mentioned in this context did involve the five constraints already discussed (showing that such constraints were normatively reinforced). Thus severe deviation from the loss of freedom constraint was seen as grounds for separation; for example, if someone committed adultery, or was out with friends all the time, or out drinking. Not fulfilling responsibilities, such as providing one's wife with money, controlling one's budget, looking after children, was also seen as grounds for separation; the same was true for give and take constraints (such as accepting each other's faults) and for task constraints (keeping the house clean and tidy, not neglecting childcare). Sharing space constraints, being seen as trivial matters, did not feature in this list of grounds.

Yet there were some types of behaviour mentioned in this context which were never said to be personally regretted restrictions. Thus people said someone would be justified in leaving a spouse if he or she were insane, a rapist, a criminal, a bully, cruel, filthy, making the other's life a misery, nagging or rowing all the time. There appear, therefore, to be some additional identities (apart from those mentioned in the earlier sections) which are restricted within marriage; they differ from the others, however, in being identities which people generally have no wish to assume, either in or out of marriage.

So far the proportions of the sample mentioning each of the five constraints have been given, but little has been said about those who did *not* mention them. The question one would want to ask about these people is whether their failure to mention the constraint was due to the fact that they *did* behave in the ways others said they could not, or that they *did not* behave in such ways but had no regret or wish to do so. For example, did those not mentioning tasks not see marriage as having increased their task-load, or did they have the tasks but wholly enjoy them? It is unfortunately impossible to answer this question satisfactorily because the five categories of constraint were not identified until the fieldwork had been partially completed. It was not therefore possible to ask all people to talk about their reasons for *not* mentioning certain areas of constraint. However some tentative answers can be given.

Tasks are probably the easiest area to discuss. As stated earlier, the men did not appear to have assumed a substantially greater burden of tasks through being married, but the women had. So it seems that the men did not mention this constraint because they did not experience it. The two women who did not mention it were quite different; like all the other women in the sample they did experience household tasks (not having servants to do them for them). They were both older women, one middle-class and one working-class, both without young children, both without paid employment, and both with small, fairly new houses with modern furniture. Perhaps the explanation is partly that they had less to do than the other women (not having young children, large houses, etc.) and more time to do it in (since they did not work outside the home). There were no other women in the sample with a similar combination of no work and no young children. It could also be that these women found housework particularly congenial and in accord with their own sense of identity (thus not working could have been an effect rather than a cause of their satisfaction). They did not quite say this; but Mrs R said:

> Mrs R: I dinna kill myself doing housework /// But I like a nice house. I like comfort. Comfort must come first. But if you want to put your feet up, you do it, and if you are not able to do the dishes at night then you can do them tomorrow. To me, you see, I would never drive myself round the bend by saying everything had to be done before I go to bed.

And Mrs G said she had no interests outside her family and her home, and that she too liked to 'have everything just fine and clean'.

Loss of freedom was not mentioned by fourteen of the wives, and it did not appear that this was because they had the freedom to go out or away whenever they wanted, or to go out with other men, but rather because marriage caused no greater restriction than before, or because it did not occur to them to want to do these things. For example, Mrs F was asked:

> JA: Some people occasionally feel the need to get away on their own just for a little while – something like that. Does that feeling ever come over you?
> Mrs F: No, I don't think so. I think it might to Frank, but then he does, he

gets his outlet. I don't seek that sort of thing somehow or other. I think I am basically a home bird, this is it . . . it is entirely different I suppose, but och I enjoy being at home. I like to *get* out, but if I go out I prefer to be out with him, you know.

The two men with no expression of loss of freedom constraints differed from each other; one, Mr H, seemed to be similar to the women in having no wish for an independent life. He said he had been ready to 'settle down' when he got married, that his life was centred around his home and family, and that he never wished to go out without his wife (see previous chapter). Mr E, however, seemed not to complain because he was able, to a large extent, to be independent; companionship with his wife was said virtually to have ceased, he spent a lot of time out of the house, and even said that sexual needs could be satisfied outside marriage 'in this day and age'.

Deviation from the other three types of constraint is somewhat more difficult to interpret. Why, for example, did some not mention any irritation at having to put up with their spouses' habits or at having to curb their own (give and take and shared space constraints)? Were their spouses so subordinate or so kind that they never did irritating things themselves, and never complained about their partners' habits? Or were they just extremely easygoing and tolerant, and with spouses of a similar nature, so that they never had any difficulties in giving in to each other and enduring each other's behaviour? Data were inadequate to answer this question, but there was some evidence of the truth of both these explanations. For example Mr A mentioned neither give and take nor shared space constraints, though his wife mentioned both. She also talked at some length about how he was the 'boss' (see earlier section) and how she had to give in to him and not do anything to annoy him because she was frightened of him. Both Mr and Mrs C failed to mention give and take constraints, but they said a great deal about being easygoing. For example:

> Mrs C: I like all my own way I suppose . . . that's what I do . I was probably spoilt when I was little. [L]
>
> Mr C: Then, me being soft-hearted, I'll agree.
>
> Mrs C: Yes, he's very easygoing and he'll always agree . . .
>
> JA: Does he?
>
> Mrs C: Oh yes. I always get round him, mostly. Don't I?

Or:

> Mrs C: The girls at my work always said I was easygoing – 'You would never get in a rage, you would never fight with anyone' . . . if anything came up at work, you know, between unions or something, I never said anything . . .
>
> Mr C: I suppose we are fairly easygoing. When you see some other couples – they're at each other's throats the whole time really.

Finally there are those who failed to mention responsibility constraints (among whom the younger wives featured prominently). Did they in fact have fewer responsibilities than others, were they less aware of them, or did they have them but wholly enjoy them? Interpretation is difficult, and even if one considers merely the group of seven younger wives it is hard to see any pattern. Each of the seven had their own houses (though only two were being bought as opposed to being rented); all but one had a child or children; they were all largely responsible for running their households; none of them explicitly said they enjoyed responsibilities. One can only resort to the possible interpretation which postulates that men are more prone than women to see marriage in terms of responsibility, and that a sense of responsibilities is something which increases with the length of marriage. What *can* be concluded from this discussion, however, is that *not* to mention some area of activity as constraining may in some cases be due to a lack of constraint (or a relative lack), and in other cases to the fact that the modes of behaviour, seen by some people as constraint, are seen by others as quite congruent with their own preferred identities.

The third topic of this section involves a return to the individual as a primary focus of attention. First, for purely descriptive reasons, four examples are given (selected at random from each sub-group) to illustrate how constraints and the attitudes towards them were combined in any one person.

Mrs L mentioned constraints concerning give and take (that she did not always get her own way now she was married), tasks (housework), and sharing space (for example her husband being bright and cheerful and noisy 'first thing in the morning'). She said she found the constraints of give and take hard to endure because 'I just like everything to go my way', but on the other hand she accepted it because 'You've got to think of him when you are doing things', and also because 'We both give, and he [husband] probably gives more than me.' She disliked the tasks for a variety of reasons: 'Housework quite bores me', 'I'm not the domesticated type'; it also prevented her from going out and from getting a job. None the less she said that the tasks were not too much of a burden, since they had only a small flat which did not take much looking after, and since her husband helped with tasks when he was at home. Her husband's early morning alertness was irritating, she said, because she just liked to be left alone in the mornings so that she could wake up gradually; however 'it's just the way he is'.

Mr J disliked the lack of freedom (not being able to get out), the give and take ('putting up with the spouse's faults'), the responsibility (running one's own affairs, dealing with a house and with money), and sharing space (his wife's talkativeness, and her cold feet in bed). He disliked the lack of freedom because he appeared to value the autonomy for its own sake (being able to 'go out any time you like'), but he also seemed to accept it by saying that he did not miss it much and that he had built himself a home bar and could have a drink at home whilst imagining himself out at the public house. He disliked give and take because it meant he sometimes had to endure things which ran counter to his preferences, but on the other hand he accepted it for the benefit of his marriage relationship, saying that 'it'll never work' if one does not accept the partner's faults. He said he disliked responsibilities because they prevented him doing other things (such as spending his money on personal entertainment); but he accepted them as inevitable ('you've got to take it [responsibility] at some time in your life') and because even if a house was a responsibility it was still: 'your own house and no one else's'. Mrs J's irritating habits were said to 'get on my nerves', and her chattering prevented him doing other things (such as watching the television). He accepted them by saying that one 'has' to do so, and that he had learned to ignore them (for example he said he could now listen to the television at the same time as his wife was talking).

Mrs D mentioned three of the constraints: tasks (housework); give and take (not getting her own way, putting up with her husband's characteristics, not having her own earned money); and lack of freedom (not being able to get out). Of the tasks, she said that she felt 'a bit of a drudge', that there was so much to do that she seemed to be struggling on all day, that it was boring doing the same thing day after day; but she also said 'but, och, I find that I just work away', that she would be bored if she did not have the housework, and that there was nothing else she would prefer to be doing. She said she had found it hard to learn to give and take (perhaps because she had been spoiled as a girl), that some of her husband's behaviour went against her preferences, and that autonomy is pleasant ('it is nice to have something to call your very own'). However, she said that she had learned to calm herself down and be more tolerant, that her husband was placid which helped, that if you had everything you wanted there would be nothing to look forward to, that she often did get her own way eventually, and that not getting it was probably a good thing (e.g. if she had her own money she would probably squander it). Lastly, loss of freedom was mentioned with regret as something which stopped one going out and doing more exciting things; but she followed this by saying that she and her husband had been content to settle down because 'we'd had our fling, or a good bit of it anyway'.

Finally there was Mr H, whose constraints appeared to be mainly to do with responsibility (though he also mentioned some of his wife's irritating habits which, he said, got on his nerves but which he just had to endure). He mentioned both the worry of responsibilities (having enough money and being able to control what you do), and the way in which they prevent one from doing other things (thus children prevented him and his wife from going away together and from spending much time together just as a couple, and prevented them having money to spend on things like expensive holidays). He balanced these regrets partly by saying that he had been ready to assume responsibility because he had had 'a good broad life' before marriage, that the children gave him great pleasure, and in addition they would grow up and cease to be a responsibility, and that he and his wife could plan for what they would do together when that time came.

These four brief sketches show, therefore, the common themes of the kind of things in marriage which are seen to restrict one, and which are simultaneously regretted and accepted. They also show that individuals draw upon a wide range of reasons both for regret and acceptance, and indicate that for any one individual there is no particular reliance upon one form of explanation rather than upon another.

Lastly there is the question of extreme cases. The previous two chapters have asked whether it is possible to identify individuals whose reported behaviour places them towards the extremes compared with other members of the sample; that is, those reporting particularly high or low levels of talk and of separate activity. Those so identified tended, as expected, to express dissatisfaction with this situation. It would also be useful to be able to identify those who report particularly extensive imposition of behaviour patterns or modes of being, and those who report particularly little imposition. However, it is not possible to do this when the variables under study are so complex, and when the categories used have been induced from the data with the result that the necessary follow-up questions were not present in the interview schedule. For in order to make distinctions between individuals on the basis of the five types of constraint one would need to question each of them about the experience of each possible kind of constraint within each broad category (for example, within the category of responsibility one would ask about money, children, household management and so on); one would then have to ask interviewees to rate each item according to a level of regret and acceptance; one would have to ask them to rank items according to their importance to them; and finally, one would have to aggregate their answers to get unified scores which would enable one to say that one interviewee expressed more constraint than another and that the level of constraint was associated with a level of dissatisfaction. It is doubtful whether such a project is feasible.

All one can do in the present study is ask whether there were any interviewees who mentioned either *none/one* or *five* types of constraint and see whether there is evidence that they were particularly dissatisfied (even though realising that the number of types mentioned is not necessarily synonymous with the extent of overall constraint: some people, for example, mentioned few constraints but talked of those they did experience with such warmth and/or at such length that one could reasonably see them as highly constrained); and re-examine those who said they could not see anything acceptable in any one of the constraints they mentioned, in order to see if there is any evidence that these people were particularly extensively constrained or had particularly little constraint.

The former type of analysis produced (as mentioned earlier) one man – Mr A – who only mentioned one type of constraint, and none who mentioned all five (eleven mentioned two, nineteen mentioned three, and nine mentioned four). Mr A was indeed an interesting case. It may well be true that he experienced relatively little constraint since from what both he and his wife said it seemed that he exerted considerable control over what she did, but that she was unable to exert control over him. He seemed to see himself in a position of authority in the marriage, and was also seen in such a position by his wife (see previous quotations). Thus it may be that Mr A was fulfilling his identity requirements at the expense of the stability of his marriage. He did not appear to be aware of this himself at the time of interview; but his wife expressed considerable dissatisfaction about her husband and her marriage. She appeared to be losing her commitment to him; and the continued existence of the marriage may well be in some doubt. The finding in this area (inadequate as it is) was therefore in the expected direction.

The latter type of analysis – to examine those who said they did not accept constraints (that is, who expressed dissatisfaction) to see whether they were particularly highly constrained or unconstrained – produced four such people: Mr K, who did not accept either loss of freedom or give and take; Mr W, who did not accept loss of freedom; and Mrs A and Mr E, who did not accept give and take. Although, again, this question cannot be satisfactorily answered, one can make several points. Mrs A, as already stated, appeared heavily constrained by her husband; and this could well help to explain her dissatisfaction. Mr W appeared slightly *less* constrained than other men. Thus, for example, he expressed no responsibility constraints, and said that loss of freedom involved not being able to have relationships with other women, but not that he could not go out on his own (in fact he and his wife talked of relatively high levels of separate activity, as the previous chapter shows). His dissatisfaction over loss of freedom appeared to relate to his very unusual expectations or ideal preferences for a communal living arrangement and for intimate relationships with more than one person. Mr K seemed to be in a position which involved a mixture of relatively high constraint imposed by his wife's preferences (she did not like him going out on his own, and he said he thought he was 'under her thumb'), and a discrepancy between his prior expectations and his experience of marriage (for example he said he had thought he 'would be getting out more'). Finally Mr E also appeared highly constrained in the extent to which he had to endure his wife having autonomy in marital matters at his expense. This was an unusual situation in that his wife was the main income earner (unlike all the other wives in the sample); he spent a great deal of time away from his wife and family because of his occupational training course; and he said that he and his wife had grown apart so that he no longer wished to feel involved in family and marital matters. These things combined to make him feel he had little control over what happened within his marriage. Thus circumstances rather than his partner's wishes or demands had made her the one with the control rather than him. There is some tentative evidence therefore that dissatisfaction is associated with both divergent expectations and with unusually severe constraint, resulting either from a spouse's desire for dominance or from special external circumstances.

Concluding remarks

Five areas of reported marital constraint have been identified. There were few social-class or length-of-marriage differences except that responsibility and sharing space were mentioned somewhat more by working-class than by middle-class interviewees, and that responsibility was mentioned more often by older people, and sharing space by younger people. The slight class difference in the sharing space constraint may well be a product of the smaller average space per person in working-class households, and in the responsibility constraint it could be a product of the lower average wages of the working-class husbands, leading them to experience the responsibilities of the house, providing for children, and so on, as greater burdens than did the more affluent middle-class husbands. There were noticeable sex differences, with loss of freedom being an overwhelmingly male constraint and the assumption of tasks overwhelmingly female.

On some occasions, and for some people, the source of constraint was perceived to be the spouse (either because he or she dominated or because the one did not wish to annoy or hurt the other). More often, however, constraints were discussed as though the source were general rules or expectations about marriage behaviour, or internal rules agreed between the marriage partners.

Discussion of reported attitudes towards constraints showed almost everyone giving reasons both for dislike or regret and for enjoyment or acceptance. It might be that they did so because the interview situation or their expectations of what one should say about one's marriage required that it should be so. For example, it could be that people felt that in criticising marriage they were criticising their partners or implying that they did not have a satisfactory relationship; thus they might have felt the need to redress the balance. Conversely, it could be that having described how they accepted one area of marriage constraint they felt they ought to complain about it as well, because that would make their comments realistic (since 'everyone knows marriage isn't a bed of roses'). Again it could be that in asking for likes and dislikes the interviewer was merely receiving answers on both sides because she had requested them. To counter these arguments (which of course cannot be fully resolved without further study) it can be said that it was by no means always necessary to ask for both likes and dislikes in order to receive answers on both sides; the fact that people could describe, and often in some detail, both the kind of things they liked or accepted as well as those they disliked or regretted about the areas of constraint gives one some confidence that they were experienced and not merely created for the interview; and even if marriage is seen as a relationship which one ought to criticise as well as praise, it does not follow that people do not feel those sentiments in relation to their own marriages. It seems likely from what people said – as can clearly be seen in the quotes provided – that interviewees had their own marriages much in mind. It can tentatively be concluded, therefore, that (apart from the few exceptions mentioned) people did both dislike and accept the perceived constraints. Such a finding fits in well with those of previous chapters which show the balancing of the great variety of opposing situations, activities and sentiments in marriage.

The expressed attitudes suggest that marriage constraints can sometimes be accepted because of the identities which they provide as well as the marital stability which they foster: for example, being a responsible person, thoughtful and tolerant of others, a provider, a housewife, and so on. On the other hand it appears that the constraints are on the whole disliked for reasons which could be associated with loss of preferred identities: for example, the loss of ability to be a traveller, a free agent, a man with an exciting life, a carefree person, a woman in paid employment, a non-domesticated person, and so on.

Finally, although it was not possible to identify adequately the extreme cases (that is, those particularly heavily constrained or those particularly lightly constrained), and thus not possible to explore the association between dissatisfaction and the level of constraint, five people were tentatively picked out. Four were dissatisfied, and of these, three appeared relatively highly constrained. Their dissatisfaction indicated a regret at their inability to fulfil desired identities (for instance to be a free agent, to be independent, to be confident and in control). The fourth did not appear particularly highly constrained, and for him dissatisfaction seemed to be related to unusual expectations or ideals about intimate relationships. The fifth person was not dissatisfied even though appearing to bear very little constraint; however it looked as though he might soon have cause for dissatisfaction in that, by emphasising his own identity needs, he was jeopardising his wife's sense of commitment to him and thus the stability of his marriage.

All four of the people who appeared to experience either a relatively high or low level of constraint have been discussed in earlier chapters in a similar context. The As, for instance, were shown in chapter 3 as a couple who avoided conversation on some topics and who tended not to talk a great deal. Such identity-threatening behaviour was perhaps counterbalanced in Mr A's case by his apparently low level of constraint; but in his wife's case it was accompanied by what appeared to be considerable constraint, and it is not surprising therefore that she was one of the members of the sample who expressed most dissatisfaction with her marriage. Two other highly dissatisfied people were Mr E and Mr K. In this chapter they both appeared to feel highly constrained by marriage, and in the two previous chapters also to be in somewhat extreme positions. If Mr E's sense of identity was threatened by the roles he felt were forced upon him, such a feeling may well have been exacerbated by the lack of conversation with his wife; yet on the other hand the high level of separation between him and his wife may have helped him to maintain a sense of identity, even though he disliked it because it was a threat to the stability of his marriage. Mr K's sense of identity may also have been threatened by a feeling that he was constrained to do and be certain things within marriage; a particular source of dissatisfaction was his apparent inability to engage in much separate leisure-time activity. However, the fact that he and his wife seemed able to converse without avoidance of topics may have helped Mr K to maintain his sense of identity. Unlike some people, he did not seem worried that such freedom (which he said led to rows and disagreements) might threaten the stability of his marriage – in fact his commitment to the continuation of his marriage appeared somewhat tenuous in that he talked of regret at having got married and of the wish to be single again.

6

‣‣

Changes in self and in activities

The theme of this chapter is whether people perceive themselves as having been able to achieve within marriage either desired change or desired lack of change in themselves or in what they do; or whether they think they have changed in undesired ways, or failed to change in the desired ones. This theme arises from the hypothesis that the sense of stability will best be enhanced either by lack of change or by change only in ways which strengthen the bonds between the partners or the commitment each is seen to have to the other, whereas the sense of identity is likely to be best served when people feel able to change (themselves or their experiences) in whatever ways make them feel personally more fulfilled.

This chapter therefore examines what people said about how (if at all) they had changed during the time they had been married, and how (if at all) the things they did had changed; what they said they felt about change or lack of change is also examined. The data were gathered partly in response to specific questions on this subject: 'Do you think you have changed at all since you have been married / during the time you have been married?', 'Was there any change in you /your way of life after you married?', 'Are there any things you'd like to be able to do which you feel you can't do?', and so on. People also talked about change at several other points in the interview; these too have been incorporated into the findings.

Personal change

In the previous chapter some constraints involving personal change were discussed; for example, having become settled down, responsible and less autonomous. It was shown how these were said to be both regretted and accepted. In this chapter a rather broader view, not necessarily tied to expressions of the way in which one is constrained within marriage, will be taken.

The first question, therefore, is whether the interviewees said they had changed since or during their marriages. Thirty-five of the forty said that they had (two of these said that they had changed but did not know how, so only the remaining thirty-three will be discussed). Although one would not perhaps expect people to say that they had changed for the worse, the interesting thing about the kind of changes mentioned was that they involved, on the whole, morally reputable rather than neutral or negative changes. Two-thirds of the thirty-three said they had changed *only* in positive directions, and almost everyone else gave both positive and negative personal changes. Only two – and these were people already identified as dissatisfied in their marriages – described their personal change as having been for the worse.

The development of desirable characteristics

To describe what is meant by morally reputable change it is perhaps only necessary to list the kind of changes mentioned. Among the most common was that one had become more mature, grown-up, confident and independent. In this people matched Berger and Kellner (1964) who asserted that 'married people are more stable emotionally . . . more mature in their views . . . more sure of themselves'. Three-quarters of those who said this were women. For example:

> JA: Do you think you have changed at all since you've been married?
>
> Mrs K: Yes, I think I have grown up a bit, a good bit. I would do things now that I wouldn't do afore.
>
> JA: What sort of things?
>
> Mrs K: Well, like if any of Keith's family ever spoke to me, you know, and said something [i.e. something critical] I would just have sat and took it, but I wouldn't take it now. I wouldn't give them cheek, but I would just set the facts right. Like if ever I went into a shop before and the change was wrong I would just come out and complain to Keith, but I think I would turn round and *say* now. I don't know, I think you get a bit more gallas /// You just get, I don't know, hardened. It makes you not quite so feart of things.

Or Mrs S:

> JA: Can you answer that sort of question – how, if at all, you think you've changed?

Mrs S: Well, I've thought about it, so I should be able to say something about it. When I was married I certainly was immature. I didn't have opinions about politics, and I kept out of trouble, and did what I was told, and didn't argue with anybody /// So that as I've matured I've not been quite so willing to accept other people's points of view. I've developed opinions of my own, and because Sam was so dogmatic about *his* opinions I've tended deliberately to form my own opinions, to hold my end up.

She also said:

Mrs S: I think everybody has to adjust to someone else. You know, this is maturity, learning to live with somebody else, and let the other person develop one way and you develop another, and still stay together.

Next, people commented that they had become more considerate or thoughtful of others, less selfish or more capable of give and take. Again, such remarks were rather more common among women. For example:

Mrs L: I wasn't really . . . as I say I'm not really a person for making friends, never have been, but it does make me more friendly towards people we know, not so offhand. I think people maybe found me a bit offhand before [i.e. before marriage]. You know it makes you think more about other people I would say and . . . /// It makes you aware of other people more I would say. You know, I am more . . . thoughtful towards people – I try and help if I can – things like that.

Married people were also said to be more tolerant, and patient, mellower, less fussy. There was a slight bias in favour of the men in this answer. For example:

JA: Do you think that during the twenty years you've lived together that you've changed?
Mr S: Yes, yes. Oh, I'm mellower than I used to be.
JA: What does that mean?
Mr S: /// I think I'm far easier to get on with than I used to be. But of course this happens to all married men.
JA: Yes?
Mr S: Oh, indeed. I see it in youngsters in the office – youngsters – fellows of twenty who get married and they change radically.

Or Mr I:

JA: You don't think of her [wife] as being changed really?

Mr I: No. I think I've changed more than her. I think I've come more through to her.

JA: Yes, yes.

Mr I: I think she's been aye the same, but I think I've had to change /// I was still of this single . . . I was still a single man. But I just had to gradually . . . it took a long time, you know, just gradually to come round and, but the greatest thing to take me round was when I was knocked down in this accident and, er . . . that brought me round /// Yes, I think I am just mellowing with the years, I think. That's the whole story, I'm just mellowing with the years.

Married people were also said to be (as has been shown in the previous chapter) more responsible, serious, sensible, careful, cautious, settled down and stabilised. As with mellowing, such comments were found more among the men than the women. For instance:

JA: After you got married how did you feel that marriage had changed you, if at all? What difference had it made to your lives, being married?

Mr A: Oh . . . it makes you feel a bit more conscious of your responsibilities. Instead of spending my life going anywhere any time I like, or any time I feel I can do anything and just go out or off . . . when you are married you feel more conscious about your responsibility . . . You have this to do, you can't do that . . .

Or:

Mr L: I think once you're married people tend to recognise . . . think of you as being more mature perhaps, and er . . . settled down . . . I suppose this is the catch phrase – 'settled down now that he's married'. I suppose that's true to an extent, you do tend to settle down I think once you do become married.

Or:

JA: Do you think you've changed during the time you've been married?

Mr C: Well . . . as you get older you get more sensible really I suppose, do you? You take things more seriously . . . I do nowadays, than I used to. Of course you've more responsibility now.

Or:

Mr O: Now that I am married I don't rush into things /// Now, now that I'm married I notice I think more, I stop and think. You know, I don't jump into things the same.

Finally, there were a few less frequently mentioned positive qualities: having become less of a worrier or a nagger, less prudish, and more tactful. Commonsense tells one that all these are valued qualities; and one can see in the way people talked about them that they did view them favourably (with the possible exception of being settled down which can have a wide range of meaning from, on the negative side, being staid and boring to, on the positive side, being steady and reliable).

The development of less favourable qualities

Before looking at the perceived causes of personal change one should describe the more neutral or unfavourable qualities mentioned by eleven of the forty interviewees. (Of these eleven, six were women and five men; there was no clear difference by length of marriage or social class.) Nine different qualities were mentioned, and none by more than one or two of the eleven, apart from that of having become more short-tempered or of nagging more (mentioned by three women and one man). For instance:

> JA: And are there things that irritate him now?
> Mrs O: Er . . . I suppose there's nagging [L] . . . That's a thing I've found since I got married – I'm always nagging /// I think [names her child] maybe tends to make me nag more . . . you know, I just get all irritated and that, and I seem to find myself nagging at Owen . . .

Or:

> JA: Can you see differences if you try and look back and imagine what you were like, you know, in the early couple of years of your marriage say . . . and then look at yourself today?
> Mrs F: I was better tempered. [L] I don't know, I used to be a really sweet-natured character . . .
> JA: And aren't you now?
> Mr F: I'm sayin' nothin'.
> Mrs F: I'm told I shout. This is true.

Or:

> Mr M: I suppose I'm really a wee bittie mair irritable now than when I wis younger. [L] Maybe I would have accepted things more easily earlier on in life [L], easier than I would of now, you see . . .

The other negative qualities were being in a rut, being more tense or worrying more, being less lenient to one's spouse, more possessive, less confident, lazier, less independent, more resigned. For instance:

> JA: So you think you've changed over the past few years in some way?
>
> Mr E: Yeah, I think so. Not for the better either – I'm sorry to say. Well . . . I don't know what's wrong really, it's a lack of confidence.

Or:

> Mr M: Nowadays you more or less accept what's in front of you, you ken. When you were a bittie younger you could . . . if I'd accepted the opportunities that were going at the time, and things like that, things might have been different. Well I've been bothered with my back for quite a while and you're sort of resigned to what you ought to do, and that sort of thing. I canna seem to push myself on /// I just accept life as it comes.

Or there was Mr R, who having said that he thought he had become 'a wee bit staid', later said:

> Mr R: I suppose just all couples get into a rut. [L] I suppose if our daughter had lived nearer we'd be going to see her oftener. In the winter time we watch this thing [television] – which is a menace at times. I used to read a fair bit. I suppose latterly conversation *has* been drying up a wee bit.

For these eleven something had happened to give them traits which they did not wholly like. So one needs to look at what was said to have caused change, both positive and negative. First, however, one should ask whether the changes people mentioned as having occurred in themselves were recognised by their spouses. Thus each interviewee was asked how he thought his partner had changed, if at all. People were, on the whole, very positive about their spouses, either agreeing that the spouse had gained some of the favourable qualities or that the spouse had not changed, having always been relatively tolerant, considerate, mature, and so on. Of course they did not necessarily mention these qualities in quite the same way nor did they mention as many changes as people saw in themselves. It would thus be misleading to mention all the cases in which there was a lack of total concurrence between what people said of themselves and what their spouses said of them. However, it is interesting that in only three cases was there a very sharp divergence between husband and wife, such that where one saw an increase in positive qualities the other saw an increase in negative qualities. Both the As for example saw the other differently from the way they saw themselves. Mrs A said she thought she had become more possessive, selfish and short-tempered, and that she had not changed to the extent of being able to carry out the responsibilities of marriage. For example she said:

> Mrs A: Although I've been married for almost four years . . . I still don't think I accept the fact that I'm the woman in the household, and that I'm really a mother, and [names her child] has to depend on me.

Her husband, however, said he thought she had changed for the better:

> JA: Do you think Anne has changed since you've been married?
> Mr A: Er . . . well, according to me she's changed quite a lot.
> JA: In what way?
> Mr A: You know, she was a type like . . . what would you call it? . . . not used to taking responsibility on her shoulders . . . And I think she's coping fine /// She's doing it, and that's why I feel she has confidence in herself. She makes her own decisions . . .

On the other hand Mrs A thought her husband had changed for the worse, whilst he said he thought he had changed for the better. This fits in well with a finding by Shafer and Braito (1979) which showed that people's evaluation of their spouses and their spouses' marital role performance was positively related to the way they evaluated themselves, in the sense that if they valued themselves favourably they would value their spouses favourably, and vice versa. For instance, Mrs A said her husband was very much the master of the house, and that if there was something she wanted but he did not, or did not think she ought to have, she would not get it. This was compared by Mrs A with his behaviour before marriage:

> JA: Do you think Alan has changed or not?
> Mrs A: Yes.
> JA: In what ways has he changed?
> Mrs A: Well, before . . . I mean, he would give me what I wanted. If I said that I liked something he would go out and run and buy it. But now all that sort of magic, as you could say, has gone.

Mr A did not think he had changed very much, apart from losing his freedom a little and becoming more tolerant. As he said:

> Mr A: One thing I've learned from marriage is more tolerance . . . 'cos before, I used to be so hard – I was really hard . . .

Although this does not really contrast with Mrs A's views about the disappearance of her husband's indulgence towards her, none the less their
comments about each other show no agreement. The other person
whose views about his spouse did not accord with her own was Mr E.
He made critical comments about the change in his wife, seeing her as
having become less fun to be with, less capable of 'seeing the funny side
of things', and more of a gossiper. She, on the other hand, did not see
changes in herself except to say that she had become less of a nagger
than she used to be. Apart from these cases, however, there were none
where wholly positive comments about the changes in self by one interviewee were matched by negative comments (or vice versa) about that
interviewee by his or her spouse.

Causes of personal change

People saw three main causes of change. They explained it as caused by
the marriage state itself, or by learning a quality directly from the
spouse, or by the process of growing older (that is, some things were
seen as likely to happen regardless of one's marital status). Sometimes
only one type of cause was indicated, sometimes more than one; but by
far the most common interpretation of change was that it was caused by
marriage itself. In this they matched Becker's explanation of personal
change in adult life (Becker 1964), which he saw as the effect of
situational adjustment. More specifically McCall and Simmons (1966)
say that 'it is primarily within relationships that persons grow and
evolve. Most of the new identities that we acquire, as well as the
changes in those we already hold, arise from intimate association
with others.'

One may take, for example, the quality of being responsible. Those
who get married were seen as having to possess the potential for taking
responsibility, but more important (as the previous chapter showed)
was the view that when married one has to be a responsible person. Mr
A, for instance, accounted for his sense of responsibility by saying that
now he was married there were certain things one had to do, and certain
things one could not do. Another man put the sense of responsibility
down to the fact that husbands 'have to provide for' their families. He
could see exceptions, but they were very peculiar ones:

> Mr L: I can't understand people that don't work, are content to live at the
> bare minimum and sort of just survive, and anything extra that they
> get they go and have a good bucket on, or anything like this, you

know. I can't understand that, you know, because you see their children, and they know themselves it's other people's money that's buying their clothes, and half the time they're dirty anyway . . .

Not everyone mentioned the exceptions; they tended to take for granted the general view that when people get married they take on the responsibility for providing for homes, wives and children and thus they are responsible people. Thus when another man talked of feeling more responsible and was asked to explain what he meant, he said:

> Mr J: Well . . . when you were single you could go out and spend your money, things like that and not worry about it really – because you always had somewhere to go /// And you didn't have to spend your money on a house and things to run it. You could go out at weekends and spend your money.

Thus, to sum up, married people are responsible because they have responsibilities which all – except for the odd few people – have to fulfil.

Confidence and maturity could also be seen as due to marriage itself (and all that goes with that). One person said that it was due to the feeling that 'you've achieved something in life probably'; others that it was because one was coming into contact with more people than one had before. It was also seen as connected with not having other people to do things for one, having to perform tasks, take decisions, and so on, for oneself:

> Mrs J: I think you all grow up when they get married.
> JA: Yes?
> Mrs J: 'Cause . . . suddenly there's nobody there to do things for you, and everything's happening.

It was just as common, however, for this change to be interpreted as due to the inevitable passing of the years: as one becomes older one becomes more mature, grown-up and confident. This point was not described in detail; people just said such things as: 'Well, you do get more mature as you get older', or: 'When you're older you have more confidence.'

In discussing being settled or stabilised people again tended to talk about their responsibilities and how they could no longer 'get out' when they wished, but had wives, homes and families to look after. A different kind of answer was given by a man who said that one is more 'stabilised' in that: 'You have a house to come back to, and you know there's somebody waiting for you.' This is an interpretation referring not to the responsibilities of marriage but to what one might call anchors, permanent connections which hold one in place and prevent one from making frequent changes in behaviour. This quality was explained entirely in terms of marriage itself and what it does to one.

Another change explained in terms of marriage itself was that of becoming more independent. Having moved away from parents, or having to do things for oneself now that one was married, was said to be the reason why some people felt more independent. For example Mrs I said:

> Mrs I: I married for someone to lean on, you know. My impression of my husband during the time I was going with him was that he was so self-confident, you know, and I was the opposite, and here was somebody I could lean on and look up to, sort of thing. And well . . . my husband just said it himself, he can't *see* it. I never did after we got married, I mean I found I *had* to . . . you know, so I could say I was different entirely.

A group of qualities of a rather similar kind were explained partly by marriage itself, and partly by the influence of the spouse. These were the traits of having become more thoughtful, considerate, tolerant, patient, less selfish and more able to give and take. (About three-quarters explained the change mainly by reference to marriage itself, and about one-quarter mainly to the influence of the spouse.) Mrs L, for example, used the former type of explanation. After saying that she had become more thoughtful of other people, the conversation continued:

> JA: And is that due to living with another person, or is it because your husband is that sort of person himself, or what?
>
> Mrs L: No, I think it's through living with him, because everything you do is in . . . well, most things you do is in some connection with them, like . . . You know, I just couldn't go out and spend all his pay, and things like that; you've got to think . . . I found you've got to think of him when you're doing things . . .

The same kind of answer – that when you live with someone else you *have* to become less self-centred, more tolerant, and so on – came up time and time again:

> Mrs F: I would be less selfish – self-centred I should say, nae selfish – though I used to be selfish once /// but when you just had yourself to think

about, what you were going to do . . . now you have to think for several . . .

Or Mrs M:

Mrs M: Well, you've to stop thinking on yourself, you've to think of your husband and your family. You hinna' the same freedom. I mean you've got to think there's a few instead of just the one person . . .

Or Mr E:

Mr E: You just *have* to consider her a wee bit.

Of course the dividing line between an explanation which asserts that it is being married and living with another person that has led to the personal changes, and one which says that it is living with one's own particular spouse and his effect upon one which has led to the changes, is a narrow one. Sometimes respondents did not make the distinction clearly, but at least one can say that either or both of these factors were involved in people's explanation. Below are some of the comments which stressed the influence of one's own particular spouse.

Mr B: I've probably learned to consider other people quite a bit more than what I did when I was . . . which is probably one of her good points that's rubbed off on me.

Or:

JA: Do you think you and your husband have sort of learned a little bit from one another? Have you become more like one another, or not?

Mrs M: Oh, well, aye. I think I have learned patience from Mike. He's the one that is patient, and I think I've learned to be more patient off of Mike. I don't know what he got off me though, but I think I have learned that.

Or:

Mr S: And this is Sheila's influence on me – there's no doubt about it that the unkindnesses that I was guilty of when I was in my early twenties have to a great degree disappeared. I still can't suffer fools gladly, but I don't hurt them.

Mr S also mentioned one other (related) quality: that of having mellowed. This he explained as due to marriage, and the influence of women in general upon their husbands:

JA: So you say something happens to men when they get married. Can you say how this happens, or is it impossible to answer?

Mr S: Women are nicer people. I've thought this for many, many years. The prisons are full of men; there are hardly any women in prison, and the people who carry out the worst possible crimes under the sun are men /// And it's not in the nature of women to be cruel and unkind as overtly as men do. I would maintain that they are to some extent in a softer fashion.

Mellowing was also seen by two people, like becoming more confident and grown-up, as part of the process of growing older. Becoming less fussy, more cautious or careful, and less of a worrier was explained by some people as due to the influence of the spouse (e.g. 'some of him's rubbed off on me'). Finally, two people explained changes by reference to the interaction of the partners within marriage, yet not in the general sense described above but by reference to the particular type of interaction within their own marriage. Thus Mrs T talked of how she had 'learned to be terribly tactful over the years' partly because her husband was very impulsive, impatient and moody; and because he was always 'either on top of the world or down in the dumps' she felt she had had to 'steer very much a middle course'. Another woman (Mrs I) said she used to be 'a bit of a nagger' but that she had become less so in recent years because her husband had mellowed and become easier to live with.

When examining the nine negative traits one sees the same kind of interpretations, with the exception of the diffusion of qualities from spouse to spouse. Marriage in general was seen to explain some part of becoming less lenient, more stuck in a rut, and more nagging or short-tempered. For example:

Mrs P: You've never found out my faults, have you, dear?

Mr P: She's faultless! [L] No, I honestly thought before I got married that nagging was a myth . . . I discovered that it wasn't when I did get married . . .

Mrs P: Yes, of course. But the whole point is, why do women nag?

Mr P: Yes, I know. But I realise now why they nag and I sympathise with them . . .

Mrs P: Yes, *you* know that . . . lots of men don't.

Mrs P had previously explained that what they meant was that marriage, by confining women to the dependent roles of housewife and mother without an opportunity for independent fulfilment, caused them to nag their husbands. Another more negative quality (becoming less lenient) was similarly explained, by Mr L, as being due to marriage. Having said that his wife now thought he was 'rotten' to her, he explained that he could not be so lenient, could not let her have her own way as he did before they were married, because they now had a house and a child to be responsible for, and only one salary to cover the necessary expenses. The particular influence of children could also be mentioned as a cause of nagging and also of having become more possessive, more tense and more worried.

One's own particular marriage could also be seen as part of the problem. Mr E, for example, saw his growing lack of self-confidence as due to the fact that, because he had spent so much time during his marriage training for a job rather than working, he had gradually let all the decision-making pass to his wife; this he said had had a detrimental effect on him:

> Mr E: I think the thing that really bothers me most at the present time is . . . I can see it within sight of course . . . is the fact that I had plenty of confidence before I got married. I got married and still had, and then this situation of my wife sorta doing all the earning, you know, bit ·into me really, because . . . personally, for me, the way I was brought up makes this wrong, you know.

Mr K described his growing lack of independence as due to the fact that his wife did not like him going out on his own and that he was now 'under her thumb'. As he said:

> Mr K: I've changed a lot. I dinna ken what way like – the ways I've changed, but I have changed /// I dinna' go oot as much /// never go oot at nights myself. I dinna' get to . . .
> Mrs K: I dinna let him.
> Mr K: Sometimes I'll get oot – very seldom.

Finally, there was 'growing older'. This could be seen as part of the explanation of increasing irritability, tenseness and resignation. Little detail was given, people merely saying such things as: 'I think you do get more irritable as you get older'; 'As the years pass you become more accepting, more resigned'; 'I think it's my age – the time of life – which makes me more tense.'

In summary, therefore, the main interpretations of changing personal qualities were marriage in general (including children in general); marriage in particular or the influence of one's own particular spouse;

and the inevitable process of growing older. The first of these explanations was the most common. It should indeed be added that as well as the interviewees' explicit interpretations of the changes in personal character as due to marriage in general, it can also be seen that when they mentioned the changes in the first place there was a strong tendency to generalise about them (that is, to suggest that *one* becomes more considerate, etc., or *all* married people become more grown-up, etc.) even when asked specifically about themselves.

Of course, the question of whether people feel they have either been able to change in desired directions or not change in undesired directions is a very difficult thing to examine in an interview study, especially if one would like them to speculate about hypothetical situations. 'Would you personally like to have changed in other ways?', for example, is an impossible question for most people. One must therefore be content with more limited aims, and merely ask whether people seemed content with the ways they said they had changed. One can also ask whether dissatisfaction is seen as due to marriage preventing personal development or fulfilment. In the light of the discussion above the answers to these questions are relatively clear. On the whole people do appear to like the kind of selves they think they have become. How could one dislike being thoughtful, considerate, responsible, tolerant, mature, tactful, and so on? What people appear to be doing is demonstrating that they belong to a category of normal, respectable, moral people: namely those who are married. This has been suggested by other writers. Thus Morgan (1977) says that 'marriage is seen as being identified with the attainment of full adult status or, in more popular terms, with "settling down", while the single status may be regarded as less "natural", as a problem demanding sympathy and a solution, or as a source of other problems'. Similarly, Turner (1970) states that marriage 'is one of the key devices . . . for validating personal adequacy, heterosexual normality and personal maturity'. The tendency for the married to see themselves in this morally reputable light has perhaps acted as an obstruction to wider or more detailed discussion of specific types of personal change. One cannot know; it may be that this view of the married as morally respectable people is entirely the way people see themselves as changing; it may blind them to other kinds of selves they could, or could have, become; it may be that there are no other preferred selves for most of them, or it may be that they do see other selves out of reach, but are prepared to accept and be content with the qualities they have achieved, which might be jeopardised by a search for others.

For only a minority of people was marriage seen as having been accompanied by some undesirable personal changes, but for most of these people a development of the more favourable qualities was also talked about; they were thus not wholly dissatisfied with the ways in which they had changed during the time they had been married. Only two people failed to balance their comments by mention of favourable changes; one was Mrs A, who has already been mentioned as saying she thought she had become more possessive and short-tempered, and had failed to become more responsible; the other was Mr E, who said he had lost confidence and become more moody (and also implied that he had failed to become more responsible). One would like to suggest, by twisting the original hypotheses, that these dissatisfied people would fall into one of two categories: either they would be dissatisfied because they had experienced considerable personal change which, while congruent with their desires for individual fulfilment, did not assist the stability of their marriages; or they would be dissatisfied because they had not changed, or had changed only in ways congruent with marital stability and not in ways which furthered personal fulfilment. However, neither Mrs A nor Mr E could easily be placed in either of these categories; both had changed somewhat but not in ways which furthered either self-fulfilment *or* marital stability. Thus Mrs A saw her possessiveness and lack of responsibility as good neither for herself nor for her marriage; Mr E saw his lack of self-confidence in the same way. These two were therefore rather special cases, and cannot be placed among those from whom – according to the original hypotheses – one would expect to hear dissatisfaction, namely those in extreme positions as far as the experience of personal change is concerned. The only other people it is possible to pick out are the five who said they had not changed. None of them (three women and two men; three older and two younger marriages; three working-class and two middle-class) expressed any desire for personal change. But it has already been suggested that such hypothetical situations may be very difficult for people to conceptualise and to talk about. However, one of them had been married only a few months and therefore was perhaps not yet in a position to perceive personal change or lack of change. Another laid great stress during the interviews on his contentment with family life and his readiness to settle down after a 'good broad life' before marriage; it may well be therefore that his lack of personal change was quite congruent with his own perceived identity needs. The other three, while not talking of desired *personal* change, did express some fairly strong regrets about unachieved changes in activities (and change in *activities* may be much easier to talk about than change in self).

Returning to the majority view about personal change, it may well be a common belief in our society that people change for the better, or in morally reputable ways, as a result of marriage (it was certainly common in this sample). If this is so, then perhaps one should not expect people to find it easy to present an alternative or a dissenting view. Possibilities for, or restrictions of, preferred activities may, however, be a different matter, and discussion now turns to this topic.

Changes in activities and interests

Obviously there can be an enormous number of changes in both major and minor, or long-lasting and ephemeral, interests and activities. People were therefore asked to talk about their main interests and activities, and – by means of a number of different types of question – to say how these had changed if at all. For example, they were asked whether their lives had changed when they got married, in the time since they had been married, in recent years; whether their interests had changed; whether there were some things they felt they could do now or had to do now which they had not done before; whether there were some things they would like to be able to do; and of course during the general recounting of the histories of their married lives they mentioned change or lack of change.

Naturally, there had been a considerable number of changes in people's activities; it would be very odd to find a person who said that his life since marriage was very similar to his life before marriage, or that his life had remained very much unchanged during marriage (though one can imagine such situations). The changes can be divided into activities gained and activities lost; and all interviewees said they had both gained and lost. (It does not of course follow that they liked what they had gained and disliked what they had lost.)

Activities gained

People had gained a variety of activities or interests, although there were three which stood out as more common than the rest. These were an interest in, and involvement with, children; an interest and involvement in their homes or houses; and housework. Everyone who had children talked of their advent as of the coming of a new interest, and all spoke of it favourably (although many of them also spoke of childcare as a gained activity not wholly liked). For example:

JA: Do you think that the things you're interested in have changed at all?

Mrs C: Yes, well, before I was married, I never had much time for people's children. You know, if I'd to talk to children . . . but now – well, you're really interested . . .

Or:

Mrs M: When we married we just said we would have family and . . .

Mr M: And Maureen said she'd have four.

Mrs M: I said I would like four sons /// And when I fell I was fair thrilled, I couldn't believe myself.

Or:

Mrs S: I like having a lot of young children, because I'm very fond of young children, and was very interested in young children, and I liked that. I hated the pregnancies, but I liked the babies.

About two-thirds talked of the development of their interest in the marital home, and again it was mainly of an interest they were glad to have gained. As Mr I said:

Mr I: You are just as well getting a house together, and having a wee bit of comfort.

Most women saw housework as an activity gained largely since being married, and (as the previous chapter showed) they had mixed feelings about it. Other activities which seemed largely gladly gained, and which had occurred at some time since marriage, were: a change of job (eight people); community involvement (eight); a move to a new town (four); an interest in politics (three); evening classes; sport; an interest in the spouse's work; in animals, friends and holidays. Two further examples of the kind of things they said are:

JA: And when did things start improving financially?

Mrs C: Well, you always got a better . . . you got a better job – the same kind of job, but I mean . . . better bonuses and . . .

Mr C: Better money . . . I was with the same firm for a year after I got married. Then I seen there's better money . . . and once I got kinda a

foot in the town, you ken, to see what was what, I got another
job . . .

Or:

> JA: Do you think any of your interests, or the things you like to do,
> have changed?
>
> Mrs F: I dinna think so. I feel that if . . . if anything I have more interests
> now than I had when I was single /// Well, for example, they used to
> ask me to do Sunday School when I was single and I would never do
> it; so I have got that extra . . .

Gained activities which were said to be disliked, or about which people
had very mixed feelings, were (apart from housework and childcare)
watching television more, spending more time just with their spouse,
looking after elderly relatives, and joining their spouse's church. For
example, about watching television, Mr O said, when asked what kind
of things he did when he was at home:

> Mr O: I read. I don't read as much as I used to. I find this thing here . . . you
> see Olive loves tele', you see, and I find I'm lazy . . . and it
> drags me away.

Activities lost

The losses were even more various, although one activity stood out
from the rest: this was the partial loss of 'social life' (going out, going
for a drink, and so on). As the previous chapter indicated, it was mentioned particularly by men; it was talked of with regret, but most people
had something to say to mitigate the loss. The next most frequently
mentioned loss was that of women's paid employment (excluding here
those who at some stage lost the work activity but regained it later on).
Nine women had at some stage since marriage given up a job and not
returned to it; seven of them expressed regret at this loss. For
example:

> JA: Do you ever think about going back to work?
>
> Mrs O: I would *like* to go back – just part-time. But I can't really because I've
> nowhere to put [names her son] – unless I paid to put him in a nursery
> /// and it wouldn't be worth it, you know.

Or:

> JA: Have you ever felt like going back to work?
>
> Mrs T: Yes, I feel like it about three times every day /// Speaking purely for

myself, getting myself right away from it, yes, I would go back in a minute. I miss it very much. *But* I feel I'm needed more at home.

Another loss, talked about mainly by men, was that of either participating in sport, taking exercise or watching sport (about one-third said they did not miss it at all, and two-thirds that they had some regrets). For example:

Mr H: I do evening classes, and up until I got too old I used to play a lot of football, lot of sport. Now Helen, in her younger days, she used to come and watch. That was before she had three children. But after that she came . . . you can't blame her. No, I was very keen on sport, but I haven't done it for some time now. But I would say most of the things, you see, most of your life is tied up with the house, the garden and the car – there's not much time for much else. Those people who have hobbies, I often wonder how.

Or:

Mr R: It's funny, isn't it, how the wheel turns? He [Mr R's son] is mad on golf now, and I'm sort of, er, over the hill and prefer to take it easy at night, you know. [L]

A minority of the men mentioned the loss of going out with other women, ceasing to help with housework and childcare when the children grew up, and ceasing to travel in connection with their job. They had mixed feelings about all these losses.

The other more female losses, apart from work, were buying clothes, knitting or sewing, dancing, visiting friends, talking to parents, and the chance to do things on one's own without the accompaniment of children (all were spoken of with regret, though often with mitigating comments).

Other losses mentioned by only one or two people each, and without any particular sex bias, were the loss of a joint leisure activity or talking with the spouse; the additional time one used to spend in bed; reading; some of the child interest one used to have before the children grew up; playing games; and involvement in community or religious activities. Again, all were spoken of with regret (apart from the loss of religious activity), but often with resignation or acceptance.

Most people also said they had retained, or regained, some of their interests or activities during marriage. Most of the men had retained the same type of occupation throughout marriage (not always with expressions of positive enjoyment); some of the women had regained the opportunity to work after a period without a job while they were looking after children; some people had retained interests which they had had before marriage, such as sport, cars, politics, and religious activity.

The overall picture can be crudely summarised as follows:

	Total	Women	Men	Younger	Older
Gains					
enjoyed	40	20	20	20	20
regretted	17	12	5	11	6
Losses					
enjoyed, or not missed	17	9	8	6	11
regretted	29	16	13	16	13
Things retained/regained					
enjoyed	28	15	13	15	13
regretted	4	—	4	1	3

Figures refer to persons and not activities

Of course, these figures do fairly severe injustice to the data, but they can be used to show that *all* had gained some interest which they said they enjoyed; that *most* said they had lost some interest which they regretted (even if they saw mitigating factors), and retained or regained some activity which they enjoyed; and that almost *half* said they had gained some activity which they regretted as well as losing something which they had not missed. Women were more likely to say they had experienced a regretted gain (mainly housework), and the longer-married seemed slightly less likely to have any regretted gains or losses. There was no difference by social class.

To add to the picture of 'regrets', one may also ask whether people could talk of desired changes of activity which they had not been able to achieve. Such questions produced answers (regrets) from a further quarter of the sample (five men and five women; six younger and four older; eight middle-class and only two working-class). Half of the answers referred to moving house or travelling. For example:

> Mr E: I'm sorta' restless, and I want to move away from Aberdeen . . . but she [Mr E's wife] doesna want to do this really.

Or:

> JA: And you say there are some things you would have liked to do?
>
> Mr M: Well . . . well, I suppose I would maybe like to tak' up golf. I suppose, but that disna' work out. When I was younger I was workin' quite a lot, and things like that. I might of went tae sea, but then again I was workin', and then I got married, and that put a head on that.

The other answers involved having more fun or doing something more exciting, but unspecified; having more leisure to go to activities like evening classes; or wanting to live in a commune.

Thus all people appear to have been able to change in some desired or enjoyed directions; but also all except one (Mr D) appear to have some regrets: that they have not been able to change in some directions, have not been able to retain or regain enjoyed activities, or have not been able to prevent unenjoyable changes.

Causes of gains and losses

Marriage, more than anything else, appeared as the source of both desired and undesired changes. Many of the changes or retention of activities which people said they enjoyed could be seen as occurring as a direct or indirect consequence of being married: for example, having a home of one's own, and the interest one then takes in furnishing it, altering it, and so on. For instance, one of the nice things about being married was, said Mrs J:

> Mrs J: A place of our own . . . where we could put down roots.

Similarly, Mrs N said, when asked about the advantages of being married over being single:

> Mrs N: The advantages? Because you're on your own, you've got your own house, and you can do what you like.

Mrs I, too, after her husband had talked of the responsibility of marriage, said:

> Mrs I: Well, it's maybe responsibility, but it's a different type of enjoyment. I mean we had great fun getting a house together to start with, you know that.

Of course one does not have to be married to have children, but all members of this sample did have theirs within marriage (though six of the twenty couples had a pre-nuptially conceived child). They all said both that in general it was not advisable or that it was not right to have children outside marriage *and* that when one is married it is right or normal to have children. Thus such enjoyment as they have found in having children could be said to have come to them as an indirect consequence of marriage. For example:

> JA: So on the whole you have enjoyed having children – you wouldn't have liked to go through life without having had any?
>
> Mr G: Oh, aye. Oh, no – I don't know how couples can stay together theirselves unless they have children. They must be fed up without a family.

Housework, too, was seen as having been gained as a result of marriage, and of thereby having a house of one's own. As one woman said, when asked if marriage had been similar to, or different from, what she had expected:

> Mrs O: Well, I think, I think that when you're younger you think: 'It must be great to be married', you know, sort of thing . . . having a house to look after, children and that . . . but it's not like that at all. It's just like . . . getting another job, sort of thing [L] . . . cleaning and cooking and . . . looking after children, you know.

The other activities which were sometimes said to have changed as a direct or indirect consequence of marriage in general, and which were liked or accepted, were, first, spending more time at home and watching television more often. As the previous chapter showed, married people were seen as expected to go out less often. People with children often explained this as a consequence of having children to look after, but even those without said they did not go out as often as before marriage. Second, there was taking more interest in politics or the state of the country's economy, or in special-interest groups like the women's movement. For example:

> JA: Do you think the things you're interested in have changed at all?
>
> Mrs C: /// You're more interested in the state of the country I think . . . once you get married.

Third, there was also taking an interest in one's spouse's job, learning about aspects of his or her work. Fourth came losing an interest in clothes; this was again seen as partly due to marriage itself: there were other things to think about, and it was not so necessary to be well-dressed, because one was going out less often. It was also seen as related to having children to look after and not having a job of one's own, so that one had both less time and less money to spend on clothes. Fifth, there was becoming involved in child-centred activities such as Scouts, Boys Brigade, Sunday School. Again, since children were seen to follow from marriage, and participating in activities for their benefit as following from having children, then marriage itself indirectly initiated these activities. Sixth, and finally, there was not having to work. If a woman did not have paid employment, then she could either put this down directly to marriage itself, or indirectly through having children to look after. For instance:

JA: Have you worked at all since you've been married?

Mrs F: No, not at all.

JA: No paid employment.

Mrs F: No. I'd like to, but well, I keep thinking if the children are ill . . . you know, that sort of thing /// He'd like me to go back. But I think the children come first. If I got something part-time, pretty local, I think I might snap it up. But . . . I find I've a full-time job . . .

Or:

JA: In what way do you think your life has changed?

Mrs D: Well, it changed in as much as . . . I mean I stopped my work. It was into a house, and housekeeping /// I think it was more the thing [in those days] . . . you got married . . . and, you know, you just settled down to your home life.

Some of the desired or accepted activities were naturally not said to have resulted from being married. For instance, fifteen of the twenty men said that on balance they were content with, or accepted, the job they had either gained during marriage or retained since marriage. None of them said that this retention or gain had resulted from their being married: they would have done it anyway. Some people had kept or gained new interests; again some of these were said to be just things they wanted to do and not influenced either way by their marriage or their spouse (e.g. cars, politics, sport, religion). Some activities were also seen as just things one wanted to do, but they appeared to have been achieved despite marriage (rather than because of it or without its influence). They had often been achieved with the help or support of spouses, children and parents, or because children were now growing up and therefore less of a hindrance. The most important of these were women's employment, some hobbies or interests, and holidays. Very rarely were retained or gained activities spoken of as occurring in the face of opposition from the spouse, unless that opposition was mild. Only two such instances could be found: one where a woman took a job, although her husband disapproved, because she had the support of her doctor who thought it would be good for her to work; and one where a man retained his interest in football, even though his wife disliked it; however he treated this as rather a joke, and said he was 'working on her'.

Occasionally spouses were seen as directly influential, either by default or by positive influence and encouragement. Thus one woman explained her recent interest in some community activities as due to her poor relationship with her husband, which had driven her to find companionship elsewhere; one man explained how he had approached a potential employer on his wife's behalf, because he thought she wanted to go back to work; spouses could also – by their own enthusiasm for an activity – engender interest in their partners (again, for example, sport or community activities). Finally, some enjoyed activities were seen as coming about through the process of growing older. For example, people said they had come to enjoy more sedentary occupations as time passed; or that as their parents aged, they had come to spend more time helping to look after them.

In summary, apart from things which were said to happen just because one wanted them to happen, these accounts of enjoyed or accepted change or retention of activities were similar to the accounts of personal change: they were either a result of marriage itself, of one's own marriage relationship or particular spouse, or they resulted from the process of growing older (with marriage itself – and the children associated with it – bringing the greatest changes in enjoyed activity).

Turning to unenjoyable or regretted retentions or changes, one sees a similar pattern of sources (apart from the explanation in terms of purely personal choice). For although many of them could be described as multi-causal, the major influences as stated by the interviewees were: marriage and the activities which almost inevitably accompany it; one's own marriage relationship or the influence of one's own spouse; and growing older or general physical deterioration.

Just over half of the undesired or unenjoyed activities were said to result mainly from marriage itself. These were chiefly the gaining of housework and childcare, the loss of social life, and the loss of opportunity for paid employment. The first and third mainly affected women, and the second both equally. As shown earlier, men also described marriage as preventing or inhibiting their chances to engage in activities such as going out with other women, travelling, changing their job, going to sea, spending time on reading or sport; or as forcing them to change their jobs or spend more time on home-based activities like decorating or watching the television. For example:

> Mr B: I know if I hadn't married I'd still be at sea . . . I definitely would not have come ashore . . . Oh, I liked the sea.

Women also saw marriage, and what goes with it, as preventing them engaging in activities on their own, taking an interest in clothes, spending time with their parents, sewing, or visiting, or just doing something exciting but unspecified. For example, Mrs O said:

> Mrs O: I used to do a lot of sewing, but I don't have a lot of time now to do it the same as I used to /// Well, you see, I have an electric sewing machine, and with [names son] being there, he would be touching it all the time, and I couldn't, you know, sit and concentrate.

In cases where their own particular marriage relationship or spouse was mentioned as the main source of regretted change or prevention of change (one-sixth of such activities), people mentioned a variety of interests, including social life, hobbies, sport, moving house. Thus two men said they could not move to a different area because their wives would be unhappy to do so. For example:

> Mr R: I would have emigrated when I came back from the Army, but she wouldna'. She liked Aberdeen so that's that, and so I suppose I merely gave in. If she had went, it would have been under duress, so that was no use. Unless you're both thinking the same it's no use.

Another example was Mrs T, who said she could not go to evening classes because her husband often worked at night and therefore could not take care of the children.

Growing older as a reason for undesired gains or losses (mainly losses) was of course almost entirely given by the older couples (one-quarter of all the regretted activities came into this category). They included loss of sporting activities, loss of previous child-associated activities (because children had grown up), loss of employment, and the gain of more indoor, sedentary occupations like television and reading. For example:

JA: Do you think the sort of things you do have changed?

Mr G: Oh, yes. I used to do a lot of cycling, and played football and went to football matches and that when I was younger /// I still cycle round about the town. It is just a few years ago that I stopped cycling up and down to my work. I just stopped it – I am getting too old for the hill, you see /// just taking it easy now.

Or:

Mr S: Our problem has been that we've always had kids about us. This provided a beautiful vehicle for holidays, holidays that I enjoyed /// There was always something new to happen /// When they were all young, I would say that if I look back in ten to fifteen years' time, that is bound to be the happiest time /// And now we've reached the stage where they've [grown up] . . . they tend to solve their own problems.

Finally, one in ten of the regretted activities was explained by reference to a variety of quite extraneous factors. For example, there was Mr I, whose serious accident he held to account for his giving up going out drinking (though he also saw this accident as helping to bring about other, wholly desirable changes). A further two men explained their loss of opportunity to watch football as due to the fact that the side they supported had ceased to be worth watching!

In conclusion therefore, marriage – in general and in particular – was described as causing activities to change in regretted ways and as preventing opportunities to do desired things (although there were other factors which were also seen to account for these constraints). However, to balance this, marriage was also described as bringing about several desirable or enjoyable changes in activity.

Concluding comments

Apart from the interest of this chapter's findings as descriptive data, one has to be very careful, because of some evident methodological problems, about drawing further conclusions or implications. The first of these problems is that this chapter has attempted to cover a very wide range of topics, and to cover topics requiring interviewees to provide information drawn often from many years of experience. This was necessary in order to examine people's present perceptions of change, but it has meant that all substantive topics have been dealt with at a somewhat cursory level and without full acknowledgement of their complexity or the complexity of the attitudes towards them. The second problem is that, whilst the aim was to broaden the discussion away from marriage and towards the self and individual activities (i.e. changes not necessarily tied to marriage but merely taking place within that period of time during which a person has been married), the interviewees, feeling that the researcher's interest was in marriage, may well have concentrated to some extent upon those personal traits or activities which they saw as affected by marriage. It should also be added that the analysis of extreme cases, which can be a useful contribution to the exploration of the hypotheses, was not possible in this chapter because of the complexity of the data, the lack of quantifiable measures, and the failure of any self-evidently extreme cases to emerge from the data. Having said this, however, attention can be drawn to Mrs A and Mr E who emerged as unusual (rather than as extreme) cases in that they saw themselves as having changed for the worse, and in ways which they did not see as enhancing either their sense of identity or their sense of stability. Their dissatisfaction with these changes – and indeed with some of the changes in their activities – is matched in earlier chapters by other sources of dissatisfaction. Thus Mrs A was unhappy with the lack of talk between her and her husband and said that she wished for more companionship; she also appeared dissatisfied with the ways in which she was constrained to behave within marriage, for instance discussing in her interview the extent to which she had to give in to her husband, the burdens of responsibility she had to bear, and the tasks she had to carry out. Since therefore she did not have the opportunity to develop a preferred identity in conversation with her spouse, and since she appeared heavily constrained to assume certain types of identity, it is hardly surprising that she did not appear content with the ways she thought she had changed. Similarly Mr E had said he regretted the passing of 'real companionship' between him and his wife, the lack of time they now spent together, and the fact that he had been forced into certain roles in his marriage (e.g. being the one with little control over financial matters). Again it is therefore no wonder that Mr E was unhappy with the changes in himself and his activities, and had come to see himself as moody and lacking in self-confidence.

In general, marriage appeared, from what people said, to be an arena within which a considerable amount of change was experienced. Personal change certainly did not appear to be prohibited, but the fact that questions about such change led most people to demonstrate what can be called the morally reputable character of married people means that it is impossible to gain any clear evidence about whether personal change has been in individually satisfying or fulfilling directions. For, as already stated, one could not expect people to express dissatisfaction with the praiseworthy qualities they seem to see themselves as having developed. One may speculate, however, that these qualities on the whole are more stability-maintaining than identity-enhancing in that they tend to emphasise the characteristics required for living in harmony with another person rather than for seeking individual development. For instance, consideration, tolerance, responsibility, tact and so on are all qualities which would make living with another person easier. Indeed, people's own explanations of these changes indicated that they thought that these were qualities one had to have in order to achieve a good marital relationship. There were, however, a few qualities which seem more identity-enhancing than stability-maintaining: having opinions of one's own, learning to stick up for oneself, becoming more confident. As one would expect, marriage was also often seen as the source of these identities. The hypothesis would suggest that these were developed partly through conversation with the intimate other; thus one woman said she had developed opinions of her own through association with an opinionated husband. They were also seen as developing through association with other people, and through having to think for oneself and take one's own decisions. In this case, therefore, marriage can be seen as posing a contradiction; it makes one more tolerant, etc. in order to make living with another person possible; but it may also make one more independent and assertive because it helps one to develop a sense of self and forces one to take decisions for oneself.

During the period of their marriage everyone appeared to have experienced changes in activities; these involved the arrival and growing up of children, and their leaving home; the gaining and moving of house or job; the taking up or losing of sports, social activities or pastimes. Some changes – and some lack of change – appeared to be liked, some regretted, and some both liked and regretted.

Did people do things they did not appear wholly to enjoy, or refrain from doing things they would have liked to do, in order to preserve marital harmony, to please their spouse, or to avoid displeasing him or her? This is what one would expect, if the original hypothesis is to be supported. The findings show, as in previous chapters, that the situation is less straightforward than this. It is true that sometimes things were said to be avoided or carried out specifically for the sake of the marriage relationship or the spouse (e.g. not moving house, changing a job); but they were also said to be done or avoided because it was expected or taken for granted that married people should do them or should avoid them (e.g. loss of social life); or as a means to, or accompaniment of, the enjoyable things (e.g. not working as a necessary accompaniment to having children, or housework as an inevitable part of the enjoyment of having one's own house). Things were also explained in terms of factors extraneous to marriage, such as growing older, ill health or outside influences. There are obviously other influences at work either to change or not change the behaviour of married people apart from a search for self-fulfilment or marital stability (e.g. societal or group expectations, physical changes associated with ageing, the inevitable accompaniment of one change by another). This may well be one of the reasons why although people appear to be aware of competing desires they do not necessarily explain them in terms which imply a conflict between identity-maintenance and stability-maintenance.

The crude suggestion that, for the sake of stability, change itself would be frowned upon in marriage, or that any changes occurring would either not be personally satisfying or be disruptive to the relationship, is undoubtedly not the case. People expressed their pleasure in many of the changes which had occurred during married life, even though marriage sometimes appeared to prevent change in desired directions, and sometimes to prevent it for what might well be stability-maintaining reasons.

7

‣‣‣

Relationships outside marriage

This chapter turns from self and the spouse to other people. Underlying
the questions raised here is the suggestion that there may be conflict
between a desire for personal, individual friends (in order to develop
and maintain one's own sense of identity) and a desire not to have such
friends nor encourage them in one's spouse (in order to maintain the
stability of one's marriage relationship). Thus the specific questions
asked in this chapter are: Do people have friends? Is any loss or gain of
friends perceived as having been a consequence of marriage, or were
there other reasons? How do people feel about friendship, and any loss
or gain, for themselves and for their spouses?

Description of friendships

One of the difficulties in discussing 'friends' with interviewees is that
the word 'friend' has particular connotations for them. It seems to mean
people of approximately similar age to themselves, who are not relatives, and not one's marriage partner. Unfortunately there is no wholly
satisfactory alternative phraseology: one can ask people whether there
are others they are 'close to', or people they tend to do things with, or
people they can talk to, and so on. Yet each of these questions may
mean a restriction of the pool of acquaintances from which the interviewee draws his answer. One has therefore to use a variety of different
probes to get near to answering the question of whether a person has
other intimates or significant others besides his or her partner. As well
as asking people whether they had friends, therefore, they were also
asked whether there were other people they felt close to, whether there
were any people they could talk to if they had personal problems, and
whether there were other people whom they knew better or as well as

158

they knew their spouse. The latter question takes us back to chapter 3, where the subject of how well people felt they knew their spouses was discussed. In that chapter it was stated that it was sometimes difficult for interviewees to say how the extent to which they knew their spouse or were known by their spouse compared with their knowledge of others or others' knowledge of them, since spouses tended to be placed on a different continuum of intimacy from that of friends, or since different people could be known well in different ways, so that they were difficult to compare. However, twenty-four of the forty explicitly stated that their spouse was the person who knew them best, and twenty-six that their spouse was the person they knew best. Conversely, only five stated that someone other than their spouse knew them best (a mother, a sister, three friends); and only four said they knew someone else better than they knew their spouse (a workmate, a friend, a brother and a mother). Understandably, seven of these nine individuals were in the group of more recently married couples. These answers therefore account for three-quarters of the sample; the remaining quarter either could not answer, gave contradictory answers or chose someone else equally with the spouse.

Given the assumption in our society that marriage is an intimate relationship, it is not surprising that so few people chose to say that they knew best, or were known best, by someone other than their spouse. Nor is it surprising (again as reported in chapter 3) that all except two people agreed that there were some subjects they would not discuss with anyone except their partner (namely sex, money or personal worries and disagreements).

Having seen the important position in which the spouse is placed by most interviewees, one can turn to more specific discussion of friends. In addition to the difficulty this subject presents as a result of the rather restricted definition which people seem to have of the kind of others who can constitute friends, there are further problems. For instance, people do not make a dichotomous distinction whereby all their acquaintances are labelled either 'friend' or 'non-friend'; there is, of course, a continuum rather than a dichotomy of friendship. However, there is not merely one continuum but several; there are people they see more often than others; people they have known longer; those they feel they have more in common with and those they can talk to more easily. So for different purposes people may choose different kinds of other to mention as 'friends'. There is also a variety of different kinds of labels.

For example there are people one 'is friendly with', but that may not be quite the same thing as saying they are friends. Some people use the term 'mate' or 'pal', whereas others do not. But are the terms 'mate' and 'pal' equivalent to the term 'friend' as used by others? There are also 'workmates'. Are they, or are they not, friends? In addition there is the question of when people become or cease to be friends. Some people mentioned others whom they had known previously as 'friends' or 'mates'; there had been no rift between them which clearly released them from the ties of friendship, but for one reason or another they no longer saw these people very often (e.g. because they had moved to another area, or because they were too busy with other things to be able to meet each other). Did they remain friends, or should they be excluded from the list? Equally, there were people they had only recently got to know, whom they liked, and whom they felt they would like to know better. But had they yet become friends, or were they still merely acquaintances? Given these rather obvious problems, it was not possible for people easily to say either whether they had friends, or, of course, specifically how many they had. Nor, given the time limits on fieldwork, could the interviewer spend the long period of time which would have been required to explore in detail the full complexity of people's friendship patterns. However such fine detail was not really needed in order to examine how people felt about the development of friendships outside marriage.

Taking first the more inclusive definition of friends, one can ask about the existence of people the interviewees felt they were friendly with, or felt were friends but not close friends. Most of them could not give specific numbers but they could say whether they had many, several, a few, hardly any, or no such friendships. Given that this is a comparative question, and that most people would not know whether – compared with others – they had a great number or very few friendly acquaintances, it was not surprising that the most frequent comments avoided the extremes and used such terms as 'several' or 'quite a few' (twenty-four out of the forty). Eleven said they were friendly with only a few people; a further four said there were hardly any people they were friendly with, and only one (an older, middle-class woman) that she was friendly with a lot of people.

Having found that they were not completely isolated from outsiders, they were then asked whether there were any people they now felt close to or would count as close friends. This question was apparently somewhat easier for people to answer, although it still faced them with the difficulty of knowing where to draw the line between close and 'non-close' or 'less-close' friends. Most people, however, seemed to know what was meant and answered with relative ease.

Seventeen of the sample classified themselves as people with no other intimates. Of the others, two-thirds said they had more than one, and one-third just one, such friend. Of those saying they had no other intimates, only five were women, and only six were working-class (there was no difference by length of marriage). So middle-class men seemed particularly bereft of close friends. For example:

> JA: Can you count up the number of people you would consider as friends, or is that too difficult?
>
> Mr D: Yes, it's difficult because there's a degree of friendship . . . Err, I've nobody that close but my wife. Probably my brother would come next. Or my family. Then there's a gap . . . and then you've friends – people you can get along with . . . I would call friends. I'm . . . well, I think I'm easy to get along with. I've a number of friends, I wouldn't say a great many friends, but I get along well with most people . . .

Or:

> Mr T: Socially our number of friendships would be more limited because of the fact that because of the nature of my work I don't have, you know, a very social life. So that we don't have, like some people we know, a group of two or three families who always go out together regularly. I mean we don't have anything like that.

Or there was a working-class man who similarly said:

> Mr C: Friends . . . I don't have very much friends.
>
> JA: Have you ever had anyone whom you definitely called a friend?
>
> Mr C: You mean afore, or you mean just now? Oh well . . . nae really *good* friends, no . . . Quite a lot o' . . . one or two maybe, you ken, you've worked with and so on . . . You aye seem to . . . be mair friendly wi' one than with the other . . . you talk wi' one mair than the other, it would seem to be.

Or a woman:

> Mrs L: Well, to tell you the truth, I haven't got very many close friends, you know, or anything like that. I just had one particular friend when we left school, but when I got married, you know, we very rarely see each other now, if at all /// I really haven't got any . . . I wouldn't say I have any very close friends at all, nobody that I see, you know, a lot of – it's just the way I am, I'm not very . . .

Of the twenty-three who did have close friends, fifteen were women, and fourteen were working-class. In fact no working-class woman admitted to having no other intimate, and eight of the ten said they had more than one such friend. (Again there was no difference by length of marriage.) The reasons why working-class women are particularly likely to say they have close friends (and it will be seen below that they are also the most likely to say that they have confidantes) are probably complex. Using the hypotheses one could suggest that it is because they get less assistance than others from their husbands, in the way of intimate conversation, in developing a sense of identity. Yet chapter 3 does not suggest that they talk less to their spouses than do others. Another reason commonly put forward is the cultural one: it is the custom for working-class women to have, and to think of themselves as having, close friends. Mrs I described them as follows (in the quotations used in this chapter the names of friends have been changed):

JA: Are there some people you think of as friends as opposed to neighbours, acquaintances, people you just happen to know?

Mrs I: Oh yes, there are real friends. I find that I have been very, very lucky in that respect, you know. I have few, but they are very good friends.

A middle-class woman also described her close friends:

Mrs T: I have acquaintances, and people I'm friendly with, and some real friends.

JA: Can you count the number of people you would call real, close friends?

Mrs T: Er . . . really close friends – yes, I suppose. Yes, I would say five or six at the very most – really /// I think all my really close friends I've known for a very long time /// and they have more or less the same sort of background, social standing as myself.

So did some men:

JA: Do you have some people you think of as friends?

Mr K: I've got a mate – one mate /// one good mate, one really good . . .

Or:

JA: Who do you think, out of all the people you know, you know best of all? ///

Mr L: Oh now . . . male or female?

JA: It doesn't matter.

Mr L: . . . I suppose I know Laura pretty well one way or another. Er, but if you are still on the aspect of friends, I would consider Jim, actually, the chap I work with /// because as I say I've seen him socially and business-wise.

As these quotations suggest, most of the intimates mentioned were non-relatives; of the twenty-three with intimates fourteen mentioned only non-relatives, five mentioned only relatives (two parents, one sister, one brother and one sister-in-law), and four some of each (the relatives here were all siblings or siblings-in-law). The vast majority of these friends were in a similar age-group to the respondent, the only exceptions being, of course, the two sets of parents, and one married couple whom Mrs H referred to as an 'older couple'. Most intimates were also of the same sex as the respondent; eighteen out of the twenty-three mentioned only people of the same sex: no one mentioned just one person of the opposite sex, but five talked of a mixture of sexes.

Thus the typical intimate is a person of the same age-group and sex as oneself and a non-relative. However, we cannot know for certain whether these answers reflect the actual situation in which people are more likely to see themselves as intimate with such kinds of people, or – as stated earlier – whether they merely show the kind of people respondents thought they were being asked to talk about in discussing friends and close acquaintances. Since their answers were so ready and so detailed one suspects that on the whole they reflect reality quite closely.

There was a wide variety of answers on what was meant by a close friend, with people sometimes emphasising one element, sometimes a mixture of elements. For example Mr K, who had talked of his 'one good mate', said when asked what makes a good friend:

Mr K: Just someone who'd do anything for you. He would do anything for me – and I'd do anything for him, ken within reason /// And we never argue, never had an argument.

The theme of help in time of need, as expressed by Mr K, was a repeated one. For example Mrs H said:

Mrs H: A friend is someone who would help you if you needed . . .

And Mrs I, in talking of her close friends, said:

Mrs I: They expect you to be the same as themselves – I mean we are all of a

type, you know. If they can help you, well fair enough, it is a taken-
for-granted thing.

An even more common theme was that a friend was someone one
could 'say anything to', and say it knowing that it would not be repeated
but would be treated in confidence. For instance:

> JA: In what way is a friend different from someone you just know – that
> you're just acquainted with?
> Mrs C: Oh . . . I don't know really.
> JA: It is a bit difficult.
> Mrs C: Well, a friend . . . you could say anything to them. You know, secrets
> and things.

Or:

> Mrs J: I wouldna say I was as close to her [Mrs J's mother] as to them [Mrs
> J's sisters] . . . Like there was things I wouldna tell *her* . . . I wouldna
> tell her about them . . . I'd tell me sisters rather. I'm closer that way
> to my sisters.
> JA: What kind of things?
> Mrs J: Oh just about anything. Oh, when we were younger, if we were
> going out with any boys, or anything.

Or:

> Mrs F: I could sit and talk to her [names friend] about practically anything,
> whereas others . . . well, my personal life I just don't go into, well nae
> deeply, you know what I mean, but with Freda I feel I can, and she
> has done to me, you know, if she is worked up about anything.

Or:

> Mrs H: You could turn and say, you know . . . tell them anything. And you
> know damned fine that when you go out that door it's not going to be
> spoken about, you know. And that's the kind of friends both Mary
> and Ethel are.

Other lesser themes were that close friends were people one got on
very well with, had a lot in common with, had known for a long time, or
(said by Mr S) were people who would tell one the truth about oneself.
For example:

> Mr S: These people [two close friends] would tell me the truth at all costs
> and at all times – So they'd ensure I was behaving honestly to myself
> – they would never fall out with me about it either.

Or:

> JA: And what do you think it is about them that makes them particularly good friends?
>
> Mr J: Well, we just get on well together.

Or:

> Mrs F: This is one of Frank's friends, his wife – I think we have got a lot in common. She has got four children – I've my three, and the same sort of problems seem to crop up . . .

Many of the definitions given fit in well with the suggestion that friends as well as spouses assist people in the development and maintenance of their sense of identity: with friends one can discuss common interests, private or intimate matters, and so on. For instance the comments of Mr S are particularly revealing when he says that friends ensure that he behaves honestly to himself.

Although answers varied, they were similar in that in all cases people were choosing others on the basis of extreme criteria: close friends were people who were *entirely* trustworthy, whom you could talk to about *anything*, whom you knew *very* well, whom you would do *anything* for, and so on. These are laudatory comments, and lead one to ask whether such paragons were ever the cause of jealousy or trouble with the spouse. This will be asked in a later section.

Before ending this description of friendships, however, one can ask whether there were any intimates holding such favoured positions that they would be talked to if the interviewee were worried about his or her relationship with the spouse. Berger and Kellner (1964) have suggested that in general one talks to one's spouse about one's friends but not to one's friends about one's spouse. This was not entirely supported, although only a third (thirteen) of the sample said there was someone they could talk to in such a case. This also matches the finding of Babchuk and Bates (1963) that many people do not have a friend with whom they exchange intimate confidences. Interestingly, one of the sample mentioning a confidante was a person who had said elsewhere that she had no close friends, and two were people who did not choose one of their close friends to confide in over such a matter. Most, however (ten out of the thirteen) did choose someone whom they had mentioned elsewhere as a close friend. The kind of things they said are illustrated in the following quotations:

JA: I don't know if this will make sense to you, but if you were worried about Keith or your relationship with Keith, is there anybody that you feel you could go and talk to about that, or would it be something you would have to work out for yourself?

Mrs K: I would just go to either my chummie, or his [husband's] chum's wife, because they are both young and understanding. I suppose, because they . . . well both of them sees him different from the way I do; I suppose I would work out so much for myself as well; but I don't think I would go to my Ma.

JA: Why? Because she wouldn't understand or she wouldn't give you the right sort of advice, or . . .?

Mrs K: She would sort of lecture me: 'Well, you shouldn't do this' – and I'm not home every night to make his tea, and my mother is home to make my father's and brother's tea every night. It's a case of: 'Well, you see, you should have been home every night, all this makes a marriage' . . .

After a similar question Mr N said:

Mr N: Ah, well . . . the boy that was my best man would be my favourite for that /// If I was worried at all you would be able to talk to him. It's not like people [who] say: 'Oh, aye'. He takes it in. Some of the things he can't give you advice on because he's not married, but . . .

Mr F said:

Mr F: It's never cropped up like. I don't know who I'd go to. I think I'd go to one of my pals though. Just the kind of things you'd speak to him about, you could trust him wi' it, kind of thing /// 'Cos they [friends] have told *me* things, like, that I would never pass on, like.

Two men chose their mother-in-law as a confidante even though she was not a close friend (Mr A and Mr G), and one woman (Mrs R) chose her daughter or her minister, depending on what the problem was. Apart from the minister as a professional confidant, the doctor was also mentioned occasionally (again depending on what the problem was). Altogether nine women said there was someone they could confide in, as opposed to only four men (matching the finding of Komarovsky (1962), that wives have more confidantes than husbands); similarly nine working-class people chose someone, as opposed to four middle-class. (There was little length-of-marriage difference.) The main point, however, is that most people chose no one as a confidant in the event of any marital problem. They said such things as:

Mr D: Nobody, no.

JA: No? You would work them out for yourself?

Mr D: Well, firstly, I can't see the question arising /// If it did arise I think we would cope with it ourselves. I'm sure, yes. No, the answer is definitely 'no'.

JA: You wouldn't talk to your brother about it?

Mr D: No . . . no, no. I think I could handle it myself. Well, first, I can't see it arise . . . one never knows . . . it is extremely unlikely. But if it did, I think I'd be competent to handle things myself, or us both.

JA: So you don't feel you need outsiders for that reason?

Mr D: No . . . I don't want to feel too independent, or seem too independent to you, but . . . I haven't had to seek advice from no one except professional advice from probably a solicitor or a C.A. or banker, or somebody like that. Otherwise I've just managed.

JA: So friends are people whose company you enjoy rather than people whose advice you might seek? Or anything like that?

Mr D: Oh yes, yes. Definitely.

Or:

Mrs L: I think it's him [husband] I speak mostly to; I don't like discussing . . . like any personal problems with anyone else really /// But I should think if anything . . . nothing's really cropped up that's very personal, but if anything was going wrong with our marriage, or anything like that, I don't think I would speak to my Mum about it, I would be quite wary, you know. Of course Leslie and her get on very well. We haven't really had any serious things; I mean everything I usually tell to Leslie, and he sits and listens, whether he is any help, as I said, or no . . . I haven't got a friend that I could say anything to, no one at all.

Again, after the question on whether there was anyone in whom he could confide if he had a marital worry, etc., Mr H replied:

Mr H: No.

JA: Have you never had such worries, or if you had, would you sort of sort them out on your own?

Mr H: I have had them, and have sorted them out on my own /// I think that if you have got somebody you can really go to, you know, somebody you respect enough to help you, then I think there would be nothing better than to sit down and talk to somebody /// But as I say, myself I have never made a lot of friends /// I would say that the decisions I have made I have made on my own, not that I wouldn't have liked to talk to somebody, but there has been no one.

To summarise therefore: almost everyone had several people they were friendly with, but only just over a half had close acquaintances, and only a third had someone to confide in over a marital problem.

The influence of marriage on friendship loss

Questions about the loss of friends can be very difficult for people to answer in that one is asking them to enumerate their friends and to compare the number at some point before marriage with the number at some point (or at several points) after marriage. One is also asking them to distinguish between a net loss and a gross loss. This is very hard to do, and one can provide little more than a very crude analysis of what they said when asked to talk about any loss of friends.

Half the total sample said they felt they had lost some friends (one is here referring only to gross loss). There was little difference within the sample except that the older working-class couples were particularly likely to say they had not lost friends (only one husband and one wife in this group said they had done so). Omitting this group, 60% of the sample said they had lost some friends.

Marriage was in some sense seen to have caused these losses in all cases, but the explanation was not necessarily in line with the hypothesis that third persons would be excluded in order to preserve marital stability and not distress the spouse. In fact the main reason given for loss was that at marriage, or after marriage, the interviewee had moved away from the area where he or she had previously lived (or the friends had moved away). It was thus understandable that he or she would not be able to see as much of people who had been his or her friends before. For example:

> Mrs D: I think we tend to be . . . friendly with a few but maybe not too friendly with any in particular, you know. And it's rather difficult, I think the ones that we probably would have counted as near friends are, as I say . . . they are scattered out a bit . . . and we were very friendly with them you know, when they were nearer. But they've sort of dispersed a bit, you know, and we find we don't . . . well we're not coming into contact with them the same, you know.

Such an explanation was given by eleven of the twenty. It may indeed help to explain the very small proportion of older working-class respondents who said they had lost friends, since this group also contained the smallest proportion of people moving away from the area in which they had lived before marriage (one in ten of this group had moved more than ten miles away, compared with six out of ten in the older middle-class group).

Other friends were seen to be lost for reasons more in line with the hypothesis. Three people saw the loss as due to gaining new interests at marriage and thus having less in common with friends who remain single.

> JA: Apart from not going out as much, are there any other things that have changed . . .?
> Mrs J: Well, you don't see your friends. You don't go out with your friends. Well, like school friends, or . . . I'd say . . . this Sarah I pal about with, she's married so that's why we go out together, but I wouldn't be going out with her so much had she not been married . . . I mean I think you break away from a lot of your single friends . . .

Three said they had lost friends because they had less opportunity to go and meet third persons:

> JA: What are the reasons why you've drifted apart?
> Mr L: Er . . . marriage, I would think. Simply because friends I've got . . . well, I feel friends are built up socially. Now I'm obviously not on the *go* so much as I used to be /// now they are probably, if they are still at college, or they're working themselves, and you know . . . er, times we have available just don't seem to coincide.

One man saw the excluding coming not from him but from the actions of the third parties. He said he had enjoyed having several women friends before marriage, but now that he was married women no longer responded to him. Three people saw the loss as caused not by the fact that previous friends remained *single* (and therefore had different interests) but that they got married or engaged too and thus went out solely with their partner or became busy with their own affairs:

> Mrs F: I feel that since I've got married I have lost touch with a lot of . . . I mean really close friends ///
> JA: Why do you think you have lost touch with them?
> Mrs F: I think it is just a case of everybody . . . I mean *they* are married now; they have got their own husband and family, and you get wrapped up in yourself.

Or:

> Mrs J: Mind you, they have all got boyfriends or husbands of their own . . . well, they have all their separate ways.

Finally, four people mentioned the influence of the spouse upon friendships, seeing some friends as not being the kind of people who would get on well with the spouse, or vice versa:

> Mrs E: Eddie isn't really one for a lot of friends. He's got a couple of friends and that's it. I tended to have quite a lot of friends really. But he doesn't like visiting, you see. So the result was . . . as a result that it would tend I would sorta drift away from my friends really /// I mean, well, one of my pals, her husband's a mason . . . well, I mean, Eddie and her husband don't have much in common /// now I just never really see them at all.

Answers of this type, and of losing friends through lack of common interests, through not going out so much or through being occupied with family interests, indicate to some extent a policy of exclusion on the part of the married person. Such policies (whether conscious or unconscious) may signify a desire to preserve the stability of the marriage by excluding others so that relationships with outsiders may not form a threat to one's own marriage.

For some of the interviewees this loss of friends was seen as a net loss; that is, the lost friends were not replaced by new ones. This was true of only seven of the sample. These were people who said such things as that one is bound to lose friends because one is not going out so much, one is wrapped up in family matters and therefore less interested in maintaining links with outsiders, one has to keep merely those friends with whom both partners can get on, and so on. A net loss of friends, therefore, was attributed to marriage. A net loss of *close* friends was similarly explained by the eight people who said they had experienced such a loss: 'I've not much in common with them now', 'I don't go out so much, so we've lost touch', and 'I could only cope with one intimate at a time – and my husband's enough for me.' With these two groups of people, therefore, marriage seemed an important influence.

The influence of marriage on friendships gained or retained

Thirty-three people said there had been no *net* loss of friends since marriage and twenty-three said they still had, or now had, close friends or intimates. In considering the influence of marriage one can see that in some cases it appeared irrelevant, or at least did not interfere with friendships; and in some cases it actually seemed to aid the gaining or retaining of friends. Neither one of these categories seemed more prevalent than the other. In the former category were, for example, the friends people said they had retained because they still got on well together, had not moved away from each other and still had an opportunity to meet. There were also those they said they had gained in a new neighbourhood because they happened to live nearby and found they got on well together (admittedly the move to a new neighbourhood might have been said to be due to the marriage, but the development of the friendship was not seen as relevant to it). Friendships were also seen as gained or retained through interests outside marriage; work friends are an obvious example. Thus Mr L chose his work colleague as a close friend:

> Mr L: Because I've seen him in all ways. I see him under different pressures of work, how he reacted; we share an office as well.

There were also friends made through sport or other community activities. For example:

> Mr F: Well, I go a lot to the club down here now, like . . . and I've met a lot of people there, like – aye, good people, like . . . which I'd never thought about before, like.

Such examples could be multiplied; but on the other hand there were some friends apparently gained or retained as a direct or indirect result of marriage itself. Some, for example, were said to be gained or retained because they too were married and therefore had interests in common with the respondent. Mrs F, for instance, has already been quoted as saying of her friend Freda: 'She has got four children – I've my three, and the same sort of problems seem to crop up.' Sometimes friends were said to be gained because they got on well with the spouse as well as with the respondent; and some were seen as having become friends because they were introduced to the respondent by his or her spouse: that is, the spouse's previous friends, his or her relatives, workmates, or friends made through his or her outside interests. For example:

> Mrs K: Then there is Keith's chummie and his wife; and they're just my chums as well, well I regard his wife as my chummie. I mean I could tell Sandra anything.

Or:

> Mrs L: When we go out we are usually on our own and . . . or Leslie's brother and his wife. I get on very well with my sister-in-law.

Or:

> JA: If you were worried about your wife or about your relationship with your wife, is there anyone whom you would go and talk to about any worries that you might have?
>
> Mr G: Well, I could talk to her mother.
>
> JA: Oh yes. You get on pretty well with her mother?
>
> Mr G: Oh yes, if there is anything wrong with us we let her know right away, or ask anything, or let her know.

Finally, there were some friends who can be seen as having been gained as a result of interests which developed as a consequence of marriage. For example, if marriage means children, and children mean helping with playschools, Boys Brigade, Scouts, Sunday School, then the friends acquired there may be seen – very indirectly – as a consequence of marriage. Or again, if marriage means becoming interested in pressure groups to enhance the position of married women then friends gained by becoming a member of a local women's movement group may be seen as an indirect consequence of marriage.

As far as close friends are concerned, marriage did not seem to account for their existence except in a small minority of cases. Of the twenty-three with close friends, eight had at least one who seemed to have been gained as a consequence of marriage or of the relationship with the spouse; but looking at it another way, out of the lower estimate of fifty-one close friends (i.e. taking the lower figure when respondents provide a choice – for example, 'two or three'), only nine were gained apparently as a consequence of marriage or through the spouse. In this category are those who were the husband's friend or the wives of the husband's friend and who had been met first through the husband (five), or who were the spouse's relatives and again first met through him (four). Incidentally, all the interviewees with close friends formed through marriage were women; men found their own close friends independently. This fits in with the Babchuk and Bates finding (1963) that husbands are dominant in the determination of close friendships within marriage.

A very mixed picture thus emerges: about half the sample see themselves as having lost friends, and about half as having gained friends, through marriage (only seven however talked of a net loss of friends through marriage). The net loss of friends or loss of close friends was generally attributed to marriage. Of those with friends, only a third saw a close friendship as having been formed as a consequence of the relationship with the spouse. In many cases friendships were not formed through marriage (though one might argue that they could have been difficult to retain if there had been strong dislike or opposition to the friend on the part of the spouse). Distinguishing those who might be expected to feel that marriage had adversely affected their friendship patterns, one finds a third of the sample with either a net loss of friends through marriage, or a net loss of close friends through marriage. There was no sex difference, but nine of the thirteen were among the more recently married, and nine were middle-class.

Feeling about the loss of friends

If the identity/stability hypotheses are to be supported one would expect those people who had lost friends to regret the loss for identity reasons, but to accept it for stability reasons.

Six of the eight people who said they had lost a close friend also said that they did not miss having such an intimate. The spouse had in all cases replaced him or her; and they all said they could talk to the spouse about anything and therefore needed no other close friend. For example Mrs D talked of keeping private affairs to themselves, and never needing to discuss any worries with outsiders:

> Mrs D: We don't sort of go and discuss our private affairs much with other people, you know. I don't think it's really . . . well, I suppose we just think it isn't other people's business to . . . there's nothing much that we can't talk about . . . but there are some things that we wouldn't discuss with . . . I mean, well I know of some people, they'll discuss their sex life even . . . well, we don't.

And:

> Mrs D: I don't think there's anything been that serious that I couldn't talk it over with my husband. You know what I mean? We tend to . . . well, maybe keep our problems to ourselves. We find that if we can't work it out ourselves, we don't . . .

Mr J, having said that he had at one time been close to his parents, also said that when you are married:

Mr J: You have a closer relationship – you can talk about things you wouldn't normally talk about – things you wouldn't discuss with your parents.

Mrs L said she did not have time to miss having a close friend, and that she could talk to her husband; although here she sounded somewhat ambivalent about whether he could fulfil her needs in this respect:

JA: What about nowadays, if you wanted someone to talk to about things? Who would you think of going to, or would you never feel like that?

Mrs L: I do sometimes. It's quite difficult really. Certain things I would speak to my mother about. But I tell . . . mostly I tell Leslie a lot, although sometimes he's not much help to me. But it's fine just to tell him things that worry me, and that. I find it's him I speak mostly to; I don't like discussing . . . like any personal problems with anyone else really . . .

And Mrs W explicitly stated that she could not cope with more than one close relationship at a time:

Mrs W: Well, I would find it a bit of a strain having more than one person – you know, an intimate, close relationship with more than one person /// I prefer to be close to, intimate with, just one person at a time . . .

It looks therefore as though these people either did not like the idea of having a close relationship with a third person (seeming either to disapprove of it, or to consider that it would be a strain), or found that all the intimate conversation necessary for the maintenance of their most intimate selves could occur within marriage. Most of them also said that they did have friends on the less-than-very-intimate level, so that if they wanted to go out on their own or talk to someone else they could do so. As Mrs L said:

Mrs L: I mean for all that I went out with Teresa a lot, but I don't miss that now, not being out a lot – and I'm quite free to go out with my friends for a night out myself if I want to.

Mrs W also said that she needed a group of her own friends in order not to feel squashed by her husband. But as in the case of Mrs L, these were not close, intimate friends; for her they were people, such as colleagues, with whom she could discuss work.

The two people who said they did to some extent miss close friends (both men: one young, middle-class; one older, working-class) were very different from each other in their reasons. The younger man was the husband of Mrs W, and – as already discussed – he argued at some length against the marital bond which he saw as constraining and not likely to be lasting. Unlike his wife, he was therefore very enthusiastic about a group family or commune. The older man had no such unconventional sentiments about marriage, but he admitted that it would have been 'helpful' to have a close friend to talk to when one was anxious about one's wife or about one's marital relationship.

As far as the net loss of non-intimate friends is concerned, none of the seven was wholly regretful, either because they said they still had some friends, or because they had less need of friends than when they were single, since their spouse now largely fulfilled their friendship requirements. For example Mrs C said:

> Mrs C: I'm quite happy on my own, and working on my own /// I think I'm quite self-sufficient.

And also:

> Mrs C: I know that I don't enjoy going out so much. Now I would rather stay at home. Sometimes, it's nice to get out sometimes, but . . . I mean before we were married we were always sort of out every night practically – at friends or something.

Mr H said that he still liked going out but he preferred to go out with his wife to going out with 'the boys', that he and his wife could talk to each other about anything, and that anyway there was not much time for friends as a home and family took up all one's spare hours. The comments from these two were typical of this group's positive remarks. However, four of the seven (all young middle-class people) also said they did have some regrets. They recognised that they now lived a more restricted social life, a less exciting or varied life and had settled down. Losing friends seemed to be seen as a part of this rather wider loss and was thus similarly regretted.

All one can really conclude is that most people appear not greatly to miss the loss of friends. In many cases this is because if one includes the spouse as a friend, one intimate has merely been replaced by another, and there has thus been no loss of an 'other' with whom one can have intimate conversations. Where a real loss of intimates seems to have occurred, there was some regret (possibly for identity reasons, in so far as people saw their lives as restricted by marriage); yet there was also acceptance. This was said to be because a sufficient number of friends were left or because there were other interests in one's life to mitigate any sense of loss.

Attitudes to spouse's friends

It should first be said that none of the intimates people talked about had those characteristics usually seen as particularly threatening to a marriage. Thus when interviewees were asked what kind of things would make them feel they could not go on living with their partner, 62% answered adultery or another man/woman (this was an unprompted, open-ended question; there were of course many other answers as well). Yet the friends mentioned were all either of the same sex as the interviewee or, if not, were close relatives or one half of a couple friendship. As stated, there were twenty-three interviewees with close friends; their spouses were always given the opportunity to talk about their reactions to any such friends. However, this was not one of the most detailed parts of the interview; nor were the interviewees told whether the spouse had reported himself or herself as having any close friend or friends (in half the cases anyway the spouse had not been interviewed separately at that stage). People were also given the opportunity to talk about sources of disagreement with the spouse, rows, irritations, and so on. It was expected that if the spouse's close friends were a problem to the interviewee he or she would have mentioned it in one of these contexts.

Men did not appear at all antagonistic towards their wives' friends, but four of the eight wives mentioned some resentment of their husbands' friends. This, it appeared, was because these friends were usually met at public houses or clubs and wives disliked this, though they found it hard to explain why. It may be that where friends are seen as supporting the marriage, or marriage in general, they are accepted or even welcomed; only where they cause a partner to spend time away which could be spent with the spouse, or where their ideas are seen as anti-marriage, are they disliked. For instance Mrs K gave a very interesting account of an incident involving a friend of her husband. The story was told to illustrate how her husband did not always know how she would react to things or people (though he thought he knew her very well). In the story she explained how she disapproved of the friend, though she said that her husband thought she would think – as he did – that the friend was 'a great guy'. The incident involved their meeting this married friend one evening going into a dance hall by himself:

Mrs K: And he said: 'I'm going in, and I'm going to get a tramp.' And he was always speaking like this.

Mrs K reacted most unfavourably to this behaviour:

Mrs K: I vowed that if I seen him again I would break his neck.

One can interpret Mrs K's dislike as caused by the fact that this friend's attitudes and behaviour (being very much against her own norms of proper marital conduct), if passed on to her husband, were seen as likely to be detrimental to their marriage. She therefore saw the man as an unsuitable companion for him. None of the wives' friends were described as having ideas contrary to the husbands' views of proper marital conduct; in addition most women saw their intimates mostly at home, with their husband, or at times when the husband was at work. So such friendships did not deprive the couple of time which they could have spent together.

More easy to ask about was how respondents thought their spouses felt about the respondent's close friends. This was easier because it could be asked in the light of information provided about such intimates. One would expect the same type of response as the spouses did actually make, or maybe even less acknowledged resentment, since one would anticipate that respondents would not want to recognise their friends as a source of instability in their marriage. This was the case. Of the four men whose wives had complained about their close friends, three did acknowledge their going out with these friends as a source of friction with the spouse, but all four also said they thought their wife actually liked, or got on well with, the friends. Mr L, for example, admitted that it sometimes annoyed his wife when he went for a drink after work with his friend; but there was also the following exchange:

JA: And does she [Mr L's wife] know your friend at work?
Mr L: Oh yes. We've all been out socially together. We've been out to his house, and the company dances, and things like that, you know. I would say we all get on very well.

Mr F, rather ruefully, admitted that rows were often about him going down to the club with his friends and 'over-staying his welcome'. However he also said that his friends were 'friends of both of us, like', even though he saw more of them than did his wife. He was also specifically asked how well his wife got on with the friends:

> Mr F: Oh aye – we usually . . . like in the evenings sometimes we go out with them . . . well, either of the three of them, like. Oh, she gets on well enough with them /// in fact we're goin' away wi' one of the couples to a dance this Friday, so . . .

All but two of the rest said that their spouses got on well with their friends, many stating that these were common friends. It is interesting that no individual chose the same intimate as his or her partner; but this does not of course mean that they could not be common friends. The usual situation was that a person would be a close friend of one spouse and a friendly acquaintance of the other. The kinds of thing these people said about how their spouse got on with their friends were:

> Mrs S: I have one very close friend, who I don't see a great deal of, but both . . . one of the difficulties is finding couples that you both get on with – and this is a couple we both get on very well with, both of them, and we know all each other's troubles, and we can talk.

In line with this statement about the need for friends who would get on with the spouse, Mrs S then went on to talk about a woman at work, of whom she had grown 'very fond', but:

> Mrs S: I would never dream of saying to her: 'You and your husband must come over for an evening.' I'm sure that my husband just wouldn't like her husband at all; I've met him twice, and didn't like him at all.

So this woman would probably remain a work friend and not become a social friend. Few other people talked specifically about *having* to find friends whom their partner would like; they merely pointed to the fact of agreement. For example, Mrs M talked about her close friend and the early days of their acquaintanceship:

> Mrs M: And we went to the dancing together. She met Sidney there, and I liked Sidney – her husband. I mean he was a nice chap. I liked Sidney, and then I met Mike, and she liked Mike, and he liked her, you know. And in fact they've similar natures.

Some people's comments were very straightforward and unelaborated:

> JA: Do you think that your friends are Keith's friends as well, or do you have separate friends?
>
> Mrs K: No, I think we're all just friends. My chummie, Keith didn't used to

like her – well, he didn't really know her that much, but once he got to know her . . .

Or:

Mr O: I can't think of many friends that we both have, that we dislike, definitely not. I can't think of any. I'd say on that score we've no problems at all. No, that's one thing certainly, you know, it's not a thing we've mentioned. I've never heard her say: 'I can't stand so-and-so.' And I can't think myself of anyone . . .

Or:

JA: The friends [down south] are friends of your husband's as well as yours. Do you think of them as common friends, or more as a friend of yours, or . . .?

Mrs H: Oh, *no*, they're both of us's now. At one time it was Harry's, but now it's both.

JA: And what about the friend in Aberdeen, do you think of her more as your friend?

Mrs H: No, it's the same again you see.

It looks as though on the whole there is little awareness of having to choose friends who will get on with one's spouse, but more of an implication that it just happens that the interviewee and his spouse (perhaps because they see themselves as so well matched) like each other's friends. There was only one forcible exception; this was Mrs E, whose marriage has already been described as one in which the spouses talked together little, and engaged in little joint activity. She, like Mrs S, seemed to be aware of the need to have friends with whom the spouse could get on, but unlike Mrs S, who was able to find such friends, Mrs E seemed to have had to sever links with most of her friends because her husband was 'not one for friends' and did not 'like visiting'. She said:

Mrs E: Quite a few of my friends which I had, well, I've never been not friendly with them, but now I just never really see them at all.

Mr S also can be classified as an exception, but only with regard to one friend. On the whole he demonstrated, as did others, the high degree of accord between him and his wife:

JA: Do you and your wife tend to like the same sort of people? If she says: 'I've got a friend and I'll bring her home', do you know you'll like her?

Mr S: Oh yes, yes. I can bank on it ///

JA: And would the same apply to her? Would she like the people you like?

Mr S: I think so. Yes.

He seemed somewhat less certain about his wife's reactions to his friends, and it can be seen below that he did not really *know* how his wife felt about the friend he describes (though he thinks she had reservations). It appears that they have not discussed her attitude towards him:

Mr S: And I think – now I don't know the truth of this – but I think she may have reservations about Malcolm Brown. I think so. Because he is a very hard intellectual type /// and I think Sheila would not admire this particular trait in his character. Plus the fact that I spent a helluva lot of time with him, and I think, maybe subconsciously, Sheila did not take too well to this /// perhaps it would be an element of jealousy, I don't know. But I imagine she would have reservations about him to some extent.

However this friend had obviously not caused 'trouble' between the spouses, or Mr S would surely have known his wife's attitude to the friend. Also, this friend had gone abroad, and therefore could not now be a source of disagreement. Perhaps for these reasons Mr S was able to acknowledge his wife's possible reservations, whilst still counting Mr Brown as one of his close friends.

Extreme cases

As suggested in earlier chapters, one would expect most dissatisfaction from among those whose reported behaviour places them at the extremes; in this case it would be those with either several close friendships outside marriage, or those without friends (the former being likely to threaten the stability of the marriage, the latter the individual's sense of identity). At the beginning of this chapter, five people were mentioned who were ostensibly extreme cases – four saying that they had hardly any friends, and one saying that she had a great number. However, when these cases were examined again in detail, it looked as though three of the four without friends did have several friendships, and the one woman with a great number did not have any close friendships. The only really extreme case appeared to be that of

Mr E. The picture painted of him both by himself and by his wife was of an isolated man. He said he was 'not one for friends', nor did he have work friends since he was on a training course which was peopled almost exclusively by men and women much younger than himself. Maybe his isolation from others helps to give a precarious stability to his marriage, which as earlier chapters have shown is one with which both partners are dissatisfied. Yet this isolation has probably exacerbated his feeling – as stated in the previous chapter – that he has become moody and lacking in self-confidence. His wife – as indicated above – describes herself also as now having few friends, and this may well assist the precarious stability of the marriage, for she says that she stopped seeing friends because her husband did not get on well with them. Yet her dissatisfaction with this situation seems to exacerbate her resentment against her husband, which cannot be good for the continued stability of the marriage. The couple therefore do fit the hypothesis, for although they do not directly express great dissatisfaction with their friendship situation they do appear highly dissatisfied with themselves and with their marriage.

Concluding comments

In conclusion, apart from the Es, friends seemed very rarely to be a source of dissatisfaction to the interviewees. Somewhat more had been expected: either a sense of dissatisfaction that marriage restricted one's own friendship opportunities, or a sense of resentment where one's spouse had friends of her or his own. Yet marriage certainly had not stopped people having friends; and more than half seemed to have close friends (though only a third said they would discuss a marital worry with a third person); in addition these close friends were highly praised and spoken of with great warmth. Never the less, marriage did appear to have led to the loss of friends for half the sample, yet most of those who said they had experienced such a loss did not appear to regret it.

Why was there such equanimity on the subject? There are several reasons. People were not dissatisfied with their own friendship opportunities because on the whole they felt no sense of restriction; if they had lost friends at all they had often been replaced by others; if they had fewer friends they often did not mind since the spouse was a replacement friend or since they had sufficient friends left to mitigate any sense of loss. The reasons why their spouses raised no objection to the existence of friendships are also various; in some cases friends were seen as joint friends, and thus perhaps became stability-maintaining factors in that anything a couple shares helps to bind them together. In most cases friends possessed non-threatening characteristics: they approved of marriage in general or in particular, they got on well with the spouse, they could not be seen as potential sexual partners, they did not draw the individual away from his spouse too often during times he felt they should be together. In fact it looked as though a careful process of selection had been carried out by these marriage partners in order to allow them some friends without causing disturbance in the marital relationship. Where extreme behaviour in other contexts has been noted, friendships have perhaps had to be particularly carefully selected or restricted in order to help maintain a stable relationship. For instance, where a couple appear to talk together very little one might expect them to seek an identity-maintaining friendship in which they can have conversations. Yet this did not appear to be the case: Mr E mentioned above 'was not one for friends' and Mrs E had ceased to see many of her former friends; the As and the Gs did have friends but they were very much of the non-threatening kind (the Gs' closest friendship was with the wife's parents, and the As restricted themselves on the whole to the wife's brother or else to joint friends). A desire not to 'rock the boat' appears to have been given priority over any needs of the sense of self. This is not necessarily conscious or deliberate; people are presumably largely obeying the expectations prevalent in our society which advocate the giving of preference to one's spouse over all other friendships, and the choice of individuals who are unlikely to be a threat to the stability of the marital relationship.

8

‣‣‣

Conclusion

The balancing act

There are good reasons for concluding that marriage is in many ways a compromise between stability-maintaining and identity-upholding behaviour, and that on the whole married people perform this balancing act very skilfully. For example, they seem to talk to each other a good deal, and often about things they would keep private from outsiders, but they also avoid talking, often because they do not wish to upset or annoy each other. Apart from when they are at work, they spend most of their time together; but they do have occasional separate outings although they seem aware of a need to limit these and to confine them to 'acceptable' activities. They are all conscious that their activities are restricted and that they are constrained to adopt certain patterns of behaviour. But while having cause for some regret, almost without exception people accept these constraints; they get used to them, they are not too heavy a burden, and they are the inevitable accompaniments of the satisfactions which marriage also brings. Again this seems to show a middle way: if the constraint were heavier or lighter dislike would outweigh acceptance. For example, if their responsibilities were greater people would feel overburdened by them, but if they were lighter they would miss the enjoyment or sense of achievement which they also bring. Marriage brings several gratifications; the major ones – apart from having someone to share time and talk with – being children, a home of one's own, and feelings of increased maturity and worth. Not all change is seen as positive, however, and, as with the other topics, there are some regrets as well as satisfactions. As far as friendships are concerned, a middle way is again evinced in the fact that, although most people have friends, they have either lost some or kept or gained only those not of a kind likely to threaten the marriage; they are people of their own sex, or a couple, or close relatives, and they are not people who take up time which the partners feel ought to be shared with their spouse or who in any other way interfere with a couple's shared life.

These are the kinds of pattern that were expected, although the reasons people give for feeling as they do often show very, very little theorising about marital activity. When people have thought about their behaviour in some detail their answers tend to fit the hypothesis, but they also tend to show that the situation is more complex than initially suggested. Thus it is worthwhile returning to the sets of conflicting conditions formulated at the start of the study. First, open and wide-ranging conversation was said to be needed for the development of a sense of identity, but requiring frequently to be avoided in order to preserve a sense of stability. A refinement of this formulation is necessary since it was found that, although generally true, talking openly to one's spouse is sometimes seen to be good for stability as well as identity. When people are aware that topics of conversation are being avoided they can become worried and uncertain about the significance of the avoidance for their marriage relationship; talking in such cases is felt to 'clear the air' and to allow each partner to reassure the other that 'everything is alright'.

Second, it was suggested that periods of privacy or independence would be necessary for each partner's sense of identity, but would need to be avoided (or denied to one's spouse) in order to maintain stability. This formulation was supported, but it should be added that – as with the other sets of conditions – an emphasis upon fulfilling the stability requirements may, contradictorily, injure stability; for if people feel that their marriage does not allow them some freedom to develop their own sense of identity, then they may lose commitment to their marriage altogether.

Third, the sense of identity was thought to require that no public definitions or expectations should impose an identity upon the individual (unless it was one congruent with the person's own preferences); but that the sense of stability would be enhanced by adherence to common expectations or standard practices for married couples (these, by making the relationship recognisable in other people's eyes, would cause it also to be seen in the couple's eyes as something solid and real and therefore not easily to be broken or abandoned). This formulation recognised the possibility of congruence between people's own identity preferences and widely held expectations of how married people should behave. No refinement is necessary, therefore, but it should perhaps be emphasised that people do in general accept (as well as dislike) the constraints they recognise in marriage not only because of the sense of stability which adherence engenders but also because they enjoy the identities they bring: they like, for example, being responsible people, possessors of homes and children, and with the maturity to 'give and take'.

Fourth, the opportunity for making changes in one's self or one's experiences was seen as necessary for the sense of identity, but as something to be avoided in order to maintain the sense of stability. Again, as far as the second half of the formulation is concerned, some refinement is necessary, for it appears that marriage can accommodate a good deal of change since much of it benefits the stability of the relationship as well as the identities of the participants. A reformulation would state that although the kinds of change which promote shared activities and possessions (e.g. children, homes, hobbies) can be encouraged in order to foster stability, changes which lead to separate possessions or activities need to be avoided or minimised for the sake of stability.

Fifth, it was suggested that individuals need people outside their marriage to help them in the creation of their sense of identity, but that such outsiders will need to be discouraged in order to preserve stability. Again perhaps a slight refinement should be suggested, namely that some outsiders may not threaten, or may even positively assist, the stability of a marriage by their support either for marriage in general or for a specific couple as a couple. (The other kind of outsider may however be needed to promote some people's sense of identity.)

To return, finally, to Berger and Kellner: the findings of the investigation reported here clearly show that it is an oversimplification to look upon marriage as a successful identity-building relationship. People certainly have a sense of themselves as married people, but to a large extent the qualities they see in themselves are those common to the married; as described to a researcher they do not present a wide variety of different identities. In addition, the 'world of individual choice' and the 'continuing conversation' as romanticised by Berger and Kellner are far from common: in reality much has to be left unsaid; much has to be accepted without choice; many options are closed and people's lives run in predictable grooves when they become married.

Differences between marriages

The fact that one can generalise about the marriages in this study does not mean, however, that they are all alike. As many have asserted – for example, Bernard (1973) – it seems that a woman's marriage is different from a man's. In the present study women are much more likely than men to talk of themselves as being constrained within marriage by the necessity to carry out tasks – namely those of housework and childcare; and less likely to think of marriage as involving a loss of freedom or the assumption of responsibilities. Since they seem to spend much more time than men at home doing housework and looking after children it is not surprising that they tend to talk more about their day to their husbands than vice versa. This is perhaps partly because the shared home and children are more likely to be of interest to the husband than his work life would be to the wife. It may also be partly because the wives have been relatively starved of adult company whilst the husbands are at work. On the other hand wives are more likely than husbands to describe themselves as having close friends, perhaps partly because the tasks of housework and childcare require women to seek support and mutual help when husbands are at work (e.g. help with the children when one is ill or must go shopping, and so on). Lacking the same strong perception of responsibilities and loss of freedom, women are not as likely as men to see themselves as having become more sensible and cautious, but they do think they have become more mature, grown-up and considerate. Perhaps this is partly a recognition of the changes required for living amicably with another person. For similar reasons husbands see themselves as having mellowed and become more tolerant and patient. A woman's marriage therefore provides her with constraints and gives her identities (and the activities to go with them) which differ from those of a man.

Social-class and length-of-marriage differences are less apparent than sex differences, although, of course, with a larger sample one might find more. However, it is interesting that the younger couples seem very similar to their older counterparts, except for such things as the more recently married being more aware of the irritations of sharing space with their spouse and less concerned with the responsibilities of marriage; they are also more likely than the older couples to feel that they have lost friends since marriage. These differences seem very understandable: the young have had less time to get used to living with a spouse, less time to feel the accumulation of responsibilities, and more recent remembrance of pre-marital friendships. Working-class interviewees are similar to middle-class ones except that they are more likely to mention the constraints of responsibilities and sharing space, and more likely to feel that they have close friends (and that they have retained these friends since marriage). Again, several factors appear to make these differences understandable: the tendency for the financial position of the working-class income-provider to be less secure than that of the middle-class; the impression given that the working-class interviewees do have less household space per person; the fact that the working-class interviewees are less likely to have moved away from their area of upbringing and are therefore more capable of retaining pre-marital friendships. However, the general picture of compromise and acceptance is as true for women as it is for men, for both older and younger people, and for middle-class and working-class couples. For example, the young are as likely as the old to feel constrained to behave in certain ways and yet to accept it; women are as likely as men to see themselves and their activities as having changed since marriage and to accept these changes; working-class interviewees are as likely as the middle-class to feel they spend most of their leisure time together, and to accept this restriction. More interesting than these differences are those which distinguish a minority of the couples from the rest by the fact that they do not possess all the common characteristics of compromise and acceptance. They are discussed below.

The consequences of compromise failure

The marriage of seven of the couples could not be wholly described as an 'acceptable compromise'. For three of these couples the situation was problematic, for the other four it was much less so. There are several reasons for this.

First, there may be couples who emphasise stability-maintaining to the detriment of identity-upholding behaviour, but for whom no problem ensues because their sense of identity seems so much in line with stability-maintaining behaviour that there is no real contradiction. This was true of Mr and Mrs G, who said they talked little and spent relatively little time away from home. Mrs G said 'we just live for each other' and neither seemed to feel much need for more conversation or wider experiences; they called themselves home-birds, and appeared fully occupied with their house and their children.

Second, there may be couples who emphasise identity-maintaining over stability-enhancing behaviour, but for whom it also causes no problem because they do not seek stability within marriage. This was true of Mr and Mrs W, who had an unusually high level of separation, and who (particularly Mr W) expressed little support for stability in marriage. Mr W said he did not think a good marriage relationship could last for long 'if people are changing, as they should be doing'.

Third, it is possible that even though people do behave in either identity- or stability-threatening ways it is not problematic because it is counterbalanced by behaviour of the opposite kind in other spheres of marriage. For example, it could be that a person who talks to his spouse without any avoidance of topics (stability-threatening behaviour) also largely avoids separate leisure activity (identity-threatening behaviour) and thus maintains the balance. Both Mr and Mrs S and Mr and Mrs T seemed to do this. For instance, Mr and Mrs S, while complaining of their inability to talk freely to each other about each other (identity-threatening behaviour), did none the less have opportunities for a certain amount of separate activity, and for separate friendships, which seemed to help them in the development of their own identities. In the Ts' marriage, Mr T talked to his wife without avoidance of topics and also spent a good deal of time away from home (both stability-threatening forms of behaviour), yet neither he nor Mrs T expressed dissatisfaction with their marriage. This was partly because Mr T was able to demonstrate his continued commitment in other ways, and partly because Mrs T behaved in such a way as to minimise conflict. Thus Mr T was said to have changed since marriage, becoming far less independent than before (Mrs T said he could not even buy a tie without her help now); and Mrs T said she always tried to avoid rows or disagreements, and that she too had changed, becoming far more tactful and wily to fit in with her husband's impulsiveness and moodiness. In ways such as these the balance was restored.

But the As, the Es and the Ks all had problems. For example, Mrs A was highly dissatisfied with her marriage; she talked of the lack of opportunity for conversation and companionship with her husband, she felt highly constrained, and said that she had changed for the worse.

These complaints show an inability to fulfil a desired sense of identity. Her marriage, therefore, emphasised stability-maintaining behaviour, but this was unsatisfactory to her because such behaviour was not – as it was with Mr and Mrs G – in line with her identity requirements. As stated earlier, overemphasis of stability needs has a self-defeating result, in that when people become dissatisfied with their own sense of identity within a marriage they may well want to abandon the marriage altogether. Mrs A's criticisms of her husband and of the marriage seem to point in this direction.

Mr K was also highly critical of his marriage (openly admitting that he did not know why he had got married and wishing that he had not). In his case, too, unfulfilled identity needs seemed to be the main cause of dissatisfaction. For example, he expressed strong regrets for his lost freedom and his inability to spend his spare time away from home with his friends. Yet again this enforced emphasis upon stability-maintenance had the opposite effect, for it made Mr K altogether discontented with his marriage. On the other hand he did not appear to emphasise stability needs to the extent of avoiding some topics of conversation with his wife (perhaps this helped him to maintain some of his sense of self). But this freedom of talk was a source of dissatisfaction to Mrs K, who felt that it made their relationship unstable, since it led to disagreements and rows. Perhaps this is why she was anxious to curtail Mr K's freedom in other respects, and why she prevented him spending much of his spare time away from home. With this couple, therefore, a mixture of types of behaviour had not so much restored a balance as exacerbated an imbalance.

This appeared to be the case also with the final couple, Mr and Mrs E. In their case free and open discussion would undoubtedly have led to disagreements, so they avoided it (for the sake of stability); they also avoided outside friendships, in Mrs E's case explicitly because her husband did not get on well with her former friends. Mr E also felt highly constrained to behave in certain ways (e.g. he had to give in to his wife in several ways) and felt he had changed for the worse. On the other hand they emphasised identity requirements by spending very little time together, each having his or her own spare-time interests. But in this case such separation did not restore a balance, it merely exacerbated their feeling that they no longer had any shared interests, and that they could no longer talk to each other. Not only were they unable to fulfil their preferred identities, but their dissatisfaction with this situation also undermined the stability of their marriage. As Mr E said, it had all become 'pretence and sham'.

To summarise the situation in a rather over-simplified way, people's marriages can be divided into several types: first, those where behaviour in the potentially contradictory areas is either a compromise in each area, or where an emphasis in one direction in one area is balanced by an emphasis in the other direction in another area; second, those in which there is an emphasis upon behaviour likely to enhance the sense of stability – these can be subdivided into marriages where there is no contradiction because preferred identities are congruent with those promoted in the quest for stability, and marriages seen as problematic because the participant feels that his or her preferred sense of identity is being thwarted; and third, there are those in which there is an emphasis upon behaviour likely to enhance the sense of identity – again these can be subdivided into marriages where no contradiction is apparent because a sense of stability is not sought within the marital relationship, and those which are problematic because the participant does seek, but does not achieve, a sense of stability on account of the overemphasis upon identity needs. Most people fall into the first of these categories, but the others are interesting because, although few in number, in a general sample of the married they may form sizeable proportions of more specialised samples, such as the unhappily married.

The wider perspective

It has been argued in these chapters that certain types of behaviour have consequences for identity-fulfilment and stability-maintenance; it has also been argued that to some extent people's behaviour can be explained simply by reference to their search for identity or stability or for a compromise between the two. However one needs to go further than this in order fully to understand people's actions. Although this was not the main objective of the study, some reference to these underlying forces is useful because it helps to highlight the implications of the study's findings. For example, if it is necessary that some sort of balance between identity-enhancing and stability-maintaining behaviour be achieved in order for people to see their marriages as satisfactory, then any change in the forces which either uphold or undermine such a balance will change the amount of marital discontent and even divorce in a society. There are also some underlying forces which although not necessarily affecting societal trends may help one to understand and therefore even influence the course of a particular marriage.

Among the latter forces are people's norms and goals, their upbringing or preparation for marriage, the influence of other people, and even their physical fitness. Thus the views people hold about how one *should* behave in the roles and relationships of social life might be in line with the kind of behaviour required to balance identity and stability needs in marriage, or they might not. If norms and marital needs do conflict, then people have the problem of deciding which of the various ways of handling the conflict to choose. Are they, for example, to deviate from what they see as the norms, or are they to upset the balance of their marriage and exacerbate their own and/or their partner's dissatisfaction? For instance, a person could carry out the tasks and responsibilities of marriage because she felt that neglect of children and housework was wrong or would arouse community disapproval, and that such matters were primarily a woman's responsibility; but on the other hand she might not like to see herself largely as housewife, homemaker and child-minder and feel that her sense of identity was thwarted by adhering to the norms. Again, a man might belong to a cultural group in which it was expected that men should have leisure activities separate from their wives: going to a public house or social club, taking part in sport, and so on. In some marriages, because of the partners' behaviour in other areas of their joint lives, a high degree of separate leisure might undermine the stability of the marriage. Such a man, therefore, must either deviate from the expectations of his friends and associates, or he must put his marriage at risk. Thus norms or expectations influencing behaviour either inside or outside marriage can upset or prevent a balance of activities within it.

As well as norms, people's other goals in life can either assist or conflict with those inside marriage. Obviously people have other (either major or minor) goals apart from the achievement of a sense of personal identity and a stable marriage. For example, a desire for material comforts could increase the amount of time a couple spends apart, by encouraging them to work overtime or to take an evening job. But such increased separation might endanger the stability of their relationship, although – if they enjoyed their work or the people they met there – it might well promote identity fulfilment. Another goal might, for example, be to improve or maintain physical fitness; and to do this people might well spend time away from their spouse taking part in sport or other exercise. Such activity would probably further their identity needs (unless of course they wanted to see themselves as physically fit but not as 'sporty' or 'active' people), but again it could endanger marital stability through increasing the spouses' separation. There is probably a tendency for people to avoid mutually exclusive goals whenever possible, and also for norms eventually to fall into line with widely favoured activities. But this will not always be so, and such contradictions are worth investigating for they may well help to explain why some marriages are problematic.

The way people are brought up will, of course, also affect their subsequent marriage behaviour, not only by instilling certain values, norms, goals and beliefs, but also by influencing personality development, and by teaching or failing to teach people about marital responsibilities and tasks. For example, a woman who has received little or no prior tuition in household management or childcare may see herself (at least in early marriage) as an incompetent or stupid person: probably not an identity which she is likely to have sought. Psychological factors may also affect people's ability to cope with the various activities of marriage; for instance, feelings of inferiority or inhibition, or lack of interactional skills, could help to account for the fact that some people do not talk much to their spouses or have few friends outside marriage (with probable consequences for the partners' sense of identity). Again, some people may have a need to dominate, and others lack the psychological flexibility to adapt easily to change or to adjust their behaviour to that of others. Such people will be likely to attempt to impose their own preferences upon their marriage and make insufficient allowance for their spouses' wishes (with probable consequences for the partners' sense of identity and eventually for the stability of the marriage). Physical as well as mental characteristics may also affect the ability of couples to achieve the acceptable compromise; for instance, illness or growing older often leads to curtailment of outside activities and interests (it stops people participating in sport or other recreations; it encourages them to avoid moving house or job). This is likely to make people feel that they are no longer adequately pursuing their identity needs; but stability needs will be enhanced by the increased amount of time probably spent at home and with the spouse. If at the earlier time identity needs had been emphasised over stability needs, then the increase in home-based activity may well restore a balance; but if a compromise situation had been achieved beforehand, then the new situation will lead to imbalance.

Because marriages do not exist in isolation there is also the influence of other people's behaviour, which again can operate either to further the achievement of the compromise or to disturb it in either direction. For example, the demands or needs of outsiders may separate a couple more than is good for either their sense of identity or of stability (children may lead them to start running Scout Troops, ageing parents may demand more of their help and company), so that they could come to feel that they no longer have enough time together just to talk to each other (and thus further each other's sense of identity), or that their separation is leading them to develop in different ways and to lose their commitment to each other. On the other hand, friends and relations may assist either their stability or identity needs: they may – as stated earlier – publicly support the marriage, treat the pair as a couple, give them possessions to share, cease to invite the partners out separately, and so on; or they may act as people to whom either of the partners can go if they want some separate activity or some interaction with an outsider in order to further their sense of identity.

Changing trends in marriage-related behaviour could occur through changes in some of the factors discussed above (such as changes in norms or goals or in the socialisation of young people). If such changes occur, it follows that they could disturb the achievement of the compromise most married people manage to attain between identity and stability needs. For example, if there were decreasing emphasis upon the training of girls in household and child-minding skills, and if changing norms meant changing expectations about the role of a housewife, then men's and women's sense of identity within marriage would change and new forms of compromise between stability and identity needs would have to be sought. This is not the place to begin discussing the complex subject of social change, but as a final point it is worth mentioning that whenever social trends or changes are recorded (whether in social structural factors or in societal or group values and expectations) it could be useful to assess the influence of these trends or changes upon the behaviour of married couples in their search for identity- or stability-maintenance. One obvious structural factor, for example, is unemployment or changes in job patterns; unemployment is likely to cause couples to spend less time apart than they would otherwise. This could undermine a person's sense of identity, which he or she might in consequence attempt to further by other means: trying to develop outside friendships, not avoiding topics of conversation with the spouse, refusing to adhere to disliked marital constraints. Periods of economic growth could have the opposite effect, for if they encouraged overtime plus high employment among married women, couples' separation would be lengthened and their stability threatened. Restoring a balance in these circumstances is likely to require considerable effort; these factors therefore are likely to have an effect (although in combination with others) upon levels of marital discontent. As topical as such structural change is the question of changing values, which are frequently said to differentiate the younger from the older generations, who have more traditional values. Although one can query the extent of such change, and the possible confusion of cohort with generational effects, none the less there appear to be some shifts in emphasis, and in particular it is often said that young (particularly middle-class) people place more stress upon the value of self-fulfilment than has hitherto been the case. This means that, if such people get married, they are likely to emphasise the pursuit of personal identity over that of stability, and to encourage separate activity, personal change and the maintenance of individual friendships outside marriage. If such values are actually put into practice the likelihood is that the marriage will not be permanent since stability-maintaining behavour will not be able to operate effectively. Such a consequence may or may not be seen as problematic by the participants for, as stated earlier, some identity-emphasisers would also like to seek stability within marriage, while some would not. This is an area in which further investigation would be very useful since it seems likely that a growing emphasis upon self-fulfilment and identity pursuit could well help to explain both the rise in divorce rates and the decline in marriage rates.

The approach developed in this study could, therefore, have wide application. In this first investigation emphasis has, of course, been placed largely upon the seeking of support for the validity and usefulness of looking at marriage as a relationship embodying a contradiction between identity and stability pursuit. This study has also been able to show that there are various ways in which an imbalance (or failure to compromise) can occur, and that some of these ways are experienced as problematic by the husbands or wives involved. Why imbalance occurs is a tantalising question. In these last few pages some tentative explanations have been suggested: for example, marital needs conflicting with other societal or group expectations, personality traits, changes in social structural factors or in social values making it either more difficult for people to achieve compromise or less likely for them even to desire it. It is hoped that the approach developed here will be used in further examinations of these wider questions.

Appendix 1 Sample selection

A sample of forty married people was decided upon (twenty wives and their twenty husbands). Although this was an arbitrary number, it was felt that many more would be unnecessary unless the aim had been to make the sample very much bigger in order to be able to generalise.

The sample characteristics decided in advance were that all should be legally married and not previously divorced; living with their spouses; and residing in Aberdeenshire or the city of Aberdeen. Other research and general knowledge of the area do not show those living in the north-east of Scotland as being markedly different from those living in other parts of provincial Britain.

A four-cell quota sample was chosen, so that there would be some variation, but not too widespread a variation, within the sample. The quotas set were that, first, half the sample should involve marriages in which the husband was at present in a manual occupation, and half should involve those in which he was in a non-manual occupation (there were to be no unemployed or retired husbands though they could be away from work through illness or on a training course). Second, half the sample should involve people married for five years or less, and half people married for fifteen years or more. Again this was in order to permit comparison and also to restrict the extent of variation by length of marriage.

Since no sampling frame of married people was available, a quota sample was necessary. It is usual when quota samples are employed to make initial contact by approaching people in the street, knocking on doors, going to places of work, etc. Such a method did not seem appropriate for a study which wanted to make what it was assumed would be seen as fairly heavy demands upon people – both in terms of time and of revelation of 'personal' matters. Contact points within the health service, to which the author had access through the Institute of Medical Sociology, were therefore used. Specifically, the Cytology Out-Patient Clinic, the Family Planning Clinic, a gynaecology ward, and the Institute of Medical Sociology itself were used as sources of initial contact with appropriate potential interviewees. These four sources yielded respectively four, five, six and five couples with whom interviews were completed. In addition, contact had been made with three where either the husband or wife refused to take part, four who were too busy or the husband was away, two with inappropriate characteristics (husband unemployed, couple separated), and one surplus to requirements. It had also been stipulated in advance to staff responsible for putting the researcher in contact with potential interviewees that they should omit any who did not fall within the quota restrictions (among these were included any people coming to the two clinics for non-routine visits, and any patients on the ward who were undergoing either major surgery or an event directly concerned with a pregnancy, such as termination; anyone personally known to the researcher would also, of course, have been excluded).

In almost all cases wives were the people first approached: the researcher briefly explained the aims of the study (saying that the interest was in marriage: people's attitudes towards it, how they organised their own marriages, whether their marriages had changed, and so on), where the researcher worked and what her qualifications were, that all information would be treated as confidential, and that she would like to come to their house and talk to both the husband and wife separately and together.

Using these procedures the required sample of forty legally married people was obtained. They were divided equally into first, couples married for five years or less, and where the husband was in a non-manual occupation; second, those married for five years or less, and where the husband was in a manual occupation; third, those married for fifteen years or more, and where the husband was in a non-manual occupation; and fourth, those married for fifteen years or more, and where the husband was in a manual occupation.

Profiles of each couple are given in appendix 3. Some of their basic characteristics are shown in aggregate below:

Present age of wife		*Present age of husband*	
21–30 years	10	21–30 years	7
31–40 years	1	31–40 years	3
41–50 years	4	41–50 years	4
51–60 years	5	51–60 years	4
61–70 years	–	61–70 years	2

Where wife spent all/most of childhood		*Where husband spent all/most of childhood*	
Aberdeen or Aberdeenshire	18	Aberdeen or Aberdeenshire	14
Other parts of Scotland	2	Other parts of Scotland	3
Outside Scotland	–	Outside Scotland	3

*Whether couple married in church or
Register Office*

Church	16
Register Office	4

Number of children

None	2
One	5
Two	7
Three, four or five	6

Number of children under 16 years old

None	5
One	7
Two	6
Three, four or five	2

Type of house

Flat or maisonette	11
Terraced or semi-detached house	7
Detached house	2

Type of tenancy of house

Council rented	7
Privately rented	5
Owner occupied	8

Husband's type of occupation

Professional or undergoing professional training	4
Administrative/managerial	6
Clerical	–
Skilled manual	7
Semi-skilled or unskilled manual	3

Wife's employment

Not working	9
Working part-time	6
Working full-time	5

Wife's present type of occupation

Professional	3
Clerical or retail trade	6
Semi-skilled or unskilled manual	2
Not working	9

Appendix 2 Interview guide

▶▶

Joint interview

1 Could you start off by telling me something about yourselves, about your background?
> Age
> Education (school and further education; where; what type)
> Jobs (what; where; for how long; reasons for changes)
> Where born and lived (place; urban/rural; housing; reasons for moves)
> Parents (where living; jobs; any experience of divorce, separation or widowhood)
> Brothers and sisters (number; ages; whether married; where living; any children; any experience of divorce, separation or widowhood)

2 Can you tell me something about your relationship?
> How did you come to meet?
> How long did you go out together before getting married?
> Did you get engaged?
> How long were you engaged?
> How did you spend your time together when you were going out/engaged?
> What made you think you'd like to marry [name of spouse]?
> What made you decide to get engaged?
> What did other people (parents, siblings, friends) say when they heard you were getting engaged/married?
> Why did you get married when you did?
> Do you think you'd always thought you would get married one day, or not?
> Did you ever break off your relationship before you got married?
> Did you ever think about living together rather than getting legally married?

The wedding arrangements and ceremony ('white wedding' or not; church or Register Office; number of guests; honeymoon)

3 Obtain details of significant events since marriage; asking for explanations of any innovation or change:

Housing
Place of residence
Jobs
Children
Health
Leisure pursuits
Household tasks

Separate interview

A *Friends or acquaintances*

1 Do you have people you would call 'friends'?

How many people do you have whom you would call friends? Could you tell me something about him/her/them? (age, sex, how met, how long known, marital status, where living)

What is it that makes this person/these persons friends?

Or What does 'a friend' mean to you?

Are they more your friends, more your wife's/husband's friends, or friends of you both?

2 Is there any person or any people whom you feel you know really well?

Is there any person or people who you feel knows you really well?

In the past has there been any person or people whom you felt you knew really well?

For any people mentioned above obtain details as at Question A1

3 Whom do you think you know best?

And who do you think knows you best?

Why do you think this is so?

If any person not already mentioned obtain details as at Question A1

4 For anyone mentioned in the above questions:

What sort of things do you and – tend to talk about?

How often do you see –?

What sort of things do you do when you're with –?

Would you like to see more/less/about the same of – ?

5 In general do you think you see about as much as you would like of other people (apart from your wife/husband/children), or do you ever think you'd like to see other people more or less often?

Why is this so, do you think?

Do you ever tend to feel lonely? When? Why?

6 Whom – apart from your husband/wife/children – do you see most often?

7 If you were worried about your wife/husband, or about your relationship with your wife/husband, is there anyone you would talk to about it?

Who would that be? And why?

Why do you think there is no one you would talk to?

8 Ask about particular intimates (e.g. those described as known really well, known best, as close friend);

What does your wife/husband think of –?

What does – think of your wife/husband?

Do they get on well together?

9 Are there any friends you used to have before living with your wife/husband whom you have ceased to see as much of?

How many?

Why do you think that is so?

How do you feel about that?

Are there any friends you used to have whom you now see more of?

Why is that? And how do you feel about it?

10 Are there any friendships which have grown up since you've lived with your wife/husband?

How many?

Why do you think this is so?

How do you feel about that?

B Wife and husband

1 How well do you feel you know your wife/husband?

And how well do you feel your wife/husband knows you?

If non-spouse was mentioned as person known best or as knowing respondent best at Question A3, ask: How does your knowledge of your wife/husband *or* your wife's/husband's knowledge of you compare with that of –?

2 What sort of things do you and your wife/husband tend to talk about, for example when you're sitting down together in the evenings or at weekends?

What sort of things do you think you talk about most?

What sort of things do you think you talk about least?

Do you tend to talk about your day, or not, with your wife/husband?

Does your wife/husband tend to talk about his/her day with you?

Would you say you are a couple who tend to talk a lot, about average, or not so much?

For each of the above questions, probe for reasons, respondent's feelings about the present situation, and what sort of situation he/she would prefer (if any)

3 Are there any subjects that you would tend not to talk about to your wife/ husband? What? Why?

Would you like to be able to talk to him/her about –?

Is there anyone you would talk to about –?

Do you ever avoid saying things because they might either lead to a row, or make your wife/husband feel upset or sad? Why is that? What sort of things would they be? Can you give me an example of something you've avoided talking about?

4 Are there some things that you would talk to your wife/husband about which you don't talk about with other people?

What sort of things?

Why is that so?

5 What about rows or disagreements? Do you have them?

About how often do you have them?

What are they about?

Can you remember what the last one was about?

C *Changes in self and in wife/husband*

1 Would you say that your wife/husband has changed or not changed since you've been married?

In what ways (if at all)?

Why do you think this is so?

How do you feel about that?

2 Do you think you've changed at all or not changed since you've been married?

In what ways (if at all)?

Why do you think this is so?

How do you feel about that?

3 Have the things you do, or your interests, changed or not since you've been married? In what ways?

What do you think led to that?

Have the things your wife/husband does, his/her interests, changed or not since you've been married?

In what ways?

What do you think led to that?

4 Are there some things you can't or don't do now that you miss or wish you could do?

What sort of things?
Did you do that when you weren't married?
Why do you think you don't do it now?
How do you feel about not doing it?
Why would you like to do it?

5 Are there any things that you do now which you used not to do?
What sort of things?
How long have you been doing –?
Why do you think you do it now?
How do you feel about doing –?

6 Do you ever get bored with what you do?
What sort of things do you get bored with? Why?
What sort of things are least boring, or most enjoyable? Why is that?
Would you like to make any changes in what you do? What sort of thing are you thinking of? Do you think you will be able to do that? Why, or why not?

7 Thinking back to when you got married, do you think people treated you any differently when you became a wife/husband?
In what ways?
How did you feel about that?
Did you feel different yourself after you became married? In what ways?
How did you feel about that?

8 How do you feel about your own job (if working)?
Would you like to make any changes?
Why have you not done so (yet)?
Do you think you will be able to do so?
Would you like to have a job (if not working)?
Why don't you?
Do you think you will be able to do so?
(Husband only) How do/would you feel about your wife working?
(Wife only) How do you feel about your husband's job?

D *Separate and joint activity*
1 What sort of things, if any, do you and your wife/husband do independently of each other?
How often do you do that?
Would you prefer to do it more/less/about as often as you do do it? Why?
How often does he/she do that?
How do you feel about him/her doing that?

Would you prefer him/her to do that more/less/about as often as he/she does it? Why?

2 What sort of things do you and your wife/husband do together? What sort of leisure activities do you do together?

How often do you do that?

Would you prefer to do it more/less/about as often as you do do it? Why?

3 Who tends to do what around the house? Does one of you tend to do most things, do you share, does it vary, or what?

Is that the way you like things to be, or would you prefer it if things were organised differently?

In what ways would you like them to be different? Why aren't they like that?

4 What about taking decisions? Does one of you tend to take most decisions, do you share, does it vary, or what?

Is that the way you like things to be, or would you prefer it if things were organised differently?

In what ways would you like them to be different? Why aren't they like that?

Do you tend to think of one or other of you as having the final say in important matters, or is it not like that?

5 Do you ever feel like getting away on your own or not?

Why do you feel like that?

Can you do that if you want to?

On the whole do you do things independently of your wife/husband as often as you like, or would you prefer it if you did things independently more or less often?

Why do you feel like that?

Why are things not quite as you would prefer?

On the whole do you think your wife/husband does things on his/her own without you about the right amount, or would you prefer it if he/she did things on his/her own either more or less often?

Why do you feel like that?

Why are things not quite as you would prefer?

E Attitudes to marriage

1 What sort of things (if any) do you think you've learned from living with your wife/husband?

What sort of things (if any) do you think he/she has learned from living with you?

What sort of things (if any) does your wife/husband do that you find irritating or annoying?

Does he/she do that more/less/about as often as he/she used to?

What sort of things (if any) do you do that your wife/husband finds irritating or annoying?

Do you do that more/less/about as often as you used to?

2 Sometimes people say that marriage ties you down. Do you think that is so, or not?

Why do you think that is so?

How do you feel about that?

3 Some people these days live together rather than get legally married. How do you feel about that? Why?

4 Can you envisage what kind of things would have to happen for you to feel you couldn't go on living with your wife/husband?

Why do you feel like that?

What kind of things do you think would have to happen for your wife/husband to feel that he/she couldn't go on living with you?

Why do you feel that?

Thinking about marriages that break up, what do you think are good or reasonable grounds for a wife to leave her husband or for a husband to leave his wife?

Why do you think that?

Appendix 3 Profiles of the couples

Mr and Mrs A have been married for four years and have one child three years of age. They have recently moved from a furnished flat to a new council house on an estate at the outskirts of the city. The wife, Anne, has not worked since she had her baby, but before that she was in a clerical job. Her husband, Alan, works in the health service and has had his present job for the past eight years. Alan is an incomer to the city, but Anne has lived in or near Aberdeen all her life. Her parents and brothers still live here.

Mr and Mrs B have been married for sixteen years. Betty is in her late thirties and Bob is in his early forties. When they first married Bob had a job which took him away from Aberdeen for quite long periods of time, but he got a local job when his second child, a boy, was born. He is now in a managerial post. Before marriage Betty was a nurse, but she gave up her job as soon as she knew she was pregnant with her first child, and had no outside employment for the following twelve years. For the past three years however she has had a part-time clerical post, which she says she enjoys very much. The couple have recently bought a small house in Aberdeen (they previously owned a flat), and talk with enthusiasm of renovating and redecorating it.

Mr and Mrs C live in a council flat with their two young sons and the wife's widowed father. They were both in their teens when they got married. They say that they have completed their family, and Clare has returned to part-time work (cleaning). Her husband, Colin, is a skilled manual worker, in what he sees as a secure job. It gives him plenty of overtime, which he is glad to work so that they can afford to run a car, buy equipment for the house, and have holidays and the occasional night out.

Mr and Mrs D have been married for twenty years. Don runs a farm near Aberdeen, where they have lived since shortly after marriage. Dora gave up work at marriage and has had no outside employment (apart from some help on the farm) since then. They have three children, two of whom are now working. All three still live at home. Dora's job before marriage was in a shop, but she says she would not want to go back to that now. She is forty-five years old, and Don is in his early fifties.

Mr and Mrs E have been married for five years. They have two children, one at school and one at nursery school. Ellen works full-time (a professional job) and Eddie is in full-time training for professional work. They have a privately rented house in the country near Ellen's parents, though both travel into the city to work and study. Ellen says she tries to be involved in village life. She was brought up in the country, unlike Eddie, who, before they got this house, had always lived in the city.

Mr and Mrs F. Frank left school at fifteen and has been in semi-skilled work ever since (many changes of employer but always the same kind of job). His wife Fiona, however, stayed on at school until she was seventeen and then trained to become a primary school teacher. Her husband would very much like her to go back to work but she has not taught since she was expecting her first child. They now have three children, and Fiona says that looking after the family is a full-time job. They live in a council house just outside the city. Fiona's mother, who used to live with them, has recently died.

Mr and Mrs G. George has been in the same job with the same firm for the past thirty years. He has what both he and his wife see as a low wage, and they say they have never been able to afford luxuries. Gladys has had a variety of part-time jobs on and off throughout her married life, all of an unskilled nature such as cleaning. They have been married for twenty-five years, and have three children; the eldest has just got married and the youngest is still at school. They have had several changes of accommodation (though always remaining in Aberdeen where they have both lived all their lives); they now live in a three-bedroomed council flat.

Mr and Mrs H. Helen is ten years younger than Harry; they married when she was nineteen. She is an Aberdonian but Harry is not. They met and married in the south of England, but eventually moved to Aberdeen which they both liked and where they could buy a house (a small inter-war detached house). They have been married for seventeen years, and have three children, two now at secondary and one at primary school. Harry is a skilled manual worker, Helen is a part-time shop assistant. She has only recently gone back to work after several years at home, and expresses delight in her 'little job'.

Mr and Mrs I. Irma is in her late forties and Ian, her husband, in his early fifties. They have been married for twenty-two years, and have two children, one living with them at the moment and one living away (both children are working; neither is married). Ian has had a number of different skilled jobs during his married life, but is now in semi-skilled work (this is because he is slightly disabled following an accident). Irma did not work while the children were very young, but has had a variety of part-time jobs since then. She now works full-time for the social services. Last year they were able to afford their first 'real' holiday together since they got married. They say that having the children 'off their hands' and getting on together much better since Ian's accident has given them 'a new lease of life'.

Mr and Mrs J are buying their own small tenement flat, but would like to be able to move to a bigger place when they have children. They were born and bred in Aberdeen, left school at sixteen, and went out together for three years before getting married, when Jenny was nineteen and Jim was twenty-three. They have been married for two years, and would like to start a family in 'a year or so'. Jim is a skilled worker employed in the building trade, and Jenny a full-time clerical worker.

Mr and Mrs K have been married for two years and have a one-year-old baby. They live in a two-roomed privately rented flat, are on the council house waiting list, but say they do not expect to be offered a flat for some while yet. Keith was twenty-six when they got married and Kathy eighteen. Kathy now has a one-day-a-week clerical job, and Keith has recently moved to a new semi-skilled manual job (only his second job since leaving school).

Mr and Mrs L have been married for two and a half years, and have one two-year-old child. When they first married they lived with Laura's parents, but when they found they were beginning to get on each other's nerves they moved to their present very small privately rented flat. They say they are hoping to be offered a council house before very long. Leslie was a commercial course student when he got married, but soon afterwards gave this up and took an executive job, in which he says he intends to remain. Laura had a technical post, but she has not worked since shortly before she had the baby. She is now looking for a part-time evening job.

Mr and Mrs M went out together for five years before marrying when Michael was twenty-five and Maureen twenty-three. They had their silver wedding anniversary three years ago. Michael is a skilled worker although he has to do less skilled work nowadays because of a back injury. After two privately rented homes they moved to a council flat, where they have lived for the past twenty-two years. They have tried to move because the building is old and damp, but with no success. They have two children, one recently married, the other working but still single and living with them. Maureen gave up work when she got married, but a few years ago took a part-time job, partly because her doctor told her it would be good for her. She says she enjoys it, and her husband now accepts it, having been rather against the idea to start with.

Mr and Mrs N have been married for less than a year, and are still doing up the two-roomed flat they bought a year before their marriage. Nicola has been a shop assistant since leaving school five years ago. Neil, her husband, is a year older; he is a skilled worker. The couple were engaged for eighteen months before their white, church wedding. They say they want to have children, but not for a while.

Mr and Mrs O have a three-roomed tenement flat rented from Owen's employer (he is a skilled manual worker). They both say that this is big enough whilst they have just one child (a three-year-old), but they would like to move to a bigger place before having another child. They have considered buying their own place but cannot afford a mortgage. Owen works a great deal of overtime; at the moment they are saving to buy a car. Olive would like to work part-time but does not think she would be much better off because she would have to pay someone to look after the child. Before she gave up work she was a clerical worker. They have been married for three and a half years.

Mr and Mrs P. Phyllis and Pete have two children aged four and two. They have been married for five years, during which time Phyllis has not had outside employment; but she is now very anxious to get a job, or at least to have some outside interest. Pete has a managerial job; before marriage Phyllis had a clerical post. They own their own fairly spacious first-floor flat, but say they are thinking of moving because they would like a house with their own garden.

Mr and Mrs R have both lived in Aberdeen all their lives apart from Ronald's Army service. Most of their family live here too, except for one of their children who now lives in the south of England. Both their children are married, and Rhona and Ronald have three grandchildren. Ronald started his working life as a tradesman in a factory (where he met Rhona) but was gradually promoted until he reached a managerial position. He is now close to retirement. The couple have been married for thirty-five years, and live in a council house. Rhona has had no outside employment since she got married, and says she has never wished to have any.

Mr and Mrs S. Sheila and Sam have lived in Aberdeen for five of their twenty years of marriage. They met and married in their mid-twenties, and had four children before Sheila went back to work (in the health service) eight years after marriage. Sam is in an administrative post, and expects that it will move him on from Aberdeen in due course. They own their own house. Two of their children have left school, and all still live at home.

Mr and Mrs T. Tom has been in the same professional post in Aberdeen for the past twenty-five years; it involves a considerable amount of travel away from home. He moved into Aberdeen from elsewhere, but Teresa was born and brought up here. They have been married for nineteen years, and have three school-age children (two still at primary school). They bought a flat when first married, and then more recently a house in the city. Teresa went back to work (teaching) for a while between her first and second child but has not worked since then. She says she hopes to return to work when the children are older.

Mr and Mrs W. William was born and brought up elsewhere, but Wendy has always lived in Aberdeen. They met when they were both still studying. Wendy had to interrupt her training because of pregnancy, marriage and then having a baby to look after. Three years later, however, she had completed her course and is now in a professional post. William also has a professional job. They have one child, and live in a three-roomed privately rented flat.

Glossary

Terms used by interviewees

awa	away
bairn	child
bide, biding	live, living
canna	cannot
dinna	do not
frae	from
gallas	bold, daring
ging	go
greeting	crying
hae	have
haim	home
hinna	have not
ken	know
mair	more
maist	most
nae	no, not
newsing	having a chat
sae	so

Symbols used in quotations

. . .	short pause
(pause)	long pause
///	omission of part of transcript
words in italic	emphasis given by interviewee
[L]	laughter
[words in brackets]	author's elucidation of part of transcript

Bibliography

Anshen, R. N. (ed.) 1959. *The Family: Its Function and Destiny.* Harper, New York

Askham, J. 1976. Identity and Stability within the Marriage Relationship. *Journal of Marriage and the Family,* **38** (Aug.), 535–48

Babchuk, N. and Bates, A. P. 1963. The Primary Relations of Middle Class Couples: A Study in Male Dominance. *American Sociological Review,* **28**, 377–84

Becker, H. S. 1964. Personal Change in Adult Life. *Sociometry,* **27**, 1 (March), 40–53

Becker, H. S. and Geer, B. 1970. Participant Observation and Interviewing: A Comparison. In W. J. Filstead (ed.), *Qualitative Methodology,* Markham Pub. Co., Chicago

Bell, R. R. 1971. *Marriage and Family Interaction.* The Dorsey Press, Homewood, Illinois

Bell, N. W. and Vogel, E. F. (eds.) 1960, revised 1968. *A Modern Introduction to the Family.* Routledge and Kegan Paul, London

Benson, L. 1971. *The Family Bond: Marriage, Love and Sex in America.* Random House, New York

Berger, P. and Kellner, H. 1964. Marriage and the Construction of Reality. *Diogenes,* **46**, 1–24

Berger, P. and Luckmann, T. 1966. *The Social Construction of Reality.* Allen Lane, London

Bernard, J. 1964. The Adjustments of Married Mates. In H. Christensen (ed.), *Handbook of Marriage and the Family.* Rand McNally and Co., Chicago

Bernard, J. 1972. *The Future of Marriage.* Souvenir Press, London

Bienvenu, J. 1970. Measurement of Marital Communication. *Family Coordinator,* **19**, 26–31

Blood, R. O. 1958. The Use of Observational Methods in Family Research. *Journal of Marriage and the Family,* **20** (Feb.), 47–52

Blood, R. O. 1976. Research Needs of a Family Life Educator and Marriage Counsellor. *Journal of Marriage and the Family,* **38** (Feb.) 7–12

212

Blood, R. O. and Wolfe, D. M. 1960. *Husbands and Wives: The Dynamics of Married Living.* The Free Press, New York

Blumer, H. 1962. Society as Symbolic Interaction. In A. Rose (ed.) *Human Behaviour and Social Processes.* Routledge and Kegal Paul, London

Bott, E. 1957, 1971. *Family and Social Network.* Tavistock, London

Bradburn, N. M. 1969. *The Structure of Psychological Well-Being.* Aldine, Chicago

Brenner, M. 1978. Interviewing: The Social Phenomenology of a Research Instrument. In M. Brenner, P. Marsh and M. Brenner (eds.), *The Social Context of Method.* Croom Helm, London

Brown, G. and Rutter, M. 1966. The Measurement of Family Activities and Relationships: a Methodological Study. *Human Relations, 19*, 241–63

Burr, W. R. Hill, R. Nye, F. L. and Reiss, I. L. (eds.) 1979. *Contemporary Theories about the Family*, 2 vols. The Free Press, New York

Burr, W. R., Leigh, G. K., Day, R. D. and Constantine, J. 1979. Symbolic Interaction and the Family. In W. R. Burr *et al.* (eds.), *Contemporary Theories about the Family.* The Free Press, New York

Chester, R. and Peel, J. (eds.) 1977. *Equalities and Inequalities in Family Life.* Academic Press, London

Christensen, H. (ed.) 1964. *Handbook of Marriage and the Family.* Rand McNally and Co., Chicago

Cicourel, A. V. 1964. *Method and Measurement in Sociology.* The Free Press, New York

Coser, R. 1964. *The Family: Its Structure and Functions.* St Martins, New York

Cromwell, R. E. and Olson, D. H. (eds.) 1975. *Power in Families.* John Wiley and Sons, New York

Cuber, J. F. and Harroff, P. B. 1965. *The Significant Americans.* Appleton–Century–Crofts, New York

Cunningham, K. and Johannis, T. 1960. Research on the Family and Leisure: A Review and Critique of Selected Studies. *Family Coordinator, 9*, 25–32

Dohrenwend, B. S. and Dohrenwend, B. P. (eds.) 1974. *Stressful Life Events: Their Nature and Effects.* John Wiley and Sons, New York

Filstead, W. J. (ed.) 1970. *Qualitative Methodology.* Markham Pub. Co., Chicago

Fletcher, R. 1962, 1977. *Family and Marriage in Britain.* Penguin, London

Gavron, H. 1966. *The Captive Wife.* Routledge and Kegan Paul, London

Glenn, N. D. 1975. The Contribution of Marriage to the Psychological Well-being of Males and Females. *Journal of Marriage and the Family, 37* (Aug.), 594–601

Goffman, E. 1971. The Insanity of Place. In E. Goffman, *Relations in Public.* Allen Lane, London

Gordon, C. and Gergen, K. J. (eds.) 1968. *The Self in Social Interaction*. John Wiley and Sons, New York

Gorer, G. 1971. *Sex and Marriage in England Today*. Nelson, London

Gurin, G. Veroff, J. and Feld, S. 1960. *Americans View Their Mental Health*. Basic Books, New York

Henry, J. 1972. *Pathways to Madness*. Jonathan Cape, London

Hicks, M. W. and Platt, M. 1970. Marital Happiness and Stability: A Review of Research of the Sixties. *Journal of Marriage and the Family*, **32** (Nov.), 553–74

Komarovsky, M. 1962. *Blue Collar Marriage*. Random House, New York

Levinger, G. 1968. Task and Social Behaviour in Marriage. In R. F. Winch and L. W. Goodman (eds.), *Selected Studies in Marriage and the Family*. Holt, Rinehart and Winston, New York

Lewis, O. 1962. *The Children of Sanchez*. Secker and Warburg, London

Lewis, R. A. and Spanier, G. B. 1979. Theorising about the Quality and Stability of Marriage. In W. R. Burr *et al.* (eds.) *Contemporary Theories about the Family*. The Free Press, New York

Lively, E. L. 1969. Toward Conceptual Clarification: The Case of Marital Interaction. *Journal of Marriage and the Family*, **31** (Feb.), 108–14

Lofland, J. F. 1971. *Analysing Social Settings*. Wadsworth, Belmont

Mansfield, P. 1982. Article in *Guardian*, 9 February 1982

Marini, M. M. 1976. Dimensions of Marriage Happiness: A Research Note. *Journal of Marriage and the Family*, **38** (Aug.) 443–8

McCall, G. and Simmons, J. 1966. *Identities and Interactions*. The Free Press, New York

Mead, G. H. 1934. *Mind, Self and Society*. University of Chicago Press, Chicago

Miller, B. C. 1976. A Multivariate Developmental Model of Marital Satisfaction. *Journal of Marriage and the Family*, **38** (Nov.), 643–57

Morgan, D. 1975. *Social Theory and the Family*. Routledge and Kegan Paul, London

Morgan, D. 1977. Alternatives to the Family. In R. Chester and J. Peel (eds.), *Equalities and Inequalities in Family Life*. Academic Press, London

Morgan, D. 1981. Berger and Kellner's Construction of Marriage. Occasional Paper no. 7, Dept of Sociology, University of Manchester, Manchester

Navran, L. 1967. Communication and Adjustment in Marriage. *Family Process*, 6, 173–84

Oakley, A. 1974a. *Housewife*. Allen Lane, London

Oakley, A. 1974b. *The Sociology of Housework*. Martin Robertson, London

Office of Population Censuses and Surveys. 1981. *General Household Survey 1979*. HMSO, London

Orden, S. and Bradburn, N. 1968. Dimensions of Marriage Happiness. *American Journal of Sociology*, **73** (May), 715–31

Orthner, D. K. 1975. Leisure Activity Patterns and Marital Satisfaction over the Marital Career. *Journal of Marriage and the Family,* **37** (Feb.), 91–101

Pahl, R. E. and Pahl, J. M. 1971. *Managers and Their Wives.* Allen Lane, London

Palisi, B. J. 1977. Wife's Statuses and Husband–Wife Companionship in an Australian Metropolitan Area. *Journal of Marriage and the Family,* **39**, 185–99

Parsons, T. 1959. The Social Functions of the Family. In R. N. Anshen (ed.) *The Family: Its Function and Destiny.* Harper, New York

Parsons, T. and Bales, R. F. 1955. *Family, Socialisation and the Interaction Process.* The Free Press, New York

Platt, J. 1969. Some Problems of Measuring the Jointness of Conjugal Role-Relationships. *Sociology,* **3**, 287–97

Poster, M. 1979. *Critical Theory of the Family.* Pluto Press, London

Rapoport, R., Rapoport, R. and Bumstead, J. (eds.) 1978. *Working Couples.* Routledge and Kegan Paul, London

Rausch, H. L., Barry, W. A., Hertel, R. K. and Swain, M. A. 1974. *Communication, Conflict and Marriage.* Jossey Bass, San Francisco

Rausch, H. L., Greif, A. C. and Nugent, J. 1979. Communication in Couples and Families. In W. Burr *et al.* (eds.) *Contemporary Theories about the Family.* The Free Press, New York

Richardson, S., Dohrenwend, B. S. and Klein, D. 1965. *Interviewing: Its Forms and Functions.* Basic Books, New York

Rimmer, L. 1981. *Families in Focus.* Study Commission on the Family, London

Rock, P. 1979. *The Making of Symbolic Interactionism.* Macmillan, London

Rose, A. (ed.) 1962. *Human Behaviour and Social Processes.* Routledge and Kegan Paul, London

Safilios-Rothschild, C. 1970. The Study of Family Power Structure: A Review 1960–1969. *Journal of Marriage and the Family,* **32** (Nov.), 539–52

Safilios-Rothschild, C. 1976. A Macro and Micro-Examination of Family Power and Love: an Exchange Model. *Journal of Marriage and the Family,* **38** (May), 355–62

Scanzoni, J. 1972. *Sexual Bargaining: Power Politics in the American Marriage.* Prentice Hall, New Jersey

Scanzoni, J. 1979. Social Processes and Power in Families. In W. Burr *et al.* (eds.) *Contemporary Theories about the Family.* The Free Press, New York

Scanzoni, J. and Scanzoni, L. 1976. *Men, Women and Change: A Sociology of Marriage and the Family.* McGraw Hill, New York

Schutz, A. 1971. *Collected Papers. Vol. 2. Studies in Social Theory. Edited and introduced by Arvid Brodersen.* Martinus Nijhoff, The Hague

Schwartz, B. 1968. The Social Psychology of Privacy. *American Journal of Sociology,* **73** (June) 741–52

Shafer, R. and Braito, R. 1979. Self Concept and Role Performance Evaluation among Marriage Partners. *Journal of Marriage and the Family,* **41** (Nov.), 801–10

Skolnick, A. 1973. *The Intimate Environment: Exploring Marriage and the Family.* Little, Brown and Co., Boston

Smith, D. 1971. Household Space and Family Organisation. *Pacific Sociological Review,* **14** (Jan.), 53–78

Spanier, G. B. 1972. Romanticism and Marital Adjustment. *Journal of Marriage and the Family,* **34** (Aug.) 481–7

Spanier, G. B. and Cole, C. L. 1974. Toward Clarification and Investigation of Marital Adjustment. Paper presented at National Committee on Family Relations, October 1974, Toronto

Sprey, J. 1972. Family Power Structure: A Critical Comment. *Journal of Marriage and the Family,* **34** (May), 235–8

Sprey, J. 1975. Family Power and Process: Toward a Conceptual Integration. In R. E. Cromwell and D. H. Olson (eds.), *Power in Families.* John Wiley and Sons, New York

Sprey, J. 1979. Conflict Theory and the Study of Marriage and the Family. In W. R. Burr *et al.* (eds.), *Contemporary Theories about the Family.* The Free Press, New York

Tharp, R. G. 1963. Dimensions of Marriage Roles. *Marriage and Family Living,* **25**, 389–404

Thornes, B. and Collard, J. 1979. *Who Divorces?* Routledge and Kegan Paul, London

Turner, R. H. 1968. The Self Conception in Social Interaction. In C. Gordon and K. J. Gergen (eds.), *The Self in Social Interaction.* John Wiley and Sons, New York

Turner, R. H. 1970. *Family Interaction.* John Wiley and Sons, New York

Udry, J. R. 1966. *The Social Context of Marriage.* Lippincott, Philadelphia

Walker, C. 1977. Some Variations in Marital Satisfaction. In R. Chester and J. Peel (eds.), *Equalities and Inequalities in Family Life.* Academic Press, London

Waller, W. and Hill, R. 1951. *The Family: A Dynamic Interpretation.* Holt, Rinehart and Winston, New York

Williamson, R. C. 1966. *Marriage and Family Relations.* John Wiley and Sons, New York

Winch, R. F. and Goodman, L. W. (eds.) 1968. *Selected Studies in Marriage and the Family.* Holt, Rinehart and Winston, New York

Young, M. and Willmott, P. 1962. *Family and Kinship in East London.* Routledge and Kegan Paul, London

Young, M. and Willmott, P. 1973. *The Symmetrical Family*. Routledge and Kegan Paul, London

Zicklin, G. 1968. A Conversation Concerning Face-to-Face Interaction. *Psychiatry,* **31** (Aug.), 236–49

Index

218